Fifty Hikes in New Jersey

Ice on bedrock.

Fifty Hikes in New Jersey

Walks, Hikes and Backpacking Trips
from the Kittatinnies to Cape May

Bruce Scofield
Stella J. Green
H. Neil Zimmerman

Photographs by the authors

Backcountry Publications
Woodstock,
Vermont

An Invitation to the Reader

Over time trails can be rerouted and signs and landmarks altered. If you find that changes have occurred on the routes described in this book, please let us know so that corrections may be made in future editions. The author and publisher also welcome other comments and suggestions. Address all correspondence to:

Editor
Fifty Hikes Series
Backcountry Publications
P.O. Box 175
Woodstock, VT 05091

Library of Congress Cataloging-in-Publication Data

Scofield, Bruce.
   Fifty hikes in New Jersey : walks, hikes, and backpacking trips
from the Kittatinnies to Cape May / Bruce C. Scofield, Stella J.
Green, H. Neil Zimmerman ; photographs by the authors.
     p. cm.
   Bibliography: p.
   ISBN 0-942440-44-7 (pbk.) : $10.95
   1. Hiking--New Jersey--Guide-books. 2. Backpacking--New Jersey-
-Guide-books. 3. New Jersey--Description and travel--1981- --Guide
-books. I. Green, Stella J., 1926-   II. Zimmerman, H. Neil.
III. Title. IV. Title: 50 hikes in New Jersey.
GV199.42.N5S27 1988
917.49'0443--dc19   88-14439
                                                             CIP

Published by Backcountry Publications, Inc.
Woodstock, Vermont 05091

Printed in the United States of America by Capital City Press
Typesetting by Sant Bani Press
Series design by Wladislaw Finne
Layout by VLS Graphics
Trail overlays by Richard Widhu

Cover photographs: black & white photos by Bruce Scofield; color photograph by Arline Zatz

Acknowledgments

The authors wish to acknowledge and thank the many people who helped us with information, patience, and enthusiasm. We certainly could not have persevered without them. So, thanks to:

Thomas Berrian, Dick Bittner, Robert Britton, Jr., Gary Church, Earl Danley, Howard Dash, Nancy Diekroger, A. Ross Eckler, William Foley, John Green, Robert E. Green, Matthew Guuby, Warren and Joyce Hale, Barbara Harding, Bill Holton, Tom Keck, Jeanie Levitan, Christopher Lloyd, Ken Lloyd, Bruce Matthews, Jane McGraw, Barbara McMartin, Bill and Berte Miles, Ken Negus, Barry Orr, Daisy Orr, Leslie Presser, Bert Prol, Charlie Sanders, JoAnn Scofield, Malcolm Spector, Bob Spillane, Harry Swan, Bob Torres, Richard Warner, Jerome Wyckoff, . . . and "Fritzie" and "Sheena."

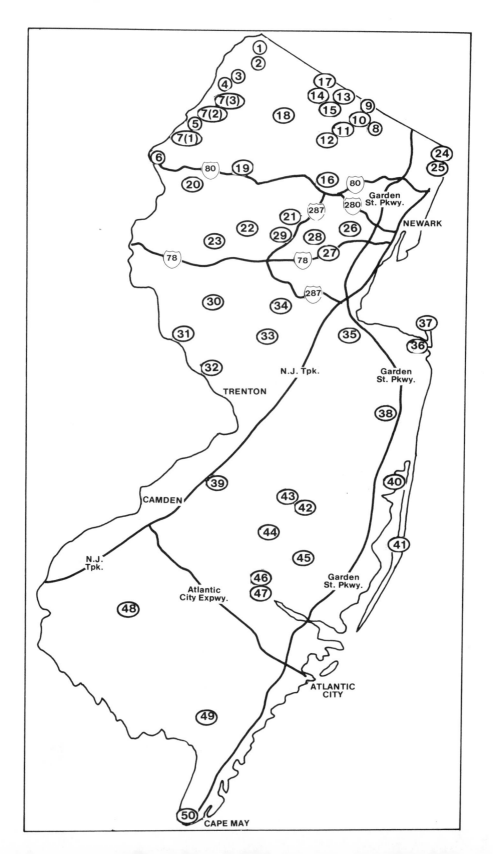

Contents

Piedmont Province

Coastal Plain

Introduction

New Jersey boasts an abundance of fine hiking trails. The famous Appalachian Trail crosses the northern part of the state; the sixty-mile-long Delaware and Raritan Canal State Park Trail crosses from New Brunswick to Raven Rock, north of Trenton; the fifty-mile-long Batona Trail traverses the New Jersey Pinelands; and the Long Path commences its journey north on the Palisades at the George Washington Bridge. Some trails are located on old roads and footpaths that existed prior to the acquisition of the land for public use, and some trails date back to the Depression years in the 1930s when a federal program to help unemployment fostered the Civilian Conservation Corps, which built park and recreation facilities still being used today. Many trails, including the Appalachian Trail, are maintained by volunteers whose dedication is evidenced by the fresh paint marks, water bars, and trails cleared of blowdowns and other hazards.

Hiking in the Garden State is varied, from the flat, sandy trails in the southern section to the hilly and rocky highlands in the north. There are swamps and beach areas, woods and grasslands. Nine-tenths of New Jersey borders on water, and of its 480 miles of boundary, all but 48 miles are either along the seacoast or a riverbed. Except for the northwest section, the typical New Jersey landscape is a low, flat plain filled with meandering streams; four-fifths of its area is no more than 400 feet above sea level and most of it is less than a quarter of that in elevation. The high point in the northwestern corner of the state is 1,803 feet above sea level.

New Jersey is divided by geologists into four primary provinces. In the northwest, running roughly southwest to northeast, is the Appalachian Ridge and Valley Province, containing the highest elevations in the state. Here, in what was once a major mountain range (since leveled by erosion) are a series of parallel valleys and ridges composed of Silurian and Devonian sandstones and conglomerates, 375 to 435 million years old. The Ridge and Valley Province extends for over twelve hundred miles from Alabama to Canada and, because of its regularity, is used as a navigational landmark by migrating birds. Hawk sightings along the main ridges are frequent during the fall migration. The Delaware Water Gap National Recreation Area, Worthington and Stokes state forests, and High Point State Park together preserve nearly all the mountainous portions of this province. The Appalachian Trail follows the crest of the main ridge, Kittatinny Mountain, for over forty miles on its way from Georgia to Maine. The hiking in this province can be challenging due to steep inclines and extremely rocky footing.

Southeast of the Ridge and Valley Province, and paralleling it, lies the New Jersey Highlands Province. This mountainous area is composed primarily of Precambrian gneisses and schists, which formed 600 to 800 million years ago as the core of mountains even more ancient than those of the Ridge and Valley Province. The elevations of the flat-topped summits characteristic of this province lie only a few hundred feet lower than those found in the Kittatinny Mountains. The range extends north into New York State as the Hudson Highlands and south into Pennsylvania as the Reading Prong. The term Reading Prong actually refers to the whole range south of the Hudson in New York, New Jersey, and Pennsylvania. Hikers will find not only more trails in this province than in any other in the state but also numerous lakes and reservoirs. The province includes the large Wawayanda State Park and the vast holdings of the Newark Watershed Conservation and Development Corporation, the latter of which supplies drinking water to New Jersey's largest city. A number of other state and county parks and forests preserve segments of the natural features of the area.

Comprising most of northeastern and central New Jersey, the Piedmont Lowlands Province is a low-lying plain composed mainly of Triassic and Jurassic sandstones and shales dating back 190 to 215 million years. In places, old lava flows from these periods have withstood erosion better than the shales and sandstones and now stand as mountain ridges. Just across the Hudson River from New York stand the Palisades, the eastern edges of a sill of igneous rock that rise over five hundred feet in places above the river. Farther west are the Watchung Hills, roughly parallel ridges made up of the resistant edges of westward-sloping, basaltic lava flows, that also rise about 250 feet above the surrounding plains. Cushetunk Mountain, and others near it, are somewhat similar features called dikes, composed of diabase, not basalt, and are found in the

southwestern portion of the province where it extends into central New Jersey.

Extensive development has marred much of the natural aspect of the Piedmont Lowlands Province, though a few parks offer an opportunity to explore what was once the forest frontier of the New York region. Palisades Interstate Park preserves much of the northern portion of the rock ramparts overlooking the Hudson. Several reservations along the crest of the first Watchung Ridge and the Round Valley Recreation Area on Cushetunk Mountain preserve some of the remaining high woodlands. In this province are also found several tracts of land that, although low and flat, offer some interesting hiking possibilities. The federally owned Great Swamp Wildlife Refuge and neighboring county parks have miles of trails, some on boardwalk, that penetrate the wetlands of a former glacial lake of immense proportions. From Raven Rock on the Delaware River to New Brunswick on the Raritan, the towpath of the old Delaware and Raritan Canal, now a state park, offers the hiker sixty-six miles of wooded walkway along a quiet, but very alive, body of water. During its heyday, the canal was the scene of intense activity. In fact, for a while, the Delaware and Raritan Canal did more business than the much better-known Erie Canal in New York State.

Encompassing nearly all of New Jersey south of a line drawn between New Brunswick and Trenton is the Coastal Plain, the largest geomorphic province in the state. This entire area is composed of ocean and stream deposits of sands, silts, and clays laid down during late Cretaceous and early Tertiary times, 50 to 80 million years ago. Here are the lowest elevations in the state, ranging from water level on the seashore to only a few hundred feet elevation inland. From the gently rolling topography of the Pine Barrens to the sandy beaches along New Jersey's 127-mile coast, this province offers the hiker an environment very different from that in the rest of the state. The Pine Barrens, a sparse pine and scrub oak forest of about one million acres, has been saved in large measure from the pressures of development. The heart of the Pinelands is preserved in several state forests, the largest being Wharton State Forest, headquartered at the old, bog iron-mining town of Batsto. The Batona Trail, named for the BAck TO NAture Club of Philadelphia, penetrates the forest for some fifty miles from Lake Absegami to Ong's Hat, including a recent seven-mile extension. This marked footpath passes deep cedar swamps, parallels rivers of cedar water, and climbs Apple Pie Hill, the highest summit in the Pine Barrens. Throughout the Pinelands are sand roads, some over two hundred years old, that make for excellent walking through this wilderness of pines.

Several areas along the Jersey coast have been preserved in their original state, in tremendous contrast to the overdevelopment that has occurred elsewhere. Here, dunes, marshes, and moving sands pushed by the ocean currents present interesting walking opportunities. The New Jersey coast lies along the Atlantic Flyway, the route migrating birds take as they wing their way toward warmer climates during the fall migration. To avoid crowded conditions, it is recommended that hiking along the coast be done during the off-season.

What is the difference between hiking and walking? *Webster's Dictionary* defines walking as "to go along or move about on foot at a moderate pace, ... to go about on foot for exercise or pleasure" and follows with the phrase "to hike." To hike is defined as taking "a long, vigorous walk, to tramp or march through the country, woods, etc." Hiking can, therefore, be interpreted to mean a long walk, through woods, mountains, or fields at a brisk pace. Every hiker develops a pace at which he or she feels most comfortable. The slow amble with frequent rest stops that most beginning hikers adopt soon gives way to a more rhythmic stride. It is usually best to adopt a pace that is reasonable enough to be maintained whether the trail ascends, descends, or is level. The hikes described here have been given an average hiking time with an edge towards a slow speed. Begin with short walks on a regular basis and, as skills and muscle-power build, move on to the more challenging hikes. In addition to the physical elation of exercising in the outdoors, hobbies such as bird watching, tree and flower identification, wildlife observation, photography, and local history can be made a part of almost any hike.

To enjoy the outdoors requires a certain amount of planning. Study the route and allow sufficient time to complete the trip before darkness falls. It is not sensible to hike alone. A group of four people is safe and enjoyable. If someone is injured, two of the hikers can go for help while one stays with the injured party. However, large groups tend to destroy the feeling of isolation obtainable in wild lands. If you are going to hike alone, tell someone dependable where you are hiking and when you expect to return, and do not deviate from the established plan.

The hiker's body is his or her resource. Your body needs adequate food to keep energy levels high; it needs water, and above all, it should not be pushed to the point of exhaustion. Hiking is pleasurable if adequate preparations are taken to make it so. Your body should be kept at a comfortable temperature, neither so warm that excessive perspiration occurs nor so cold or wet that hypothermia becomes a problem. Getting wet, whether from rain or from being over-dressed should be avoided. Hypothermia, previously called exposure, can creep up unawares. The outdoor temperature does not have to be very low. It is possible to become hypothermic in a temperature of fifty degrees if there is rain and wind and the hiker is unprepared for inclement weather. Watch your companion for the first visible signs of poor reflex actions, such as excessive stumbling, the need for frequent rest stops, or a careless attitude towards clothing and equipment. Once uncontrollable shivering has started, it may only be a matter of minutes before the body temperature has cooled beyond the point of recovery. Immediate warmth for the afflicted person is the only solution.

Suitable clothing and equipment are essential as safeguards against emergencies. It is assumed, and highly recommended, that new hikers will start their hiking career during the warmer months of the year, so the pieces of equipment discussed here are only basic items. Winter hiking is superb, with fewer people in the woods, no bugs, and a completely different feeling from summertime hiking, but we emphasize that rocks may be icy, wet leaves and lichen make rocks slippery, and clothing and equipment must be adjusted accordingly for the different conditions.

Clothing: Clothing is largely a matter of personal choice and the temperature of the day. We do not recommend jeans or other all-cotton pants. When cotton becomes wet, it is heavy, does not dry quickly, and does not retain warmth. Breathing will be impaired if the waistband or belt is too tight. Some hikers prefer suspenders to a belt for this reason. We prefer layering as the method of dress, possibly a long-sleeved shirt over a short-sleeved T-shirt for the upper body. Be certain that clothing is loose enough not to chafe. Whatever is worn, it is important not to become wet with perspiration, but to remove some layers to avoid becoming damp and to add a layer at rest stops to prevent being chilled. For emergency use it is recommended that you carry a wool shirt or sweater; wool or polypropylene hat and gloves; a small flashlight; a simple first aid kit, including a pocket knife, toilet paper; and, in summer, bug repellent. For hikers who would be helpless if their eyeglasses were lost, an extra pair should be carried.

Boots: First of all, feet must be comfortable. A few hikes in New Jersey can be walked easily in sneakers, and for young people, these may be their preferred footwear for all grades of hiking in the Garden State. However, it is strongly recommended that most hikers wear a lightweight hiking boot with effective ankle support. If new boots are required, to ensure a good fit take along to the store the socks (see below) you plan to wear on the trail. There should be ample room in the boots so the toes are not cramped, and there should not be much forward movement of the foot in the boot. Most good outdoor stores will have salespeople on their staff experienced enough to advise a new hiker on the boot choice. Walk around at home or in the office for several days before deciding that this is "the pair." The first hike in new boots should be a short one, and should a "hot" spot develop, immediately stop and protect the area with moleskin or molefoam, obtainable from the druggist.

Socks: Wear two pairs to prevent blisters, the inner one being lightweight polypropylene or wool, and the outer one, thicker wool.

Rain/wind protection: Ideally, your coat should have a hood and be waterproof.

The hood will prevent cold wind from penetrating between your collar and neck. There are many varieties in the stores. Remember, though, that hiking will generate perspiration, and some parkas will generate rain inside the garment even if it is not raining outside. Waterproof, breatheable fabric such as Gore-tex® is favored by many hikers.

Pack: A lightweight day pack is an indispensable item for carrying those pieces of equipment essential to happiness on the trail. The following is always in our pack *even for a short hike:*

Water: The time has passed when the hiker could be refreshed at that beautiful stream by drinking the pure, cold water. *Giardia lamblia* and other bacteria in the water that may look so pure have destroyed that pleasure. Always carry a minimum of a quart of water per person, and drink it, even if you are not aware of thirst. Monitor your urine, and if it is dark in color, water intake should be increased, particularly in colder weather when feeling thirsty is not as apparent as in hot weather.

Lunch: Even if lunch is not planned on the trail, take an emergency ration—a chocolate bar or gorp (good old raisins and peanuts) will do.

Maps: The maps printed in this guide, along with the written text, are all you need for these hikes. As you become experienced, you may want to explore areas in more depth. Each hike gives map references as keyed at the end of this introduction. These sources can be contacted for maps of additional hiking areas. For hiking in New Jersey, it is not usually necessary to carry a compass, particularly if you are on a described hike; however, if you stray from the trail, a map and compass can return you to the path or to civilization, if you know how to use them. You *will* need a good

New Jersey road map to find your way to the trailheads. The directions for each hike focus on reaching the trail itself, but getting to the nearby town is often up to you. New Jersey, like most states, issues an "official" highway map, and it is free. Write to New Jersey Division of Travel and Tourism, CN 826, Trenton, New Jersey 08625; 609-292-2470.

Ticks: These are a problem in New Jersey and other nearby states. Lyme disease is not to be trifled with. Learn to look for and remove ticks after hiking in an infested area. Long-sleeved shirts and pants with the legs tucked into socks are a must in these areas. A flier on Lyme disease is available from the New Jersey State Department of Health, CN 360, Trenton, New Jersey 08625 or from the New York–New Jersey Trail Conference.

Parking Fees: Some state parks and forests have moderate fees for parking, especially in summer. New Jersey residents over age 61 can obtain a free parking pass, good at any time. Apply at any park or forest office. New Jersey has a short deer hunting season, usually in December. Avoid hiking in hunting areas during firearms season. Check with the local park office, the New Jersey Department of Environmental Protection, or the New York–New Jersey Trail Conference for specific dates. There is no hunting in New Jersey on Sundays.

There is a certain etiquette to hiking. Two of the most important phrases to remember are the familiar "take only photographs, leave only footprints" and "carry out what you carry in." If every user of our woods followed these guidelines, litter would not be a problem. Many concerned hikers carry empty garbage bags in their packs and, towards the end of the hike and where litter is prevalent, pick it up and carry it out. Some trails border, or actually cross, private property. No Trespassing signs should be honored and care should be taken to respect private landowners by not damaging fences or trees and by not littering. A few, thoughtless walkers can damage good relations built up over the years with trail neighbors.

If there are trail registers, complete the record in an informative manner at the first register on your hike and sign out at the last one. On an overnight hike with plans to use an existing shelter, remember that the lean-to should be available for all who need to use it and, on that wet and windy night, make room cheerfully for that latecomer. Pack away all evidence that you have been there and vacate the lean-to exactly as you would wish to find it on arrival.

Check before beginning the backpack if fires are permitted in the area. Rules are changing, mostly leaning towards banning them. No live trees should be cut for firewood, and the fire should be contained in the fireplace provided at many shelters. When fires are permitted, it is courteous to gather enough dead wood to leave the next occupant at least enough to get another fire started. Wood is in short supply in frequently camped areas. Keep fires small and safe, whether for atmosphere or smudge (keeping mosquitoes away). A small, lightweight backpacking stove is preferred for cooking. They are inexpensive, cook quickly, and keep pots unblackened.

There are certain areas in the United States, for instance on the beaches of the Colorado River in the Grand Canyon, where human body waste began to be such a problem that now it is required for all such matter to be carried out. With the increasing number of people using New Jersey trails, it is not unthinkable that in the future we should all be required to carry out our personal waste. To avoid this inconvenience, use the outhouse where one is provided, otherwise, be "copy cats"—act as a feline does. Choose a spot far away from any water and the trail, remove the layer of leaves and twigs, dig a hole at least three inches deep in the soil, either with a rock or a sturdy stick (some hikers carry a special trowel for this purpose), take care of your business, and cover the whole mess over so that no disturbance is apparent.

The umbrella organization for hiking in New Jersey is the New York–New Jersey Trail Conference, a nonprofit federation of five thousand individuals and seventy hiking and environmental organizations working to build and maintain trails and to preserve open space. Formed in 1920, the founders built the first section of the Appalachian Trail in 1923. Today, their trail network covers more than 850 miles. The Conference is supported by dues, publication sales, and donations— along with thousands of hours of volunteer time. Members receive the bimonthly *Trail Walker,* can purchase their maps and guides at discount, and can avail themselves of the Conference Library. Dues start at $15 ($10 for students and retirees); $20 for a family. We encourage you to support the people who support the trails. They can be reached at GPO Box 2250, New York, New York 10116.

There are many fine hiking clubs in New Jersey, catering to all grades of hikers in many areas of the state. These clubs are an excellent way to meet people who share your love of the outdoors. The clubs are your ticket to the special, natural sections of your area and will help you learn the special ins and outs of hiking in the Northeast. For a listing, send a self-addressed, stamped envelope to the Trail Conference at the address above.

Many of the trails used are maintained by volunteers. Respect their work and their tender loving care and do not cut corners on switchbacks or otherwise erode the trail unnecessarily. If you'd like to help maintain a trail, contact the New York–New Jersey Trail Conference.Trail markers, or blazes, ideally are spaced so that the walker can easily see the next marker as he moves along the trail. At times, these markers are obscured by new growth or blowdowns, and their clarity also varies from time to time. The hikes described in this book are mostly on marked trails, and a notation has been made where markers are indistinct or missing. Markers tend to be prolific where the hiker needs to be alert, and whenever there is an abrupt change of direction, the trail is marked with two standard markers, one above the other, the upper blaze indicating the direction of the turn. The beginning or the end of a trail is indicated with three markers. *Remember that a trail is a dynamic entity and rerouting takes place frequently.* When rerouting occurs, old markers are painted out, and a new route is marked and trimmed.

Map Key:

USGS: Topographic quadrangle maps are available for all parts of the United States. For a New Jersey index, write to United States Geological Survey, Distribution Branch, Box 25286, Federal Center, Denver, Colorado 80225; 303-236-7477. The maps used in this guidebook are all 7½' maps. These maps were not designed with hikers in mind and often do not show the trails or show them incorrectly. The exception to this generalization is in the Pinelands. Here, USGS topos are very useful, for they clearly show nearly all the sand roads of the area. In spite of the drawbacks, the depiction of general topography is superb, which is why we have used them as the base maps for the hikes in this book. The New Jersey index also lists retail stores throughout the state that sell these maps over-the-counter. They are also available from the New Jersey Geological Survey, Map Sales Office, CN 402, Trenton NJ 08625; 609-292-2506 or 229-2578. Catalog available.

NYNJTC: Waterproof, color topographic maps, usually sold in sets, published by the New York–New Jersey Trail Conference, GPO Box 2250, New York, New York 10116.

WB: Topographic color maps printed in the rear of the *New York Walk Book,* 5th edition, by the New York–New Jersey Trail Conference and published by Doubleday in December 1984; available in many bookstores or directly from the Conference.

HRM: Topographic Hiker's Region Maps published by *Walking News,* PO Box 352, New York, New York 10013.

DEP: Sketch maps, usually free, from the various state park and forest offices; or, write to New Jersey Department of Environmental Protection, Division of Parks and Forestry, CN 404, Trenton, New Jersey 08625; 609-292-2885.

NPS: Park maps, usually free, from individual park offices. Addresses in hike text.

Recommended Books:

Bennett, D. W. *New Jersey Coastwalks.* American Littoral Society (Sandy Hook, Highlands, New Jersey), 1981.

Dann, Kevin. *Twenty-five Walks in New Jersey.* Rutgers University Press, 1982.

Kjellstrom, Bjorn. *Be Expert With Map and Compass.* Scribner's, 1976.

Kobbe, Gustav. *The New Jersey Coast and Pines. Walking News* (PO Box 352, New York, New York 10013), 1982.

Mack, Arthur C. *The Palisades of the Hudson.* The Palisades Press (Edgewater, New Jersey), 1909.

McClelland, Robert J. *The Delaware Canal.* Rutgers University Press, 1967.

McPhee, John. *The Pine Barrens.* Farrar, Straus and Giroux, 1968.

New York–New Jersey Trail Conference. *The Daywalker.* Doubleday, 1983.

New York–New Jersey Trail Conference. *Guide to the Appalachian Trail in New York and New Jersey.* 10th ed. Appalachian Trail Conference, 1986.

New York–New Jersey Trail Conference. *Guide to the Long Path.* 2nd ed. New York–New Jersey Trail Conference, 1987.

New York–New Jersey Trail Conference. *The New York Walk Book.* 5th ed. Doubleday, 1984.

Nixdorf, Bert. *Hikes and Bike Rides for the Delaware Valley and South Jersey.* American Youth Hostels, Delaware Valley Council (Philadelphia), 1981.

Otten, Iras, and Eleanor Weskerna. *The Earth Shook and the Sky Was Red.* Bicentennial Committee (West Milford Township, New Jersey), 1976.

Ransom, James M. *Vanishing Ironworks of the Ramapos.* Rutgers University Press, 1966.

Scheller, William B. *Country Walks Near New York.* Appalachian Mountain Club (5 Joy Street, Boston, Massachusetts 02108), 1980.

Scofield, Bruce. *Circuit Hikes in Northern New Jersey.* 2nd ed. New York–New Jersey Trail Conference, 1987.

Thomas, Lester S. *The Pine Barrens of New Jersey.* New Jersey Department of Environmental Protection, 1983.

Wyckoff, Jerome. *Rock Scenery of the Hudson Highlands and Palisades.* Adirondack Mountain Club (174 Glen Street, Glens Falls, New York 12801), 1971.

Ridge and Valley Province

1

Cedar Swamp and High Point

Total distance: 4 miles
Hiking time: 3 hours
Vertical rise: 300 feet
Rating: Moderate
Maps: NYNJTC North Kittatinny Trails #18; WB #18; HRM
#52A; DEP High Point State Park; USGS Port Jervis South

In the far northwestern part of New Jersey is High Point State Park (RR4, Box 287, Sussex, NJ 07461; 201-875-4800), where the highest elevations in the state are found. The entire park is quite large, 14,000 acres, and offers good hiking along the Appalachian Trail and on a number of other marked trails and woods roads. The hike described here is in the section of the park north of NJ 23. This part contains the highest elevation in the state at 1803 feet, the High Point monument, and also Cedar Swamp, New Jersey's first natural area. The area is the most visited and used section of the park, and an off-season or midweek hike is suggested if solitude is desired.

The land making up High Point State Park was donated to the public by Colonel and Mrs. Anthony R. Kuser of Bernardsville, New Jersey. The park itself was created in 1923 and has long been a favorite mountain retreat for native New Jerseyites. The most obvious feature of the park is the monument itself, an obelisk that towers 220 feet above the high-

High Point Monument.

est piece of ground in the entire state. The views from the mountaintop around the tower, and from the tower itself, are without a doubt the most expansive in the state.

On October 12, 1965, the Dryden Kuser Natural Area was dedicated in memory of the late Senator Dryden and Colonel Kuser. This area contains a unique cedar swamp, the present-day remains of an earlier glacial lake. Here are found hemlock, rhododendron, and even Atlantic white cedars—far from their usual habitats in southern New Jersey.

To reach this interesting area from NJ 23, turn north on the park road opposite the park office. Proceed straight into the park following signs to the Cedar Swamp Natural Area. Lake Marcia will be passed on the right, and after 1 mile, a left turn will lead to the natural area. Travel down this road for .25 mile and park on the right-hand side, just after a Dead End sign and just before a gate that closes off the road to vehicles.

Begin the hike by walking north past the gate on a paved road. After about five minutes of walking, another gate appears by a park bench, one of several seen on this hike. Again, walk past the gate on the road, which becomes narrower and gradually heads downhill towards the swamp. At the plaque set in stone, bear left on a walkway of slate chips onto the perimeter path encircling the swamp. The walking is very pleasant and easy. The heart of the swamp will always be on your right, and soon pines, hemlocks, and cedars appear above rhododendron groves. The swamp is deep and dark and, upon close inspection, supports mosses, ferns, and even the carnivorous pitcher plant and sundew.

Soon after entering the swamp area itself, the path swings sharply to the left and temporarily heads south. The trail rises slightly now, allowing a few views over a somewhat dryer section of the swamp. Here there are standing dead trees and occasional pines. After only about five minutes, the trail makes a sharp turn, this time to the right, and begins to head northward again, returning to the wetter section of the swamp. Stay on the main path for another few minutes, passing a bench located where a footpath comes in from the left. Just after this intersection, a particularly wet and dense section of the trail is reached. The swamp is now on both sides of the trail, and the footing is sometimes slippery in spite of the boards providing a dry walkway. The swamp is intensely green and dense in this section; moss is plentiful and ferns flank the sides of the path. Notice also some very large white cedars.

At the end of this wet section, a little over a mile into the hike, a trail junction is reached near another park bench. Turn left here and continue heading north on a much drier path. There are a few large hemlocks along this section of the hike. Walk approximately another five minutes to a junction with the Monument Trail. There is a circular clearing immediately before this junction, and at the

junction itself there is a small bridge over a brook on the left. Turn right on the Monument Trail, a footpath marked by metal tags painted with a red and green circle. The New York/New Jersey border is very close at this point.

The Monument Trail almost immediately begins to climb and leads to the highest summit in New Jersey. The trail, built by the Civilian Conservation Corps in the 1930s is well constructed with large blocks of stone placed along the edge. The trail is steep here, quite a change from the level walking so far encountered. The ridge is reached after about ten minutes of continuous climbing, with views to the east and west appearing through the trees. The trail now heads southward on a narrow ridge of Kittatinny Mountain and continues to gain elevation. There are no markers on this section of the trail, but it is easy to follow since it wanders in the scrub oak between the eastern and western sides of the ridge. Soon a number of viewpoints appear on both sides of the trail, each one better than the last. This section is about 2.5 miles into the hike.

The footing is now quite rocky in places and is typical of the higher elevations on Kittatinny Mountain. Just after the trail makes a short jog to the left, there is a good lookout to the east out over the Wallkill River Valley, containing some farms and much forest. The first big ridge visible beyond the valley is Pochuck Mountain, and beyond that can be seen the long Wawayanda Ridge where the Vernon Valley and Great Gorge ski areas are located. Ahead, among bare rock outcrops and pitch pines sculpted by the high mountain winds, is an overlook to the west. The bend in the Delaware River, I-84, the Pocono plateau, portions of Port Jervis, and in the distance to the north, the Catskill Mountains are all visible.

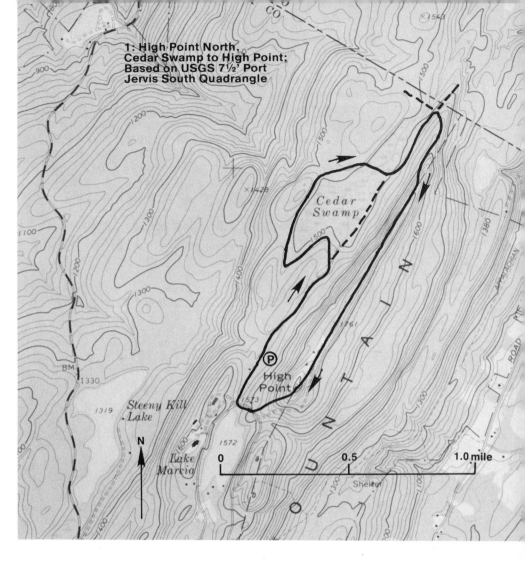

Continuing south on the trail, which now rises gradually, glaciated outcrops of rock topped with pitch pines are seen. This sedimentary rock is known as the Shawangunk conglomerate and was formed by deposits in an ancient sea. After folding, faulting, and uplifting, these erosion-resistant sediments remained to make the ridge when the weaker, surrounding rocks were worn down and washed away. The trail soon levels off and becomes easier to hike and then, quite suddenly, comes out to a huge parking area and the gigantic monument. Here is the end of the Monument Trail, indicated by its unique white pipe marker. Welcome to civilization.

Walk directly toward the monument through the parking area and past the rest rooms. The views are fantastic, particularly at the monument itself or from within it during the summer. The monument is 220 feet high, on a base 34 feet square that tapers to 19 feet at the base of the apex. It was built of local quartzite and faced with New Hampshire granite.

Cedar Swamp and High Point **21**

A plaque on the monument indicates that it was "erected by Colonel and Mrs. Anthony R. Kuser to the glory and honor and eternal memory of New Jersey's heroes of land, sea and air in all wars of our country." To the south is Lake Marcia, the former Kuser residence, and the long spine of the Kittatinnies (forty miles to the Delaware Water Gap). West is the Pocono plateau (some call this eroded plateau "mountains"), and the Catskills are to the north.

From the monument, find a path that begins near the southwest side of the foundation and head downhill. This walkway, apparently a utility line, provides an easy path downhill and is a far better alternative than the road it parallels. Monument Drive and Lake Marcia are reached after only a few minutes. Pass the rest rooms and turn right onto the road leading to the Cedar Swamp picnic area. It should take only five or six minutes from here to reach your car.

BCS

2

South of High Point

Total distance: 6 miles
Hiking time: 4 hours
Vertical rise: 300 feet
Rating: Moderate
Maps: NYNJTC North Kittatinny Trails #18; WB #18; HRM
 #52A; DEP High Point State Park; USGS Port Jervis South

South of the monument and the popular Lake Marcia is a section of High Point State Park (RR4, Box 287, Sussex, NJ 07461; 201-875-4800) that is wild, expansive, scenic, and lightly used. The Appalachian Trail (AT) passes through this area, and the Rutherford shelter, one of the few New Jersey AT trail shelters, is also found here.

To reach the trailhead, take NJ 23 to the High Point State Park ranger's office located at the top of Kittatinny Ridge on the south side of the highway. Stop in at the office for a map or to pick up a permit if leaving your car overnight. Park your car at the Appalachian Trail parking area, which can be reached via a driveway found about 200 feet east of the office on the same side of the road.

Enter the woods on a path marked by two large granite blocks. In about 50 feet, a junction with the white-blazed Appalachian Trail is reached. Make a left here and walk about 200 yards to a trail junction, marked by a painted, vertically placed pipe. Leave the AT, turning left onto the Iris Trail, a woods road marked with occasional red tags nailed to trees.

The Iris Trail descends through a mixed oak forest with an understory of ferns. In places the trail can be quite grassy. Cross a small brook on planks, then begin a short uphill section. After this rise, the trail gradually descends through a more open forest filled with small blueberry bushes. Low rock outcroppings line the trail in places. Forest birds, such as the rufous-sided towhee often seen in the bushes and the seldom seen veery with its ethereal call, inhabit this woods. The trail, used in the winter by snowmobiles and cross-country skiers, gradually widens in this section.

After about forty-five minutes of walking, the trail, now covered with a fine gravel, enters a darker and denser woods. Ahead through the trees is Lake Rutherford, a reservoir that meets the water needs of the town of Sussex. Where the Iris Trail comes closest to the lake, look for a side trail that will take you to a rocky overlook near the shore of the lake. Lake Rutherford is quite large and, except for one distant building, is uninhabited and quite wild. Unfortunately, swimming is not permitted.

Return to the Iris Trail and continue, crossing over one of the small brooks

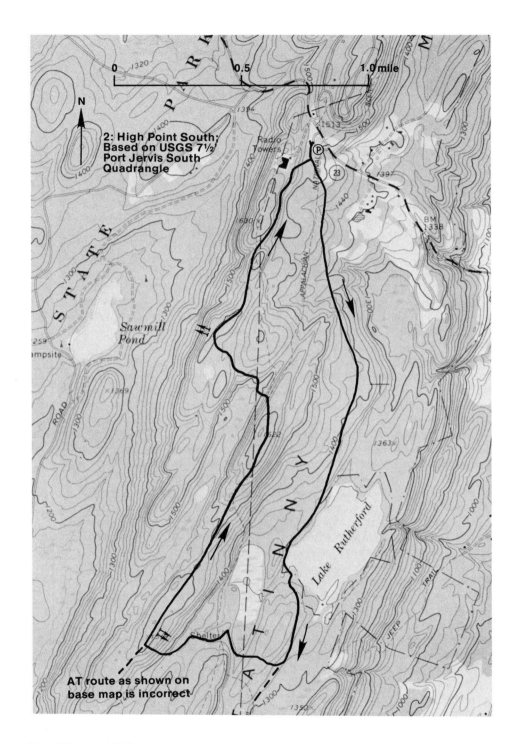

2: High Point South;
Based on USGS 7½
Port Jervis South
Quadrangle

AT route as shown on
base map is incorrect

that feed the lake. Here the bright red cardinal flower, a type of *Lobelia,* blooms during the summer. After crossing the stream and leaving the area of the lake, the trail swings sharply to the left and then to the right. The trail climbs gradually, descends, and once again, this time more gently, swings to the left and then the right. Cross a low, and possibly wet, area and soon after come to a junction with an unmarked path that comes in sharply from the right. Turn right here leaving the Iris Trail.

The unmarked path, actually an old woods road, you have turned onto is not often used. At the time of this writing, parts of it were grassy and mossy, and there were a few blowdowns blocking the path. After a few minutes of walking, the trail gains elevation quickly, this ascent being the steepest so far on the hike. The climb ends shortly and you'll descend and swing around a wet area. As you follow the path out of the wet area on a gentle, uphill grade, you'll notice through the trees a large marsh to your right, the remnants of which are shown on older maps as a lake. Walk ahead through the high grass to find a footpath, turn right, and you'll find the Rutherford shelter. It should take you under thirty minutes to walk from Lake Rutherford to the shelter.

The Rutherford shelter is one of the more remote Appalachian Trail shelters in New Jersey. The presence of large lilac bushes around it reveals that it was built on land that was once farmed. In back of the shelter are a number of attractive campsites at the edge of the marsh you saw earlier. This remote area is a good place for lunch or a snack.

When you leave the shelter, follow the footpath straight ahead (keep to the right), heading roughly west. This path is the access trail, marked occasionally with blue markers, to the shelter from the Ap-

palachian Trail. In a few hundred feet, you'll come to a rock-lined spring that feeds a small brook. Continue past the spring on the rocky footpath, cross a small stream, and find your way through a section of trail that was not clearly marked at the time of this writing. Swing around to the left and begin to climb the ridge, first through ferns and then, just before the junction with the Appalachian Trail, over the glacially scraped eastern face of the ridge. The view from the trail junction is good, but we suggest that you bear right (north) on the AT and walk about 150 feet to the first viewpoint on your right.

From the viewpoint, over the large, glacially polished rock slab known as Dutch Shoe Rock, a tremendous vista to the east presents itself. Lake Rutherford and, in front of it, the large marsh near the shelter are just to your left. In the distance are Pochuck Mountain and Wawayanda Mountain, both traversed by the Appalachian Trail. A short walk farther north on the AT leads to yet another vista.

After enjoying the views, continue north on the AT, which turns away from the cliffs and begins a gradual climb into the ridge-top forest. The trail, quite rugged and rocky in places, passes through an oak and maple forest before it reaches the sparse pitch pines and scrub oak of the high western ridge. Here are views of a parallel ridge to the west. From these outcrops, the trail descends steeply over rocks into the valley below and then climbs the next ridge. At the top of the climb there are views over the Delaware River into Pennsylvania.

Continue heading north on the AT past the junction with the Blue-Dot Trail, which descends steeply and reaches Sawmill Lake below in about .5 mile. After following the western side of the ridge for a short distance, the AT swings over to the

The Appalachian Trail in High Point State Park.

eastern side, where there are partial views, and then begins a long descent. This section is a beautiful stretch of trail and forest. In places pine needles cover the trail, which winds through huge fern fields under oak, maple, and large white pines. You'll walk along a man-made embankment with a large cliff on your left for a while, drop to a lower level, and then, in about 200 yards, meet the Iris Trail with its white pipe marker. After just a short distance straight ahead, you'll find the turn-off trail to the parking area.

BCS

Stokes State Forest

Total distance: 10 miles
Hiking time: 7 hours
Vertical rise: 340 feet
Rating: Moderately strenuous
Maps: USGS Culvers Gap/Branchville; NYNJTC North Kittatinny Trails #17 and #18; WB #17 and #18; HRM #52A; HRM #52B

Acquisitions of land for Stokes State Forest (RR 2, Box 260, Branchville, NJ 07826; 201-948-3820) began in 1907, and the state now owns fifteen thousand acres, with more than seventy-five miles of roads and well-defined trails. The area is named in honor of Governor Edward Stokes who donated the first five hundred acres. Some of the early tracts were acquired for one dollar per acre, much different from present-day land prices. Routes used for this hike will be the Swenson (red), Cartwright (red and brown), Bannon (unmarked), Appalachian (white), and Tower (dark green) trails, as well as Crigger Road.

The entry to Stokes State Forest is on US 206, 3 miles northwest of Branchville, New Jersey, and 10 miles south of Milford, Pennsylvania. The park sign is on the east side of US 206. Drive to the forest office to pick up literature and then follow the signs to Stony Lake via Courson Road. Courson Road passes Kittle Field on the left. Turn right at the T-junction onto Kittle Road and proceed to the Stony Lake parking area.

The Stony Lake parking area is divided into two lots, but it is immaterial for this hike which one is used. Walk to the signboard between the two lots, and facing the woods, look for a wide, gravel road leading uphill past a metal barrier labeled "Entrance to Snowmobile and Dogsled Trails." This road is the starting point for the hike and is marked with light green, dark green, blue, and brown markers. Be wary of the poison ivy at this point. Walk uphill for five minutes until the road crosses a metal drainage pipe, and immediately afterwards, turn left on the red-marked Swenson Trail. This trail is named after the family who had a subsistence farm in the area until it was abandoned in the late 1920s or early 1930s. From Stony Lake, the trail meanders up a low ridge through areas of mixed white pine, mountain laurel, and oak. Portions of the land here were logged fifty to sixty years earlier, and there is also evidence of the chestnut forest that covered the area prior to the 1920 blight.

Within about thirty minutes, the forest changes, becoming more open as the trail leads down to a low-lying, wet area with a seasonal stream. Look around in

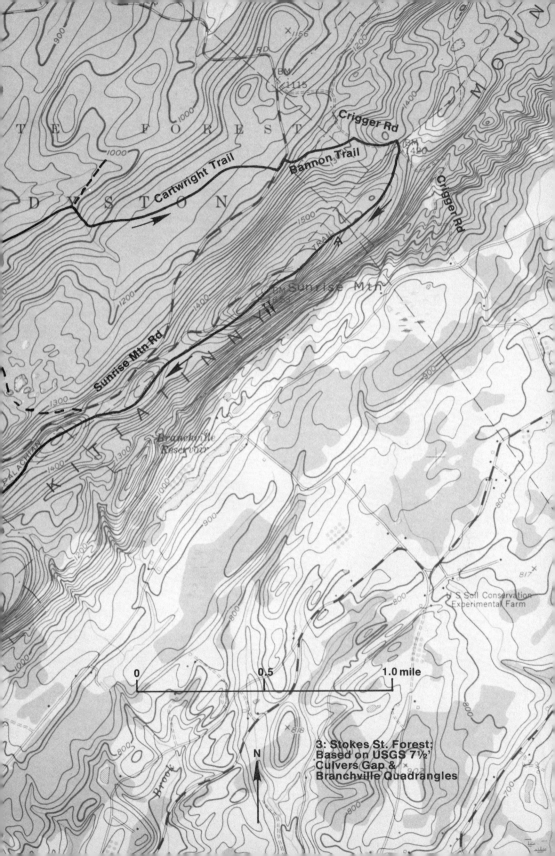

3: Stokes St. Forest;
Based on USGS 7½'
Culvers Gap &
Branchville Quadrangles

spring for many violets, trillium, jack-in-the-pulpit, wild cranesbill, and the showy pink flowers of rhodora, reminiscent of the cultivated azalea. Skunk cabbage and false hellebore are also found here. These two plants can be distinguished by the way in which the leaves grow from the stem. Wildflowers flourish here because of the rich soil and moist atmosphere. After the brook crossing, the trail parallels the stream for a short distance and gradually climbs to an area of blue paint markers at right angles to the Swenson Trail. These markers indicate the boundary of a forest management study area, which may eventually lead to a harvesting operation. In spring the woods are crowded with many species of birds on their way north after the winter migration.

Follow the red trail as it moves through the woods to reach the junction of the Tinsley Trail which goes steeply uphill to the right. Tinsley Trail was at one time called Tinsley Road, for it crossed over the mountain to Wantage Township where the Tinsley family lived. Three yellow markers indicate the joining of the Swenson and Tinsley trails. Markers at this junction have been considerably damaged by porcupines chewing around the painted edges, and their teeth marks may be clearly seen. (The Stony Brook Trail is incorrectly shown on the map as joining the Swenson Trail from the right. Do not look for this trail as a point of reference while you are walking.)

Continue on the red trail, going steeply down to the left. When the leaves are off the trees, the ridge to the left is clearly seen. The red markers of the Swenson Trail and the yellow of the Tinsley Trail are both visible in this short section. Three red markers soon indicate that the Swenson Trail travels off downhill to the right, leaving the yellow marker for the Tinsley Trail visible straight ahead.

Turn right onto the Swenson Trail, which descends and then climbs over a minor rise to Spring Brook cabin. The trail is now narrower and much rockier and care is needed to walk safely on the rocky footing.

The attractive Spring Brook cabin is located near a small pond embellished by a large white dogwood and takes about an hour to reach. Spring Brook is often dry here and it appears almost as though the pond has no inlet. There are remnants of old walls in the area, and the trail goes past a substantial wood pile to the right of the cabin. The cabin is used mostly in summer for recreational purposes by employees of the Department of Environmental Protection.

Walking becomes easier again after leaving Spring Brook cabin. At about this point in the hike, numbers of young beech and black birch trees are encountered, and it is interesting to note the similarity between the leaves of these two trees. The leaves can be distinguished by the tiny serrations on the edges of the black birch leaf, while the edges of the beech leaves are less jagged, with larger serrations. A forest resource plan for Stokes State Forest has been prepared by the Division of Parks and Forestry and the Division of Fish, Game, and Wildlife. Stokes State Forest has lost over one-half its trees to drought and to three seasons of gypsy moth defoliation. The forest resource plan incorporates a method of harvesting the dead trees for profit while simultaneously encouraging the growth of new, healthy trees. The New Jersey Bureau of Forest Management has four methods of reproducing forest areas. Two of these, called the "shelterwood harvest" and the "clear-cut harvest," have been applied farther along on the Swenson Trail, and when the leaves are off the trees, this bare area is visible from Sunrise Mountain. Fifteen acres were cleared in this section in 1985. Shelterwood harvest produces new forest areas in the shelter of older trees. The stand is gradually removed in a series of partial cuttings, the last one resulting in what looks like a clear-cut harvest when all stems larger than two inches in diameter are cut. Denning trees for birds and other wildlife are usually left at the edges of a shelterwood harvest area. Normally, five years are needed to improve the visual shock of an area within a shelterwood or clear-cut harvest. In the center of the cut on the Swenson Trail a wire enclosure is installed, designed to determine what impact deer have on clear-cuts.

The trail here is located on a shelf, with the Appalachian Trail ridge visible through the trees on the right. After about ten minutes from the cabin, the path dips down to a low-lying area, with higher ground on the left-hand side. Watch carefully now for the Cartwright Trail that you will take on the right. The Swenson Trail passes through a wide, wet area, with several small streams and a round mud flat area to the left. One of the last stream crossings to be negotiated is easily identifed by an eight-inch diameter tree bearing a red marker immediately at the point of crossing. Negotiate the stream on rocks behind this marked tree and, 20 yards beyond, find the beginning of the Cartwright Trail, indicated by three distinct red and brown markers on the right. The junction is also emphasized by a small cairn on the right-hand side of the trail. Walking from the beginning of the wet area to the trail junction takes approximately three minutes, and you've missed the turn if you encounter in the trail a large, felled tree about two feet off the ground.

At first the Cartwright Trail footway seems to ascend a streambed, and the path is indistinct. The markers can be easily followed, however, and after a level start, the trail climbs moderately. Seventy-five years ago, old farmlands were abandoned in this area. The stumps of chestnut trees, victims of the blight, are numerous, but Solomon's seal, white violets, many varieties of ferns, together with very tall trees now make this trail very pretty. After leveling out and crossing a stream, the trail widens and then narrows again before emerging onto Sunrise Mountain Road. The end of the Cartwright Trail is indicated by three red and brown markers on a tree by the roadside.

Turn left onto Sunrise Mountain Road and walk three minutes to where the road bends sharply to the left, just after an unpaved pullout on the left-hand side. On the right is the unmarked Bannon Trail. Look for an orange paint blob on the first large tree a few yards into the woods and follow a narrow, uphill trail until it shortly opens into a wide woods road. After the uphill section, the trail enters a marshy area. Halfway across, on the right-hand side, look for a tree growing over a rock slab and forming an interesting spring. The marshy area continues for several yards, and the trail reaches a T-junction with Crigger Road after about seven minutes from Sunrise Mountain Road. Confirm your location by looking to the left upon reaching the wide T-junction to see the wooden sign, "Bannon Trail."

Turn right onto Crigger Road, which is unpaved and unused by motor vehicles, crossing a metal drainage pipe that is buried and almost completely hidden in the road. The wide and grassy road bends slightly uphill to the left and ascends toward the ridge, crossing another metal drainage pipe. Towards the top of the hill, the road makes a left detour around a large boulder and dead tree trunk, which is signed "dead end" from the other direction in an attempt to deter road traffic. Soon after by-passing this obstacle, climb over a large pile of slate and rocks to reach the white, rectangular markers of the Appalachian Trail. Exceptionally large wild strawberries are rampant here in season, and there is also a patch of May apple, with its attractive white flowers that curiously appear only at the junction of two leaves. Only the fruit of the May apple is edible—all other parts are poisonous.

Turn right onto the Appalalchian Trail, which is narrow and rocky here and parallels an old stone wall for a short way. Within about five minutes, a good rest stop can be found by leaving the main trail on a path to the right leading to a pleasant, rocky outcrop.

As the Appalachian Trail climbs, a view to the left becomes more apparent, and within about ten minutes, a junction on the right is reached with a trail leading uphill towards wooden steps. This side trail accesses the Sunrise Mountain parking lot, with rest rooms and garbage cans, and should be ignored unless there is a need to use the facilities. Walk straight ahead, up rock steps to a man-made scenic overlook with wooden benches. The rain shelter and cairn at the top of Sunrise Mountain is reached by walking another few minutes along the ridge. Sunrise Mountain is 1,653 feet above sea level. High Point monument can be seen eight miles to the north, and you can also see the Catskills on a clear day, just to the left of the monument. The New Jersey Topographic Survey maintains more than eight thousand markers within the state, and one can be found just south of the shelter on Sunrise Mountain. It takes the form of a stone monument, with a bronze marker embedded in the top.

Turn left, downhill, from the rain shelter and ignore the turnoff to the right that appears within a few minutes. The rocky trail undulates, and at one point, other white rectangular paint markers appear. This path may be the remains of a temporary reroute. Follow the correct trail uphill to the right, ignoring the downhill direction. Following the white markers south will bring you to the junction of the Tinsley Trail in approximately thirty minutes, and shortly afterwards a viewpoint to the west among white pines is found just to the right of the trail. High Point is again visible, and Sunrise Mountain Road is startlingly close at the bottom of the hill.

The terrain does not change very much in this section. The trail undulates, sometimes on the top of the ridge and sometimes just below it, through an abundance of tall mountain laurel. The sharp-eyed will see a metal marker on a tree to the left of the trail with posted signs close behind it and, by stepping just off the trail, will discover an eighteen-inch-high cement block with NJ 15 engraved on the top. The Branchville Water Company owns the land to the east of this boundary marker.

The trail detours slightly to avoid a wet area, passes by two flat depressions to the left, which are sometimes quite full of water, and arrives at a shelter sign with three blue markers on a tree to the left. The shelter is .3 mile distant. This wide junction is also that of the brown-marked Stony Brook Trail, which could be used to shorten the hike by about thirty minutes.

Proceed south on the Appalachian Trail across a stream and uphill, very soon looking down onto another clearcut. A sign by the right-hand side of the trail indicates that this area is a tree harvest location, with information obtainable from the Forestry Information Bureau of Forest Management or the New Jersey Department of Environmental Protection's Division of Parks and Forestry. The sign indicates that diseased and weakened trees have been selected by foresters for removal in an effort to improve the growing space for the remaining trees and, generally, to protect the forest and its wildlife. This section of eighty-five acres was a clear-cut/salvage harvest area that, because of an eighty percent mortality, was cleared of dead stems and cull trees in 1986. Salvage harvest is designed to utilize dead and dying trees for their commercial value before rot and insects render them worthless. Two vistas to the west were created by making two small, pie-shaped clear-cuts into the corridor, which actually stop short of the trail. If it is agreed that these man-made vistas are successful, it is possible that more will be incorporated when planning future cuts.

Thirty minutes from the Stony Brook Trail there is a definite trail to the left. The white-marked Appalachian Trail is routed to the right and climbs uphill on a rocky path. The alternative trail rejoins the correct route farther on and offers an easier path to the same point. Fifteen minutes more, and the first sighting of the Normanook Fire Tower is obtained. The tower is reached by a short climb on some rock slabs. A few yards after beginning the ascent, look to the right to find a green marker on a tree (sometimes obscured by new leaf growth). This spot marks the beginning of the Tower Trail, to be followed on the way out.

Normanook Fire Tower is manned during times of greatest fire hazard, although the range of visibility is only about thirty miles. It is well worth climbing the six flights of steps (at your own risk) to the top of the tower, though the sight of New York City is barred by distant hills. There is an exceptionally long picnic table at Normanook where the weary traveler can rest.

Backtrack to the beginning of the Tower Trail; turn left and then immediately right across a large rock slab to the footway on the opposite side. There are no markers actually on the rock. Caution should be exercised, for this trail travels downhill over highly polished boulders that are slippery even when dry. The path switchbacks steeply downhill towards the left, levels out on a dirt section for a while, and continues to descend until it reaches Sunrise Mountain Road about fifteen minutes after leaving the fire tower.

Go straight across Sunrise Mountain Road, angling slightly to the right, and re-enter the woods. For a short way, the trail descends, then immediately enters a low-lying area with many wet sections, some of them requiring considerable detours or stepping-stone stream crossings. In spring, this part of the woods is carpeted with the common blue violet. In addition, keep a look out for the tiny, magenta-colored flowers of the fringed polygala; the flowers resemble a tiny, tailless airplane and flourish in rich, moist woodlands such as this area. If the leaves are off the trees, it is possible to see a magnificent stand of red pines to the left of the trail. The next stream encountered is deep and must be crossed on stepping stones. Shortly after passing an old wall, a wide T-junction is reached where brown, two dark green, and light green markers on a large tree opposite the emergence of the Tower Trail are seen. There is a slight confusion of markers at this junction. In addition to the markers already identified, there are brown and light green markers on a tree to the left, and two dark green ones on a tree to the right.

Turn left onto this wide woods road, enjoy the flat, easy walking through deciduous trees on the left-hand side and evergreens on the right, and follow the mixture of brown and dark and light green markers. A short distance along

View from Sunrise Mountain.

this woods road are two enormous lilac trees on the right. This square, grassy area is the site of the old Coursen subsistence farm, abandoned in the late 1920s or early 1930s, and used as a ranger station until the late 1950s when it was demolished. A few steps down the road on the opposite side of the clearing, where the brook is running, look for the foundations of the old milk house where milk and other perishables were kept cold. All that remains now is a square hole supported on one side by a cement slab.

Shortly after passing the site of the old farmhouse, the junction with the Courson Trail is reached. Do not go straight ahead but turn right, noting that the blue markers of the Courson Trail have been added to the existing dark green, light green, and brown ones. Walk on the wide road up the slight incline, on the right, passing first the light green loop and then the red trail on which you began the hike. Walk back down to the car.

SJG

Tillman Ravine

Total distance: 1 mile
Hiking time: 30 to 40 minutes
Vertical rise: 200 feet
Rating: Easy
Maps: USGS Culvers Gap; NYNJTC North Kittatinny Trails
#17; WB #17; HRM #52B; DEP Tillman Ravine Stokes State
Forest Booklet

Stokes State Forest (RR 2, Box 260, Branchville, NJ 07826; 201-948-3820) has cabins available for rent in addition to campsites. The Tillman Ravine expedition is gentle enough to be walked in sneakers and makes an admirable follow-up trip to a more strenuous hike undertaken the previous day, such as that in Stokes State Forest. The ravine is an exceptionally versatile area, attractive in all seasons. When the rhododendrons are blooming, it is a delight, and it is utterly fascinating in winter when ice transforms the stream. Tillman Ravine is maintained as a natural area, and several bridges have been constructed to make walking easier. The temperature in the ravine itself can be several degrees colder than at the parking lot, especially in summer, and the change can be noticeably distinct during the tour. Tillman Brook rises from a spring along the side of the Kittatinny Mountains about 1.5 miles east of this gorge, which it has created along the joints and beds of the shale bedrock.

To reach the area, drive in a northerly direction on US 206 past the entry sign to Stokes State Forest. This sign is 3 miles northwest of Branchville, New Jersey, and 10 miles south of Milford, Pennsylvania. Take the next left turn at the wooden sign towards the 4H camp and the Sakawawin Boy Scout Camp. Continue towards Wallpack Center on Struble and Dimon roads to the first parking lot for Tillman Ravine. The distance from US 206 is approximately 4 miles.

Face the wooden notice board and enter the woods to the right down three or four stone steps and onto level ground. The path is wide, travels through large evergreens, and is intermittently bordered by logs. The American chestnut was destroyed by a blight that was first discovered in 1904 in the New York Zoological Park. Stumps in this area are sprouting, but, although the root of the tree is not affected by the blight, the new growth will be destroyed before it reaches any size. The American chestnut is a particularly decay-resistant tree whose timber was very valuable, and, unfortunately, so far no remedy has been found for the blight.

A short way along the path, a tree has fallen over a rhododendron, which is still

Tillman Brook.

growing strongly, illustrating the tenacity of natural things. Some of the rhododendrons are large and form arches over the path. The trail descends gently, and to the right the remains of an old water system are visible. At the bottom of the incline there are seven or eight rock steps to climb with two dead trees at the top of the flight, and from here on it is possible to hear the sound of the water. Watch down the gully to the left, through the huge hemlocks, to catch the first glimpse of Tillman Brook.

The U-turn for the return journey connects from the left, and the next trail to the right, encountered almost imme-

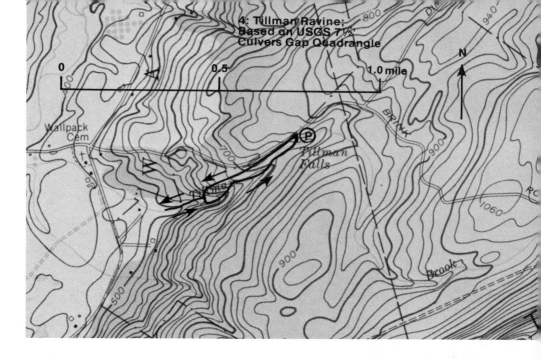

diately, should be ignored as it leads to the second parking lot. Continue slightly downhill on a trail about seventy-five feet above large rhododendrons and the brook, until the gradient becomes steeper and leads down to water level. There are several large blowdowns, and it is easy to walk closer to admire the rushing stream.

The route now climbs a natural rock wall, made interesting by the trees growing from it, and traverses over to the Lower Falls and the pothole called the Teacup. Many violets and ferns grow amongst the boulders, which provide good seating for admiring the rush of the water. Potholes such as this one are formed by the swirling action of the water as it scours away the rock walls with stones and sand caught in the current.

Retrace your footsteps across the wall and up the hill to where the trail down which you came forks. Take the right-hand turn down into the ravine and notice the change in temperature. The first bridge across the water is in an area of extreme wind damage, with at least one large tree felled across the ravine. Rhododendrons and hemlocks both like an acid soil with cool and moist temperatures and thrive in this ravine.

The walk is against the flow of the water, so the many cascades and rock formations are distinctly seen. Watch for the unusual fungus called varnish conk, which is aptly named and normally grows on fallen hemlocks. There are a few stepping stones to cross in the vicinity of a geological formation called an anticline, caused by slippage or pressure. After the last stream crossing, the trail bears right and up about a dozen stone slab steps, moves away from the water, levels out, and parallels the stream until turning left towards the parking lot. The hemlocks now give way to a stand of mixed red and white pine, planted by the Civilian Conservation Corps in 1932. The constant water movement is so captivating that repeating this walk in the opposite direction gives a completely different perspective.

SJG

5

Rattlesnake Swamp to Catfish Pond

Total distance: 5 miles
Hiking time: 3.5 hours
Vertical rise: 500 feet
Rating: Moderate
Maps: NYNJTC South Kittatinny Trails #16; WB #16; HRM
 #43; NPS Millbrook Area Trails map; USGS Flatbrookville

This loop hike in the heart of the Kittatinnies skirts the edge of a swamp, passes a lake, and then climbs to an excellent ridge overlook. The area is underused, if anything, and, if hiking during the week, the chance of encountering others is minimal. Though you will probably not see a rattlesnake (which are on the endangered species list and very rare), you should prepare for a very rocky trail by wearing sturdy boots.

From exit 12 on I-80, take County Road 521 north to Blairstown. After about 5 miles, you'll come to a junction with NJ 94. Make a left here and, after another .2 mile, turn right at the blinker. Drive through part of Blairstown on Bridge Street—do not make the sharp right on 521. When you come to the end of Bridge Street, at the top of a sharp rise, bear right and then make the next left. This road, the Millbrook–Blairstown Road (County Road 602), will take you in 6.2 miles to a trailhead for the Appalachian Trail (AT), which is at the top of the ridge. You'll see the ridge and the fire

Catfish Pond.

tower looming in front of you as you approach the area. Parking for a few cars can be found near the gate on the left side of the road. Additional parking is located on the right about 150 yards west, in a small area just off the road. Start the hike at the gate, heading south on the Appalachian Trail.

Begin hiking south on a gravel road, following the white markers of the Appalachian Trail. Pass an AT trail sign and register and, after that, cross a small brook. In an area of many clearings and tent sites, the gravel road veers to the right, entering a corridor through a jungle of immense rhododendrons. Rattlesnake Swamp appears on your right with its hemlock, mosses, and skunk cabbage. Take note where the Appalachian Trail turns left off the gravel road, heading uphill through the rhododendrons. Continue straight ahead, past Rattlesnake Springs on the left, and look for the orange markers of the Rattlesnake Swamp Trail. At a signed junction, the orange markers will lead you to the right, off the gravel road and onto a cut footpath. The footing, typical of trails on the Kittatinny Ridge, becomes extremely rocky almost immediately.

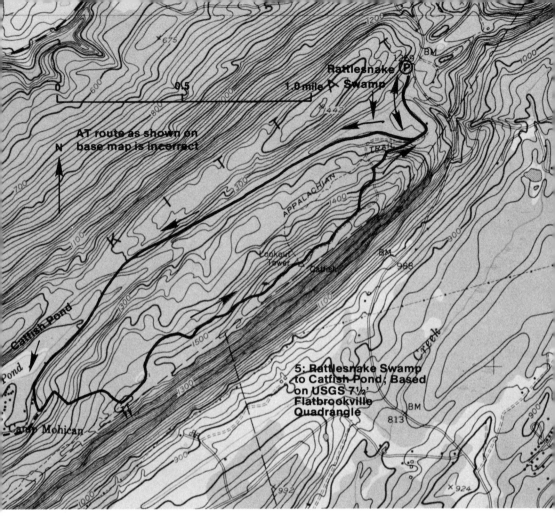

The map image contains the following labels:

- ×675
- 0   0.5   1.0 mile
- **AT route as shown on base map is incorrect**
- N
- Rattlesnake Swamp
- BM
- 1443
- APPALACHIAN
- 1400
- Lookout Tower
- Catfish
- BM
- 986
- Catfish Pond
- Pond
- **5: Rattlesnake Swamp to Catfish Pond, Based on USGS 7½' Flatbrookville Quadrangle**
- BM
- 813
- Camp Mohican
- ×992
- ×924

The Rattlesnake Swamp Trail continues to the left of, and slightly above, Rattlesnake Swamp. Some sections are deep and dark, dominated by hemlock and other shade plants, while other sections, with dead trees and high ferns, are open to the sun. As you leave the swamp, the trail, now traversing thick mountain laurel growth, enters a deep hemlock grove. Farther along, the footing becomes mossy and, in places, quite wet. Cross over a small brook and begin to climb toward higher ground. Don't be surprised if you startle a deer in this section, sending it crashing through the brush. After a stretch of much dryer woods, the trail descends and crosses a small brook twice. Immediately after the second crossing, notice a large swamp, part of the drainage that feeds Catfish Pond, to your right. After about forty-five minutes to an hour of walking, Catfish Pond appears through the trees on your right.

As you walk past the northern end of the pond, enjoy the views of lily-covered water against the steep western banks, some of which are completely bare of foliage due to rock slides. The sounds of frogs fill the air in spring and summer. The trail follows an old road lined with both low and highbush blueberries. The highbush blueberries, ripe in late July and early August, are delicious. Catfish Pond is the centerpiece of Camp Mohican, which has several buildings and is leased from the government by a state college. Near the camp is a swimming area, the water here being free from plant life, deep, clear, and clean.

The trail will gradually veer away from the pond and soon come to a junction where a sign indicates a turn to the left. After only a few hundred feet, the orange markers will direct you to turn left again onto a grassy road leading uphill. Just after the road swings to the right, the trail turns off the road onto a footpath and begins to climb the Kittatinny Ridge in earnest. The ascent is quite steep and takes you over large rocks and through clumps of laurel. After a few minutes of work, there is a temporary respite where the trail levels off before it resumes climbing, this time not so steeply. After meandering through another level section, the trail climbs once more, leading to the flat, level summit of the Kittatinny Ridge. Here, in dense blueberry bushes, a vast vista of forest and farmland is seen through the trees. Just a few steps ahead is a junction with the Appalachian Trail and a magnificent view, over cliffs, to the east and south.

After resting from the climb and enjoying the spectacular view, turn left and head north, following the white markers of the AT. The trail twists and winds along the broad summit, through an open area of dead trees killed by gypsy moths. To the right are vistas out to the horizon. After about a half hour of walking, arrive at the Catfish Pond fire tower.

Currently, the fire tower is not manned due to radio frequency radiation. The antenna for a local radio station was placed here by arrangement with the government, yet its signals endanger anyone occupying the observation cabin at the top of the tower. A forest ranger explained that, even in times of severe fire danger, the tower must remain unmanned until some kind of metal shield, which will supposedly deflect the radiation, is installed. He also explained that if the radio transmission was ceased during a fire alert, the radio station may have legal grounds to sue for lost air time. In front of the fire tower is a sign that reads, "Closed to public—Warning: RF Radiation."

Continue straight ahead on the AT, which now follows the grassy utility road allowing access to the fire tower. Watch where the AT veers off to the left from this service road and begins to descend the ridge through an open area covered with blueberry bushes and ferns. The AT joins the service road again, now gravel, for a few hundred feet before turning right, back into the woods on a cut trail. After a descent through dark woods on a very rocky trail, come to a T-junction and bear right. After another 200 yards, the AT joins the gravel road once again, this time near Rattlesnake Springs, which you passed early in the hike. A right turn here will lead, via the AT, to the gate and your car.

BCS

Mount Tammany

Total distance: 4 miles
Hiking time: 3 hours
Vertical rise: 1,200 feet
Rating: Moderately strenuous
Maps: USGS Portland, Bushkill; NYNJTC South Kittatinny Trails
  #15; WB #15; HRM #43; NPS Kittatinny Point Area Trails
  map

Overlooking the Delaware River on the New Jersey side of the Delaware Water Gap stands Mount Tammany. This mountain, a portion of the Kittatinny Ridge and located within Worthington State Forest, offers one of the steepest climbs in all of New Jersey as well as spectacular views from its summit. Because of its easy access from I-80, the trail to the summit is heavily used year round, though particularly so in summer. Also in the area is Dunfield Creek with its many falls and cascades, the Appalachian Trail, and Sunfish Pond, making this location a major natural area in the state.

To reach the trailhead, take I-80 west to the Delaware Water Gap. As the highway enters the gap itself, turn off to the right following signs to a rest area. If you miss this turnoff, take the next exit off the highway, the last exit in New Jersey, and follow signs to the Delaware Water Gap National Recreation Area Kittatinny Point Information Center (Bushkill, PA 18324; 201-496-4458). You will be able to find

The Delaware Water Gap.

the rest area by passing the visitors center, crossing back under I-80, and bearing right. The trailhead is in the rest area, not at the parking area for the Appalachian Trail and Sunfish Pond.

Begin the hike on the River Ridge (or Red-Dot) Trail, which leaves the rest area heading east. It is found on the far side of the parking area just to the left of a small cascade that flows during wet periods. The trail, marked with red/orange on white painted on trees, begins climbing almost immediately, a foreshadowing of things to come. After this brief elevation gain, the trail levels off, temporarily paralleling Dunfield Creek well below on the left. Where the trail turns sharply to the right, it begins a steady climb on a well-used, rocky path lined with evergreen hemlocks and rhododendrons. The sounds of the falls on Dunfield Creek, even further below now, are still heard in the distance. Watch for where the trail turns to the right, climbing over tilted but parallel beds of sedimentary rock.

After this last climb, you'll arrive at the first of several overlooks. Here, at the edge of a steep cliff and exposed to the

6: Mount Tammany
Based on USGS 7½'
Portland &
Stroudsburg PA/NJ
Quadrangles

elements, cedar trees struggle for survival. Below, looking south, the Delaware Water Gap opens in front of you. Mount Minsi, on the Pennsylvania side, is to the right, and Mount Tammany, to the left. Mount Minsi, which rises 1,463 feet above sea level, is named after the Indians who lived in the area. Mount Tammany, at 1,527 feet, is named after the Lenni-Lenape chief, Tamenund.

The Delaware Water Gap, certainly one of the scenic wonders of New Jersey, is a deep, twelve hundred-foot gorge carved by the waters of the Delaware River through the long, wall-like Kittatinny Ridge. Back in Cretaceous times, roughly 100 million years ago, the Water Gap did not exist. The entire area, which was once very mountainous, had been worn down by erosion to a flat plain that gently sloped toward the Atlantic Ocean some forty miles away. Streams, which drained

the land, meandered through this landscape on their way to the sea. In the late Cretaceous period, the land began to rise, and the streams began cutting deeper channels through this landscape.

As the land rose, the ancestral Delaware River found itself confronted with a major barrier, the relatively resistant rock that makes up the Kittatinny Ridge. This rock, known as Shawangunk conglomerate, occurs as a horizontal layer, except in a few places where it dips down and then rises back to its former level. One of these dips occurs at the Water Gap. Also at this location, the ridge crest axis is fractured, the New Jersey crest lying about seven hundred feet from the crest in Pennsylvania. Because of these structural weaknesses, the river successfully maintained its course through this particular section of the Kittatinny Ridge. Today, the river continues to cut and remove rock as the land continues to rise slowly.

After skirting a few more viewpoints, the trail crosses a brook and then passes, on the left, a reliable spring. After this brief respite, the trail once again begins seriously climbing the mountain ridge. Because of the rocky terrain, climbing this section is difficult in any season but can be particularly challenging, and even dangerous, in icy conditions. First a boulder field is crossed, and then, through a beautiful forest of hemlock and rhododendron, a steep rock slab must be navigated. One must use both feet and hands in many places while still paying attention to the markers so as not to lose the trail. After leveling off temporarily through a more open forest, the trail begins climbing again on a rocky footpath high on the ridge. From here to the summit, the forest is sparse, offering little protection from the winds. Along the way, a cedar-lined viewpoint is found on the right.

Just before reaching the summit, notice that the area to the left is very open, a fire having occurred here some years ago. The former oak forest is being replaced by thick laurel growth. Finally, the summit is reached. Here the oak forest stops at the edge of a twelve hundred-foot cliff overlooking the Delaware River. Only scrub oak and pitch pine survive in this rocky, exposed environment. At the summit area, walk to the right and down over the exposed rocks, which offer the hiker an incredibly expansive view west to Mount Minsi and the Blue Mountain Ridge behind it. The Pocono Plateau of Pennsylvania stretches out to the horizon in the north, and the plains of the Great Valley and, beyond it, the Reading Prong section of the highlands extend to the horizon in the south. If one walks down the exposed rocks of the summit, the Indian Head profile, located on a portion of the cliff below and to the north of the viewpoint, may be seen staring out over the river.

From the summit, follow the trail, now marked with blue, away from the overlook area. Now heading in a northeasterly direction, the trail meanders along the summit ridge for about a quarter of a mile and then, near a viewpoint through the trees to the east, bears sharply left. Do not continue straight ahead on the grey markers. There is a sign posted here indicating that you are on the Blue-Dot Trail.

After a long, steady descent from the ridge over rocks, the trail swings to the left towards the river, following a nearly level walkway. Finally, after a long walk, the Blue-Dot Trail arrives at Dunfield Creek near one of its many falls. The trail bears left and then right, crossing the creek on a wooden bridge. Here, in this dark hemlock gorge, are numerous cascades and plunge pools, the white water creating a sharp contrast to the dark rock it glides over. After following the right bank of the creek for a short distance, the Blue-Dot Trail reaches its terminus as shown by three markers on a tree. From here, follow the white markers of the Appalachian Trail downhill along the stream, and cross the creek again on a wooden bridge. After crossing the bridge, leave the AT, which bears to the right, and follow the pathway out to the parking area. To reach the rest area and your car, walk along the parking area keeping to the left. Look for and take a very small footpath that leaves the area heading south just past the last parking spot. This small path parallels the road below it on the right and leads to the rest area and its picnic tables.

BCS

7

Appalachian Trail Backpack

Total time allowed: 3 days, 2 nights
Total distance: 26.75 miles
Hiking time: 17 hours
Rating: Strenuous
Maps: USGS Portland/Bushkill/Flatbrook/Culvers Gap; NYNJTC
   North and South Kittatinny Trails #15, #16, and #17; WB
   #15, #16, & #17; HRM #43; HRM #52B

Most hikers are aware that the Appalachian Trail is a marked footpath extending two thousand miles north from Springer Mountain, Georgia, to Mount Katahdin, Maine. The summer of 1987 marked the fiftieth anniversary of the completion of the Appalachian Trail. The last section to be completed was on a remote ridgeline in Maine between Spaulding and Sugarloaf mountains and was cut by a crew from the Civilian Conservation Corps. Trail markers are white rectangles, with side trails to water, viewpoints, and shelters marked in blue.

The Appalachian Trail is often rerouted, and if there is a discrepancy between the markers, the guide, or the map, follow the markers. This backpacking trip begins at the Delaware Water Gap and follows the ridge of the Kittatinny Mountains, generally north through Worthington State Forest and the Delaware Water Gap National Recreation Area. The terrain is rocky, and it is recommended that sturdy hiking boots be worn instead of sneakers. The hike is rated as strenuous because of the need for a backpack.

Squirrels and chipmunks are numerous and are always attracted to campsites where food scraps are available. Their sharp teeth can do a tremendous amount of damage to tents and packs. To avoid such damage, whenever the campsite is unattended and at night put all food into one, large plastic bag and string it on a line between two trees, remembering that, because these little animals are adept climbers, the bag should be a minimum of six feet away from the nearest tree or large branch.

Most natural water sources along the trail are liable to be contaminated and should be purified before use, either by boiling, by filtering, by chemical treatment, or by a combination of these purification methods. Open ground fires are not permitted in the Delaware Water Gap National Recreation Area, so a portable camp stove is essential. Camping is permitted along the trail with certain restrictions, and you should check on regulations with the ranger at the Delaware Water Gap Visitor Center before setting out.

Because the term "rattlesnake" is used

frequently in these parts, it is assumed that timber rattlesnakes are numerous, but, in fact, this snake is on the New Jersey list of endangered and rare wildlife species. Do not meddle with any snake encountered during the expedition since most retreat quickly unless interfered with.

This hike requires transportation at each end. One car should be left at Culvers Gap, at the parking lot on Sunrise Mountain Road. To reach this parking lot from US 206, turn east onto Upper North Shore Road just north of Culvers Lake, 3.4 miles northwest of Branchville, and then immediately left onto Sunrise Mountain Road. The parking lot itself is at the first bend on the left-hand (west) side of the road. When cars are needed at both ends of a hike, the best arrangement is to leave the majority of cars at the end point, using as few cars as possible to transport all the hikers back to the other trailhead. The other car should be positioned at the Delaware Water Gap, either at the Delaware Water Gap National Recreation Information Center (Bushkill, Pennsylvania 18324; 717-588-6637), south of I-80 at the gap or at the Dunnfield Creek Natural Area. The Dunnfield Creek Natural Area lot is often crowded, but can be reached to the east of the information center by turning left at the underpass under I-80 and making a second left onto a paved road. Go to the parking lot on the right with the sign "Dunnfield Creek Natural Area."

First Day

Delaware Water Gap to Catfish Fire

Total distance first day: 11 miles
Hiking time: 7 hours
Vertical rise: 1,000 feet

Hoist your backpack and enter the woods at the far end of the parking lot for the Dunnfield Creek Natural Area. Follow the stream's right bank until the trail crosses a substantial wooden bridge and parallels the stream on the opposite side. The trail leads steadily upwards, away from the stream, through a mixture of deciduous and coniferous trees and ferns. Look to the right where distinct layers of rock can be seen on the opposite bank of the stream. Look down, as you climb high above the stream, to numerous pools and waterfalls and enjoy this delightfully cool section.

Follow the signs to Campsite #1 and Campsite #2, although these sites are too close to the start of this trip to be useful for overnight accommodation. In a half mile the woods road forks. There is a metal sign with a painted map at this junction, and the blue trail to Mount Tammany leads away to the right. Follow the left-hand trail through small, sweet chestnut trees, which will probably not reach maturity because of the blight that practically destroyed these sweet chestnuts in the 1930s. The blue trail and Dunnfield Creek are visible below.

Still climbing, the woods road changes dramatically into a rocky trail, and at 1.5 miles reaches the intersection of the Beulahland Trail. Campsite #1 is a half mile to the left of our trail, which continues to climb until leveling out, paralleling the ridge of the Kittatinny Mountains to the right. By now you have been on the trail for about an hour, and after another thirty minutes of walking through an open area on a rocky trail with tall mountain laurel, the intersection for Campsite #2 is reached. Another forty minutes brings you to the southern tip of Sunfish Pond. Just at the left of the trail here is a stone monument dated 1970. Walk straight ahead to the shore of Sunfish Pond, then turn west to follow the trail around the left-hand shore. The no camping regulation is strictly enforced at Sunfish Pond.

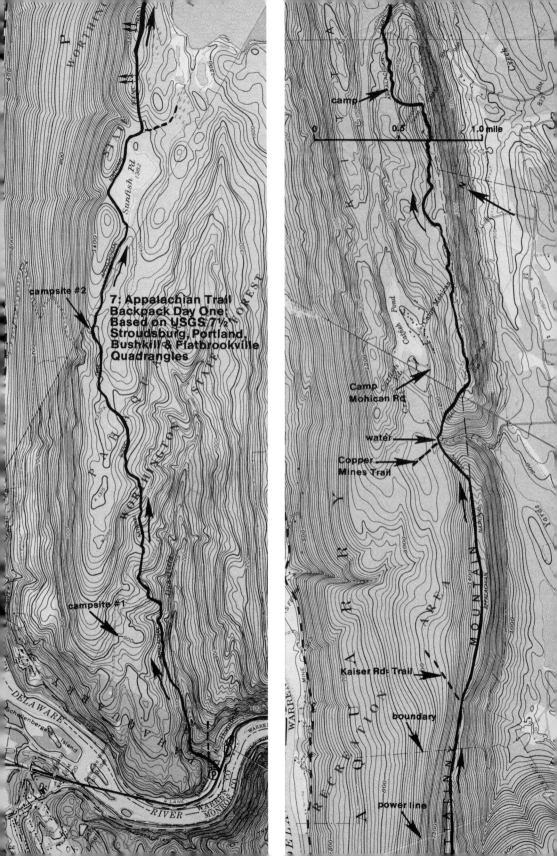

7: Appalachian Trail
Backpack Day One:
Based on USGS 7½
Stroudsburg, Portland,
Bushkill & Flatbrookville
Quadrangles

campsite #2

campsite #1

camp

0   0.5   1.0 mile

Camp
Mohican Rd

water

Copper
Mines Trail

Kaiser Rd. Trail

boundary

power line

The center of much controversy, this glacial lake is 1,380 feet above sea level and is regarded a natural, geological oddity. In 1954, six thousand acres containing the lake were acquired by the state for $420,000 from the Charles Worthington family in the hope that this old mountain estate would be preserved in its natural state. However, the Department of Conservation and Economic Development sold 715 acres, including the pond, to power companies in 1961 for $250,000 and some land, without the knowledge or approval of the legislature. A private citizen, Casey Kays, and a conservation group, the Lenni-Lenape League, joined to agitate for the return of the illegally sold acreage and pond. Their efforts included letter writing, publication and distribution of fliers, and pilgrimages to Sunfish Pond itself, but they achieved no success except to bring publicity to the situation.

In 1968, when it seemed that the New Jersey legislature was about to pass a law requiring repurchase of the disputed acreage, the power companies donated the pond and some surrounding acreage back to the state and, at the same time, unveiled plans for pumped water storage on Kittatinny Ridge about one thousand feet from the pond itself. Three hundred seventy acres east of the pond still have not been returned, and there is still concern that these acres are required to ensure that the pond's natural watershed is protected.

The trail is now rocky and narrow. It shortly crosses a small outlet from the pond, climbs above the pond's level, turns right, and descends again to the water's edge. Many rocky areas on the shore of the pond invite the traveler to rest. In one area, we came across a stony beach where industrious folk had built many Stonehenge-like edifices. This nondestructive graffiti must have kept someone busy for many hours.

At the end of Sunfish Pond, the trail moves back deeper into the woods, and a dependable spring can be found 600 feet to the left of the trail. In this section, there are two blue-marked trails, one entering the main trail from the right and another from the left. Watch also for black markings on a boulder in the middle of the trail, signaling the way to the orange trail and to "WSF Pond."

The trail levels out after a short climb, turns left and descends again through magnificent mountain laurel. Two and a half hours after the commencement of the hike and at about the 4.5-mile point, cross a small brook. After climbing a short way, it is possible to make a detour to the left of the trail to see the Delaware River and the Pennsylvania Mountains. Within thirty minutes, the trail is crossed by a power line, and, slightly further ahead where the trail reaches the crest of the ridge, there are views in both directions. Walking slightly to the left improves the view of the river and Pennsylvania. Directly ahead, Catfish Fire Tower is visible, and to the right, Yards Creek pumped water storage ponds can be seen.

The Yards Creek Pumped Storage Electric Generating Station began operation in 1965, and the station is owned jointly by Jersey Central Power and Light Company and Public Service Electric and Gas Company. The concept for this type of power generation was developed in 1947, but it was not until 1956, with the development of modern, large, reversible pump-turbines, that the project became feasible. The upper reservoir was created from two, small, swampy areas on the mountaintop, and the lower, about a mile east and approximately seven hundred feet below the upper reservoir, is located on Yards Creek (a small tributary of Paulins Kill, which flows into the Delaware).

The auxiliary reservoir, now part of a Boy Scout camping area, is situated just to the north of the lower reservoir.

The lower reservoir is the largest, and the three together cover 519 acres and hold almost 3.5 billion gallons of water. The reservoirs are connected by a pipeline (or penstock) that runs through a pumping–generating station on the lower reservoir level. The powerhouse holds the reversible pump–turbines, designed to act as pumps when operating in one direction and as turbines when operating in the other. The total plant generating capacity is 330,000 kilowatts. The water flows down from the upper reservoir to supply electricity at peak periods and is pumped back up in slack periods, so it is constantly reused. The only water lost is by evaporation and from being released downstream to maintain the flow in Yards Creek. Water is replaced when necessary from the auxiliary reservoir. The companies maintain an interesting facility for visitors to the generating center, including a picnic area and hiking trails.

The trail remains high on this slabby terrain for a short distance. The bow in the Delaware River, which is not visible from other places, can be seen from here, and on a clear day, the Catskills also can be seen. Just as the trail begins to drop, there is an Appalachian Trail sign on the boundary between Worthington State Forest and the Delaware Water Gap National Recreation Area. The sign is large and lists pointers on behavior while on the trail. The ridge is called Mount Mohican.

The trail continues downhill on the ridge, with glimpses of the views seen previously, until it reaches a sign for a spring on Old Kaiser Road. Continue ahead until Old Kaiser Road turns to the left and the Appalachian Trail makes a right. After about a mile from the right

turn, the trail becomes rockier and, descending steeply through mountain laurel, eventually reaches a stream crossing at Mohican Road. This stream is a dependable water source. The distance walked is now about 9 miles, and as it will soon be time to make camp, water should be collected here for overnight use.

Coppermines Trail soon enters from the left. New Jersey claims the first copper mine opened in America, by Dutch settlers in the Kittatinny Mountains around 1640. The Coppermines Trail leads to a number of mines that can still be entered and explored by flashlight, but such explorations should not be attempted while on this hike.

Cross Mohican Road and immediately enter the opposite woods. The steep climb takes about ten to fifteen minutes before the trail emerges onto a ridge with a view of an agricultural valley to the right. This section of the trail is spectacular for it travels along the side of the ridge through cedar and scrub pines. There is a sharp drop-off, and looking back, Yards Creek Reservoir is visible in the distance. A short way along this ridge to the left is a sign for Rattlesnake Swamp Trail and another for Catfish Pond, only a half mile distant. The trail turns away from the ridge and climbs slightly towards the left, then descends and passes through a more open area with many dead trees.

After the trail leaves the ledges it passes areas that could be used for camping, but we recommend you proceed to the area just after Catfish Fire Tower, to be reached shortly. Catfish Fire Tower is sixty feet high, and it is well worth climbing the eight flights of stairs to the splendid 360-degree view. The elevation here is 1,565 feet, and it is possible to see the Catskills in the distance and, closer in, Sand Pond of Camp No-Be-Bo-Sco, Bergen Council, Boy Scouts of America.

From Catfish Fire Tower, the trail descends on a old jeep road towards the Millbrook–Blairstown Road. Shortly after leaving the fire tower is the place to seek the ideal campsite. There are many good sites both to the left and to the right of the jeep trail, but it is the responsibility of the camper to comply with the camping regulations.

Second day

Catfish Fire Tower to junction with trail to Buttermilk Falls

Total distance second day: 8 miles
Hiking time: 5 hours
Vertical rise: 1,000 feet

Still heading north, the trail leaves the jeep road, turns left, and descends slightly on a rocky path overlooking a different valley from the one seen previously, until it rejoins the jeep road. Once again, the trail leaves the jeep road, veering to the left and reentering the woods to the right through a lush section. At the foot of a steep descent on a narrow, rocky trail winding through tall mountain laurel, turn right at the power line and proceed through an extensive rhododendron thicket onto a gravel road. Rattlesnake Spring is just a few feet to the left along this gravel road. This spring is delightful and can be depended upon for water for the day's hike. Walk back to where the Appalachian Trail joins the wide gravel road and continue until it shortly makes a sharp turn to the left. The paved Millbrook–Blairstown Road is reached within approximately thirty-five minutes of leaving the campsite in the Catfish Fire Tower location.

Turn left on the paved road and, after a very short walk, enter the woods again on the right where there is a sign-in register a short distance in. Take the left fork after signing in. At the beginning of this section, the trail is wide and passes a swamp on the left. The path is located high on a ridge above this wet area, with glimpses of an even higher ridge on the right-hand side. After about ten minutes of walking, watch for a sharp turn to the left detouring around the northern end of the swamp, away from the road. The trail becomes narrower, then opens out at the top of a short climb. There is a rocky bank on the left-hand side, and a careful watch is necessary for a sharp right turn leading steeply uphill. This turn was obscured by a blowdown at the time of this writing, and if it is missed, the power lines soon come into view. It is not necessary to backtrack, however. By bushwhacking underneath the power lines to the top of the hill, the trail is easily found again on the right-hand side. Views of the Wallkill Valley and Pocono Plateaus are visible from the clearing at the top of the hill. Several small cedars are scattered around this viewpoint, and the power lines march down the hill with Sand Pond (Camp No-Be-Bo-Sco, Bergen Council, Boy Scouts of America) visible below.

The view to the east continues as the route follows the ridge. Markers are not clear in this section. The main trail is shortly joined from the right by one marked with a mix of diamond-shaped red and white metal emblems. Fairview Lake is visible through the trees to the right. The wide, rocky road is high on a ridge, and very shortly, passes a large boulder on the left, from which views of the valley to the west are available. There is another sign-in register at this point.

After about 5 miles of walking, a paved road with a metal barrier is reached, Flat-

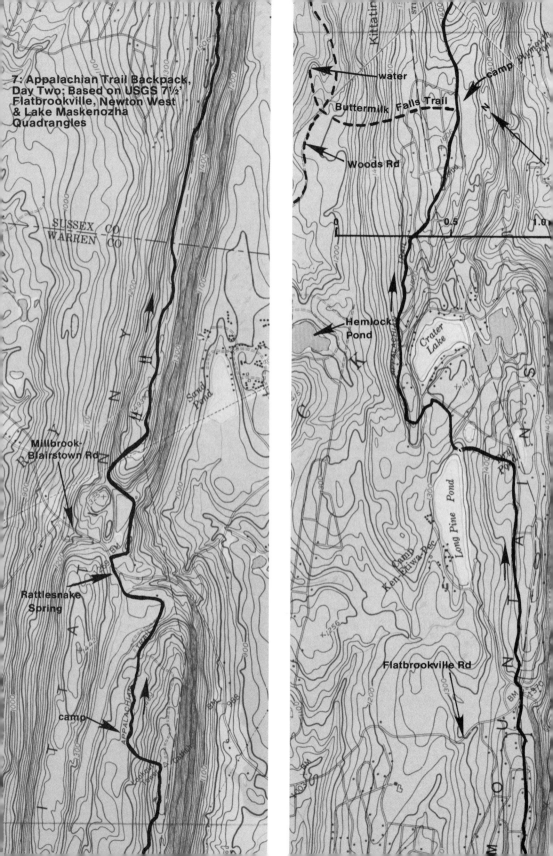

7: Appalachian Trail Backpack,
Day Two; Based on USGS 7½'
Flatbrookville, Newton West
& Lake Maskenozha
Quadrangles

SUSSEX CO
WARREN CO

Millbrook-
Blairstown Rd

Rattlesnake
Spring

camp

Sand
Pond

water

camp

Buttermilk Falls Trail

Woods Rd

Hemlock
Pond

Crater
Lake

0   0.5   1.0

Long Pine Pond

Camp
Ken-Etiwa-Pec

Flatbrookville Rd

brookville Road, and you should turn right, walk a few steps down the road, and turn left into an area of small white pines. Two or three minutes later, a woods road linking two paved roads is crossed. Walk straight ahead and register on the left.

The trail is located in a pretty area here. It is narrower and is cut through a well-wooded area with mountain laurel. The route is clearly marked and descends steeply through rock slabs until it reaches a rock-strewn bog on the right. Looking back and to the left through the trees, it is possible to see Long Pine Pond. Cross the gravel road by bearing slightly to the right and reenter the woods on the left, observing the outcrop of rock to the left up which the trail is routed. At the top of this escarpment, another gravel road is crossed, and there is the reward of a good view to the west. Within a few minutes, a view of Crater Lake (or Lake Success) can be obtained by taking a blue-blazed trail to the right. A metal post is embedded in the rock at this viewpoint.

The walking is very easy on a wide, grassy trail that soon makes a sharp left turn. Notice the pipe to the left of this turn, which indicates there may have been a spring here at one time. Views of Hemlock Pond are available at this point, and the orange trail to Hemlock Pond is marked practically at the crest of the rise.

This attractive section is still on a slightly uphill gradient, with more views of Crater Lake to the right. The trail is on a ledge, with the ground dropping down to the left and rising to the right—a rock slab slope dotted with white pines. Two other trails join the main trail here, one from the right and another from the left, and in a short time there is a marked left turn onto a gravel road, followed within 100 yards by the blue-blazed trail to Buttermilk Falls on the left. The trail is

marked by a wooden sign on the left of the trail, which indicates that the route leads to a woods road in a half mile and to Buttermilk Falls at 1.75 miles.

One of the many secluded and attractive campsites in this location should be chosen for the night. A prime site is found by proceeding down the Appalachian Trail approximately another 100 yards from the Buttermilk Falls sign and turning left onto a wide, grassy woods road. Within a minute, there is a delightful, flat, grassy opening with a beautiful white pine at each end. After setting up camp, water and a refreshing wash are available by taking a side trip to Buttermilk Falls. The trail to the falls is very steep, but, except in dry weather, it is not necessary to go all the way to the falls for water. Within ten minutes down the trail, a woods road is crossed, and within another five, the sound of water is heard. Where the trail goes downhill and makes a sharp left turn, go straight ahead a few more yards to a group of two or three pools of water. If these pools should be dry, follow the streambed down to find a suitable water-gathering spot. On the way down, the trail passes through several open blueberry patches, which in season might provide dessert.

If you prefer not to add this side trip for water to the day's walk but to camp nearer to the water supply, continue for approximately another mile until the trail descends to a stream crossing, where dependable water is available about 200 feet down a blue-blazed trail. The beautiful campsite described above, at the head of the Buttermilk Falls Trail, however, might make the extra effort to get water very worthwhile.

Third day

Buttermilk Falls Trail to NJ 206 at
Culvers Gap

Total distance third day: 7.75 miles
Hiking time: 5 hours
Vertical rise: 800 feet

After leaving camp, the gravel road
bends to the right, leaving the Appalachian Trail to turn left on a narrow footpath into the woods. Two good views
west to the Poconos are available here
(one of them via a blue-blazed trail on
the left) before the trail descends steeply
through a rocky section. At the next fork,
turn right and cross a stream (the alternate camping spot past the Buttermilk
Falls area).

The trail now goes through a mature
hemlock and sheep laurel grove. It
makes a sharp left turn a few minutes after the stream crossing to begin the
climb up Rattlesnake Mountain. This section has been burned out and conse-
quently is quite open. Rattlesnake
Mountain was once called Columbus
Mountain and is 1,492 feet in elevation.
As the mountain is approached, the route
up through the boulders and white pines
is seen more clearly, and during the ascent, good views become more and
more apparent to the left until the entire
panorama is visible from the summit. This
vista includes Normanook Fire Tower and
High Point. Walk slightly to the right to
reach the highest point, where, unfortunately, there is a telephone pole and
cement work on the rocks.

Ignore both the blue trail leading back
toward the recent climb and the woods
road and continue northwards, gently descending on a narrow, rocky trail through
many small pine trees towards a short
swampy section, easily crossed by rock-
hopping. This swamp is approximately 2
miles from the Buttermilk Falls area.

Within a half mile, the trail has climbed to
a rocky area where it turns right onto an
old dirt road and begins to descend
again. Quick Pond and Mecca Lake can
be seen. This road is wide and obviously
used by four-wheeled vehicles.

Just to the left of the road are cages
containing two types of well-fed and watered pigeons, a blind, and evidence of
trapping. This facility is operated in cooperation with the US Fish and Wildlife Service and the New Jersey Division of Fish
and Game. It is manned by members of
the New Jersey Raptor Association and
Len Soucy of the Raptor Trust, who oper-
ate two banding stations during the fall
when raptors are migrating in great numbers along the Kittatinny Ridge. Birds of
prey with strong, hooked beaks and tal-
oned feet, such as hawks, eagles, fal-
cons, and owls, are included in the term
"raptor." Bald eagles can be found in winter in the Delaware Water Gap Natural
Recreation Area as they travel to more
southerly areas, leaving behind the
frozen lakes and rivers in the northern
United States and Canada where they
nested and spent the summer. The
pigeons are used to lure the raptors into
hanging and spring-loaded nets con-
trolled by tethers operated from the
blinds. When a raptor is entrapped, various physical records are made, it is
banded, and it is immediately released.
These banding stations on the Appalachian Trail have been in operation for
about fifteen years, and injuries or mortal-
ities, either to the pigeons or raptors, during banding operations are extremely
rare. Information from the banding operations is submitted to the Bird Banding
Laboratory operated in Maryland by the
US Fish and Wildlife Service. It is used to
identify migratory routes and wintering
concentrations of raptors to afford the
birds adequate protection.

When the road bears to the left, the

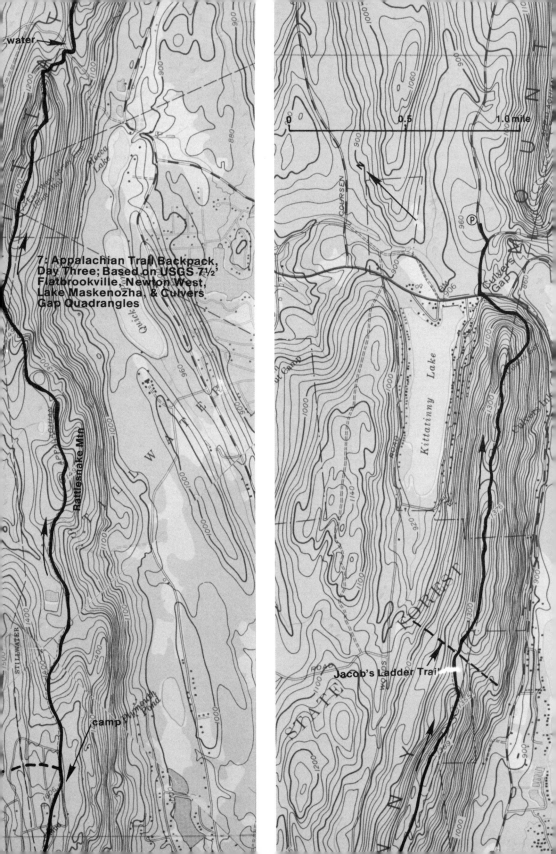

water →

7: Appalachian Trail Backpack,
Day Three; Based on USGS 7½'
Flatbrookville, Newton West,
Lake Maskenozha, & Culvers
Gap Quadrangles

Rattlesnake Mtn

camp

Kittatinny Lake

Culvers Gap

Jacob's Ladder Trail

STATE FOREST

0   0.5   1.0 mile

trail turns right and begins to climb through white pines. There are views to the left from the rock ledges, and at the top of the ridge, extensive views of the Wallpack Valley and the Poconos are obtainable before the trail moves back into the woods again on rocky terrain. This high area is commonly known as Blue Mountain, and the larger area of water glimpsed through the trees is Lake Owassa. This lake will be seen more clearly later on in the hike. The general direction is now downhill, more rapidly in the approach to Brink Road. As the trail leaves the wooded section, the next ascent can be seen ahead.

Brink Road is 4 miles from the Buttermilk Falls camping area. There is a shelter here with a spring, reached by a blue-blazed trail to the left of the road crossing. Uphill from Brink Road is a very pretty area with tall mountain laurel, white pines, massive rhododendrons, and hemlock. The climb is short, lasting only about ten minutes, and the trail remains on the crest of the ridge for a similar amount of time. Just before a rocky, wet area on the right of the main trail, watch for the first unmarked side trail leading to an overlook and, after about another half mile, for a second unmarked trail leading to an observation point of Lake Owassa.

The trail now alternately rises and falls until the final drop to US 206.

Jacob's Ladder Trail, with blue-silver markings, is reached after another half mile from the viewpoint of Lake Owassa. The first view of Culvers Lake, seen here through the trees to the right, is probably not available in summer when the trees are in full leaf. Nearing the end of the trip is a large, cleared area. From this vantage point, Culvers Fire Tower, Culvers Lake, and US 206 are apparent straight ahead and Lake Owassa, behind. The trail turns back into the woods, reaching another clearing with US 206 visible on the right-hand side, and emerges onto a gravel road. The route traverses the side of a hill, and care must be taken not to miss the turn to the right. Continuing on the gravel road will lead to US 206 but involves crossing private property.

Cross US 206, turn left for a few yards, and then turn right on Upper North Shore Road to reach your transportation in the parking lot on Sunrise Mountain Road. Walking a little farther on US 206 brings you to Worthington's Bakery. Their delicious products are highly recommended as a reward for your efforts.

SJG

Highlands Province

Hoeferlin Memorial Trail

Total distance: 13 miles
Hiking time: 7 hours
Vertical rise: 700 feet
Rating: Moderately strenuous
Maps: USGS Ramsey/Wanaque; NYNJTC North Jersey Trails
  #22; WB #23; HRM #15

The hike described here is almost entirely on the Hoeferlin Memorial Trail, although rerouting of this trail has recently been necessary at both ends. The southwestern section has been modified because of the construction of the I-287 extension from Montville to Suffern, and the northeastern part has been reduced because of a change in private ownership. The trail was originally called the Suffern–Midvale Trail, the name being changed in honor of well-known trailblazer and mapmaker William Hoeferlin. Bill Hoeferlin's interest was hiking and for over thirty years he was involved in many facets of his hobby. He was an avid trail maintainer and was the originator of the Hikers Region Maps, which he prepared and published, some of which are still available. Bill founded the Wanderbird Hiking Club and served the New York–New Jersey Conference in many capacities for over three decades. He conceived and published *Walking News*. This periodical, designed to keep the hiking public informed of trail modifications, included hike schedules and was the forerunner of today's publication the *Trail Walker* (New York–New Jersey Trail Con-

ference). He died in 1970, at age 72, while leading a small group of hikers on the trail.

Other trails used in this hike, in addition to the Hoeferlin Memorial Trail, are the Silver and Red/Silver Trails within the Ramapo Valley County Reservation trail system, and, at the end of the hike, the blue-marked MacEvoy Trail. The land on which this trail system is built was originally settled around 1720, after it was bought from the Indians. Since its purchase through the Green Acres program and federal funds in 1972, it has been administered by the Bergen County Park Commission. The end of the hike follows a long strip on the ridge approximately six miles long, purchased in 1976 from the estate of the late Clifford F. MacEvoy by the state of New Jersey, also using Green Acres and federal money. Mr. MacEvoy was a contractor involved in large public works, which included work on the Wanaque Reservoir.

During the hike, the trail leaves the Ramapo Valley County Reservation (PO Box 225, Oakland, New Jersey 07436; 201-337-0960), proceeds through Ringwood State Park, crossing land belonging to the Boy Scouts of America, and, finally, traverses the eastern section of the Ramapo Mountain State Forest. The Ramapo Mountains, though not especially high, rise no more than eight hundred feet above the bordering valleys of the Wanaque River on the northwest and the Ramapo River on the southeast. The Ramapo River Valley was the site of a trading post, established as early as 1710, which attracted squatters to this location. The ancestry of the Ramapo Mountain people has been, since colonial days, a mixture of Indians, blacks, and whites, resulting in their social isolation as a separate racial group and in their feeling that they are "different" from their neighbors. Today, they are a relatively small group of about 1,500 living in Mahwah and Ringwood, New Jersey, and Hillburn, New York.

This hike requires transportation at both ends of the trail. One car should be left at the Ramapo Valley County Reservation on the north side of US 202, approximately 2 miles from NJ 17 at Mahwah. The other car should be left at the Ramapo Mountain State Forest parking lot, accessed by turning north onto Skyline Drive from the junction of West Oakland Avenue and NJ 208. The parking lot is on the west side of Skyline Drive, 0.3 miles from that junction.

With your back to the road at the Ramapo Reservation parking lot, cross the blacktop and enter the woods at the lower left-hand corner of the parking lot. Look for three metal markers on a tree to the right of the footway leading through a gap in the fence. After a short distance through the woods there is a building and a water fountain to the right. Go straight across the road, past a small pond on the left. Camping is permitted here, and information is available from the Bergen County Park Commission at 201-646-2680. The route is on a wide, dirt road, which first crosses a wooden bridge over the Ramapo River and then immediately passes Scarlet Oak Pond on the right.

After reaching the end of the lake, the road becomes paved and climbs to the left. There is a dirt road on the right, which should be ignored, for the best route is the one that is alternately dirt and blacktop. (This dirt road runs parallel to and just uphill from the prescribed trail, which it rejoins farther up the hill.) The correct route has metal markers indicating the silver trail and is the reservation service road to Macmillan Reservoir.

Within about twenty minutes, waterfalls can be heard to the left, but, although there are paths leading down to the water, they are posted as dangerous. Just as the metal-marked silver trail bears left, the white trail and the previously ignored dirt path join. The trail being followed continues to climb, crosses several stone bridges over streams through prolific jewelweed, and bends sharply left as it approaches Macmillan Reservoir, named after the original owner of the land. Spend a few minutes at the reservoir by turning right and walking a very short distance to the water's edge.

Returning to the silver trail, climb steadily uphill on a rocky path paralleling the reservoir. Pass the yellow/silver trail and another junction on the left until, within twenty-five minutes, the junction of the blue-marked Ridge Trail is reached. The junction has several markers on a tree to the right in addition to a blue blaze on the left-hand side farther down the trail. At this point, the 1984 Trail Conference map is inaccurate, but we understand that the confusion will be corrected on the next edition of this map. Follow the red/silver trail straight ahead, winding through the woods on a narrower path. Just over the crest of the hill, red/silver markers are evident, and, farther on at

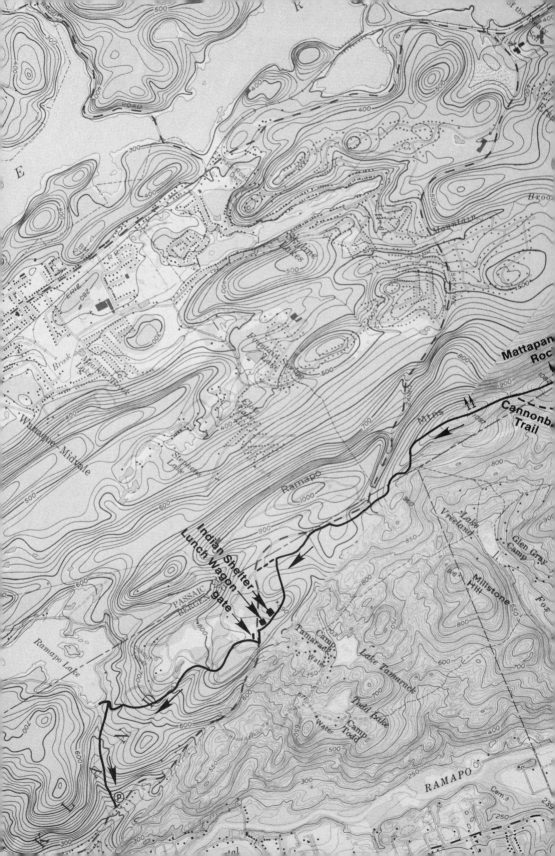

Note: The Cannonball Trail route
as shown on base map is incorrect

0   0.5   1.0 mile

8: Hoeferlin Memorial
Trail; Based on
USGS 7½' Ramsey &
Wanaque Quadrangles

Hoeferlin Trail

Erskine
Lookout

Ilgenstein
Rock

Bear Swamp Lake

Dias Hill

Monroe Ridge

Camp Yaw Paw

Cannonball Lake

Rocky Mtn

Matty Price Hill

Middle Valley

MacMillan Reservoir

falls

Scarlet
Oak
Pond

Bear Swamp

Bear Brook

RAMAPO MOUNTAIN

Hawk Rock

RIVER

RAMAPO

Immaculate
Conception
Seminary

Darlington

the lowest point in the trail, the silver trail exits, very obscurely, to the left. Ten minutes sees you through this confusing section.

The red/silver trail through here is sometimes narrow and muddy but, after about ten minutes, widens and descends to meet a wider, grassier woods road. Bear left until the pipeline is reached within a few minutes and walk straight ahead on a wide, gravel road, avoiding the poison ivy to the right of the trail. Red/silver markers are still visible and lead to a T-junction at the edge of Bear Swamp Lake. Turn right on a leisurely, wide, gravel road parallel with the water. Note that blue paint markers are visible on the first tree. The trees to the left of the road prevent a good view of Bear Swamp Lake, but where the trees thin, the road turns a little and goes uphill. Watch carefully here for an open space on the left containing a garbage can and look for the blue trail, which leads around the northern end of Bear Swamp Lake.

Follow the blue markers on a narrow trail. During the summer months, look for the yellow flowers of the false foxglove near this turn. The footway is not worn for the trail was cut only in early 1987. Within a short distance, the trail is marked for a turn, crosses the inlet stream to Bear Swamp Lake, and proceeds uphill away from the water. Very soon a grassy trail comes in on the right. Turn left and follow the route of the Hoeferlin Memorial Trail for the remainder of the hike.

Fifteen minutes from the commencement of the blue trail around Bear Swamp Lake, a fork is reached. Bear Swamp Lake can be seen to the left, and both the blue and yellow trails take the right fork. The yellow-marked Hoeferlin Memorial Trail immediately makes another right turn onto an obscure footway, again not well trodden because of its

newness. It leads uphill, through some areas that could be wet in some seasons, until the junction with a woods road is reached. Turn right on a well-marked, wider trail.

After a few minutes, leave the woods road, which continues straight ahead, cross a stream, and turn left uphill, away from the stream on a narrower and rockier trail. Continue to climb, crossing a large rock slab and watching carefully for the yellow markers that lead along a ridge. Occasionally a view is glimpsed to the left. A white-marked trail, the Crossover Trail, joins the Hoeferlin Memorial Trail from the right, after which the markers mingle and the footway is a little more distinct.

An hour's walk from the commencement of the blue trail, a viewpoint to the left of the trail is found called Ilgenstein's Rock, which makes an admirable lunch spot. The Hoeferlin Memorial Trail now goes through Ringwood State Forest. The city can be seen to the extreme right, Bear Swamp Lake immediately below, and a tremendous panorama before you. When leaving this viewpoint, take great care not to follow the white-marked trail leaving to the left. Here the trail leaves state forest property and crosses Scout property. Bear right on the yellow-marked Hoeferlin Memorial Trail, which begins by going downhill and then on undulating rocky ledges until it reaches a northwestern outlook at High Mountain, called the Erskine Lookout. The view towards the Wyanokies includes Lake Erskine, Upper Erskine Lake, and the Wanaque Reservoir, and here is an excellent place to pause.

After Erskine Lookout, many private Boy Scout trails join and leave the main Hoeferlin Memorial Trail. These trails are not generally open to the public and will not be mentioned again in this hike description. Follow the Hoeferlin Memorial

Trail along the ridge, noting the two trails that connect—the red Ringwood–Ramapo Trail and the Cannonball Trail. The Hoeferlin Memorial Trail enters the Ramapo Mountain State Forest soon after it merges with the red trail. The Cannonball Trail is marked with a white "C" on a red background and should be regarded as a white trail in accordance with trail custom. The road in the valley (now US 202) was not held securely by the Continental Army during the Revolution, and the Cannonball Trail was originally a secret military highway used by Revolutionary soldiers to transport weapons and munitions.

A wide, grassy crossroads is reached about an hour from the Erskine Lookout. The path to the left is a red-marked Boy Scout trail not open for public use; the one to the right leads to a viewpoint. This lookout, at Matapan Rock, is only two or three minutes down this wide path and has a view similar to that of the viewpoint at Erskine Lookout. Although not visible from the ledge, traffic on Skyline Drive can be heard clearly.

At the crossroads, the Hoeferlin Memorial Trail on the right is marked both in yellow and with the Cannonball sign. The first mountain laurel to be seen on the hike grows in this section, and the trees are less dense. The trail parallels Skyline Drive.

Fifteen minutes from the crossroads, the trail descends towards Skyline Drive. Cross the guard rail and turn left on the road. At the end of the Oakland Disposal Area parking lot immediately encountered on the left, the trail enters an open space between the end of the chain-linked fence and a telegraph pole on which there is a marker. Cross the pleasant, grassy area and walk back into the woods through a low-lying section, again paralleling Skyline Drive. The trail next makes a turn to the left and crosses a

small stream. Watch carefully at this point as the Cannonball Trail continues ahead, across several blowdowns, while the Hoeferlin Memorial Trail turns left away from Skyline Drive, just after a substantial blowdown. There is a double yellow blaze on the left-hand side of the trail to alert you to this turn.

The trail climbs to a level, rocky outcrop where the terrain is more open and almost immediately loses elevation as it passes the Indian cave and travels back down to Skyline Drive. On the descent, watch the rocks to the right closely to find the yellow arrow pointing to the site of the Indian shelter.

The Indian rock shelter was rediscovered in 1980, and fieldwork took place at the site during the following four years. Nearly three thousand stone artifacts were found, including an unusual effigy, which it is thought was used as a "dream stone" or a "wish stone" either to arouse the bear spirit or to conjure up a magic vision to guide the hunter's destiny. It is believed that the cave was used as a seasonal hunting shelter during the fall, probably from 5,000 B.C. to perhaps 1,600 A.D. A rock and soil wall had formed naturally in front of the cave, giving protection from the weather and also hiding the inhabitants. The area of the shelter is approximately six feet by twelve feet, which, together with the location of the hearths, leads archaeologists to believe that only two hunters were in residence at a time. Pause awhile in this sheltered spot and imagine how life was for these ancient people, before modern man disturbed the tranquillity of this cave.

Almost immediately after leaving the Indian rock shelter, Skyline Drive is reached, and Mom and Pop's lunchwagon is available to the right with a picnic table and a few annuals to brighten the scene. The lunchwagon is open every weekend and on most days during the week, except during really bad weather.

Walk away from the picnic table towards the Boy Scout sign for Camp Tamarack and cross the road, reentering the woods at the lower end of the parking lot through a gate barring the paved road. There are two yellow markers to confirm your location. Just as the road makes a right-hand bend where there is a utilities shelter on the right, the trail turns back into the woods on the left.

Soon after a large pile of boulders (with trees growing on the tops), there is a right bend in the trail and a jog across the same woods road. The trail now wanders through the woods, marked at times with yellow-painted can tops, and parallels the road, crossing streams from time to time. About forty-five minutes from Skyline Drive, the trail finally emerges onto the road. Turn left and walk towards Ramapo Lake, noticing the blue trail on the left just prior to reaching the water. This trail is the route out to the car; however, time should be allowed to sit by the lake. On our last visit there was a large black snake swimming close to the shore. Fishing is permitted in Ramapo Lake, but not swimming. There is a ranger station on the west shore, and the northern part of the shore is wild and open to hunters as well as to hikers. Ramapo Lake was formerly called Rotten Pond, probably originating from Dutch settlers who called it Rote Pond because of the muskrats they trapped there. The lake has also been known as Lake LeGrande and was originally part of the MacEvoy estate.

Turn back and take the blue-marked MacEvoy Trail on the right-hand side of the road, up over a short bank only a few feet high, after which the trail levels out. Although after the first blue marker it is ten minutes before another one is seen, the road is wide and there is not much doubt which way to go. After crossing a small stream and walking down some short, rocky descents, the parking lot is reached about twenty minutes from Ramapo Lake.

SJG

Ringwood Manor Circular

Total distance: 1.5 miles
Hiking time: 1.25 hours
Vertical rise: 250 feet
Rating: Easy
Maps: USGS Greenwood Lake (NY/NJ); NYNJTC North Jersey
   Trails #22; WB #23; HRM #15; DEP Ringwood State Park
   Summer Map

Ringwood Manor, part of the larger Ringwood State Park (Box 1304, R.D., Ringwood, NJ 07456; 201-962-7031), is located in northeast Passaic County. The history of the area is closely tied to the local iron industry, which started at Ringwood in 1740. The products of the forges and furnaces were of much importance to the colonies during the Revolutionary War. Troops were stationed here, and George Washington made Ringwood his headquarters on several occasions. Robert Erskine, manager of the mines, served General Washington as surveyor general and prepared many of the maps for the campaign against the British.

The property was purchased by Peter Cooper in 1853. Cooper, a New York philanthropist, is best known as the founder of Cooper Union Institute. The property later passed to Abram Hewitt, a famous ironmaster. He had become a family friend of the Coopers and, later, their daughter, Amelia. The greater part of the present mansion was built from about 1810 to 1930. It was always used as a summer house, the winters spent in New York City.

In 1936, Erskine Hewitt donated the Manor House and ninety-five acres to the state of New Jersey. His nephew, Norvin Green (namesake of nearby Norvin Green State Forest), made an additional gift to bring the total up to 579 acres. Later purchases, using Green Acres funds, continued up to as recently as 1978. The park now extends east into Bergen County, connecting with Ramapo Mountain State Forest and a Bergen County reservation to form a large network of public lands. An extensive network of trails in the area was developed in the 1970s by volunteers coordinated by the New York–New Jersey Trail Conference.

Ringwood Manor is on Sloatsburg Road, just south of the New York/New Jersey border. Access to this road is from County Road 511 (1.8 miles north from Skyline Drive) or from NY 17, just south of the village of Sloatsburg, New York (3.6 miles north of the New York/New Jersey border). The area has many roadside directional signs for this park and the adjacent Skyland Gardens. As in many state parks, there is a fee for park-

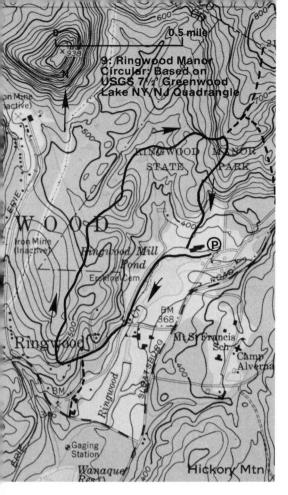

9: Ringwood Manor Circular; Based on USGS 7½' Greenwood Lake NY/NJ Quadrangle

the wrought-iron gates (standing by themselves on the lawn) and continue to the far side of the pond. Pass a row of large oak trees and come to a dirt road. Bear left and watch for the first sign of a blue-marked trail on a telephone pole. The trail is nameless, but its blue markers are followed throughout the hike. The pond is stocked with bass and pickerel, but fishing is, of course, subject to the various New Jersey laws.

Continue along the shore with the pond on your left. The road is well marked with both the blue and another blaze— a red dot on a white background. The latter denotes the Bus Stop Trail and follows the blue trail before branching off to a public bus stop. It was established for hikers coming to the region via public transit.

Start down the road and cross a small stream on a bridge. Note the rust-colored rocks, indicative of the iron ore present throughout the area. Along the shore, the route passes several small graveyards. Pause and browse. Names like Morris, Paterson, Erskine, and Hewitt are central to regional history. Many of the graves are small—children died often in the eighteenth and nineteenth centuries. Cedar trees add to the tranquility of the area (unless you made the mistake of coming late on a summer weekend!). The large building visible across the pond is the sanctuary of the Order of Saint Francis.

Pass the end of Sally's Pond and take the right fork of the road uphill, as always following the blue paint markers. The deteriorating houses passed here were acquired when the area became parkland. They are now used by various state agencies for short-term projects.

Ignore the dirt road on the left and continue uphill, following the main gravel road. As the route crests and then begins a gentle drop, watch the blazes

ing from Memorial Day to Labor Day. New Jersey residents over age sixty-one can get a pass that allows for free parking at all state parks and forests (see Introduction).

History is everywhere at Ringwood Manor, and it is a fine idea to combine your hike with a tour of the Manor House. Call ahead to determine their house tour schedule. The hike commences at the park office, where maps and brochures are usually available. Heading out towards the clearly visible Sally's Pond (a local name; the USGS and NYNJTC maps show this pond as Ringwood Mill Pond), turn right passing the Manor House porch. Walk through

Gravestones overlooking Sally's Pond in Ringwood Manor.

carefully. Two blazes together indicate a sharp right turn onto a woods road. If you go too far, you'll soon see a paved highway (Margaret King Avenue). Taking the right turn the path continues uphill along a woods road. There are some steel cables in the ground that may have been used in connection with a recreation camp Cooper Union had on the property years ago. No one we talked to really knew. The woods road is generally level with short pitches up and down. This place is good for observing the surrounding woodlands. In spring, flowers abound: jack-in-the-pulpit, rue anemone, spring beauty, and trout lily to name just a few. Watch for a large rock to the left of the trail with a green metal marker on top. This marker is called a benchmark, placed (many on the summits of mountains) by the United States Geological

Survey throughout the country. They identify key spots in connection with the government's mapping work. This one, however, is a remnant of the Cooper Union Camp.

About forty-five minutes into the hike, the trail crosses a pipeline. This area provides a nice view, marred by some illegal dumping. Littering and dumping are serious problems on state lands, and the government has a special program in operation to try to apprehend the perpetrators. Area hikers under the direction of the New York–New Jersey Trail Conference conducted a cleanup of this area in the mid-1980s but with no lasting success.

Continue across the path of the buried pipeline, as the marked trail takes a short jog to the right. The trail is narrower now, and the woods deeper. Soon a lovely stream is reached. Note the red rusty rocks—iron ore. This spot is a good place for a break. Pull up a rock and have a snack.

The trail follows the stream for a short distance then crosses it on some stones. Watch your footing here! The path is again in the woods. Note the large stumps, evidence of past logging activities. Beech, oak, maple, and dogwood abound in this area. Soon, off to the left, there is a large, water-filled rectangle. This depression is an old mine pit. Note again the rust-colored rocks. The trail continues across a small stream. Watch out for some poison ivy here. If you are not yet sure what to watch for, avoid all three-leafed plants and vines.

The trail turns right, following an old woods road downstream. There may be some wet, muddy stretches here—just walk to either side, into the woods, to avoid them. The trail passes under a canopy of ten-foot trees forming a lovely arch. More flowers are here, as well as some false helibore and skunk cabbage.

Upon reaching an intersection with a wide road, follow the blue markings as they indicate a right turn (downhill). [The white-blazed trail, which follows the road to the left, makes an interesting, if somewhat longer, alternate return route. Should you decide to take the longer route, just follow the white markings carefully. There is one sudden turn right off the road that you could miss. Although the white trail is well marked, it is easy to lose concentration when walking along such a wide and obvious footway. The white trail, which adds about half a mile to this hike, will return you to Ringwood Creek just upstream from the Manor House section of the park.] To be back in sight of the Manor House within a few minutes, follow the blue blazes right. Perhaps you have time now for a tour?

HNZ

10

Governor Mountain

Total distance: 1.5 miles
Hiking time: 1 hour
Vertical rise: 350 feet
Rating: Easy
Maps: USGS Wanaque; NYNJTC North Jersey Trails #22; WB
  #23; HRM #15; DEP Ringwood State Park Summer Map

This hike is on a peninsula of state-owned land in the southwest section of Ringwood Manor State Park (Box 1304, R.D., Ringwood, New Jersey 07456; 201-962-7031). In 1936, Erskine Hewitt deeded the Manor House and ninety-five acres to the state for preservation. His nephew, Norvin Green, gave New Jersey considerable lands. Additional purchases in the 1960s and as late as 1978 brought the park to its present-day size. Since the boundaries of Ringwood couple with those of Ramapo Valley State Forest and Ramapo Valley (Bergen) County Reservation, an extensive and varied trail network now exists. Most trails in this region are maintained by volunteers coordinated by the New York–New Jersey Trail Conference.

To arrive at the trailhead, drive along Sloatsburg Road to its junction with Carletondale Road, .4 mile south of Margaret King Avenue and south of Skyland Gardens and Ringwood State Park. Sloatsburg Road can be accessed from NY 17 just south of the town of Sloatsburg, New York (3.6 miles from the New York/New Jersey border), or by going north on County Road 511 1.8

miles from its junction with Skyline Drive. The area has many roadside, directional signs for the two parks previously mentioned. Head east on Carletondale Road a short way to a large, dirt parking area on the left. There is a bright red fire hydrant on the right side of the road and space here for a dozen cars. If you go too far, you'll almost immediately pass a township education building.

The yellow-blazed Cooper Union Trail, which starts near the New York border, enters the parking area from the north. Cross over Carletondale Road just opposite the parking lot. The trail starts downward into deep woods but almost immediately levels out. The markings are clear and easy to follow. There is some evidence of illegal trail-biking, but the trail is, for the most part, in good shape. The wide path passes through tall woods with a lush undergrowth. Indian pipe, as well as some poison ivy, is evident. In spring, wildflowers are abundant. Pass by a faint, dirt path going left to a school building yard and continue straight ahead.

In a little more than five minutes, the trail splits, and a loop begins. Both forks are yellow marked. Take the left one — a ninety-degree turn. Note the large hemlock tree in this particularly dense sector. The trail begins an uphill course here, gently at first and then more steeply. The steep parts of this hike are, however, always short-lived. At the top of the rise, the woodland thins out and gives way to more grasslands and open areas. The cedar trees here are especially lovely, large specimens with their typical, symmetrical shapes. This stretch also has patches of poison ivy, so stay on the trail and be attentive, especially if you have children or the dog along.

The footpath narrows with gentle ups and downs as a plateau of the mountain, interspersed with some dense underbrush, is traversed. There are small outcrops of rocks, blackberry bushes, more cedar groves, and moss patches. Though there is some evidence of illegal camping in this area, the moss on the

trail is indicative of the generally light use. The walking is pleasant, and the underfooting, soft. Most people go in and out to the upcoming vista using only the exit route of this hike. They see the fine view at the summit but miss this peaceful section.

After crossing a wet area on some stepping stones, the trail swings steeply up towards a panoramic viewpoint at a point known locally as Suicide Ledge, just below the true summit of Governor Mountain. At a 600-foot elevation and some three hundred feet above the water below, the view is extensive. Below and ahead is the Wanaque Reservoir. Across the water, Board and Windbeam mountains are prominent, the territory of the popular Stonetown Circular hike. Farther south are the hills of Norvin Green State Forest, described elsewhere in this book.

Unfortunately, this area also attracts people who leave considerable litter. Each spring, volunteers organized by the New York–New Jersey Trail Conference sponsor a Litter Day. Hikers cover many of the trails in the bi-state area. Governor Mountain has received special attention over the last several years and is much cleaner, at times, than it used to be. Each time we take this pleasant walk, we bring along a litter bag and spend ten minutes cleaning up. It seems that "litter attracts more litter," so if we leave it clean, we hope it stays that way longer...at least, that's the theory.

The Cooper Union Trail was originally laid out by members of the former Cooper Union Hiking Club, which owned a camp purchased by the state in 1978. Cooper Union, a New York City institution of higher learning, was founded by Peter Cooper, who became one of the largest landowners in New Jersey. His Ringwood property was almost 100,000 acres. For additional history about this area, see the Ringwood Manor hike in this book.

10: Governor Mountain; Based on USGS 7½ Wanaque Quadrangle

0   0.5 mile

According to Ringwood Borough historian Bert Prol, the name Governor Mountain is presumably a corruption of "Gouvernour," the family name of early owners (until 1764) of the Ringwood Ironworks. There was a beacon here during the Revolutionary War, part of a system linking Torn Mountain near Suffern, New York, and Federal Hill in Pompton Lakes.

Leaving the viewpoint, turn right, uphill, to the actual summit of the mountain and follow the yellow blazes straight ahead. Ignore the "local" white paint here. A large glacial erratic is soon passed on the left side of the trail. These boulders, quite common in New Jersey, were left behind as the glaciers of the ice ages retreated and melted. The large ones attest to the awesome power of nature's force.

Passing through a conifer grove and descending a little more steeply, the trail bends right, crosses another wet area on rock steps, and swings back to its original, northward course. In a few minutes, you'll be back at the trail fork, having completed the loop. Continue out, following the yellow markers, over the same route upon which you entered.

The entire hike, including some time to linger at the summit, can be walked in less than an hour. The best time to journey forth is early on a weekend morning when you may be alone on the mountain and have the trail and viewpoint to yourself—your own personal "wilderness."

HNZ

11

Norvin Green State Forest—Wyanokie Circular Trail

Total distance: 7.5 miles
Hiking time: 5 hours
Vertical rise: 1,100 feet
Rating: Moderate
Maps: USGS Wanaque; NYNJTC North Jersey Trails #21; WB
#20; HRM #37

The Wyanokie ridge, forming part of the New Jersey highlands, dates back to the Precambrian period, and many of the rocks in the area are more than 600 million years old. These hills were here long before there was a Wanaque Reservoir or a New York skyline to be seen from the viewpoints on this hike. Blue iron ore was abundant, and villages grew up around the iron mining operations and charcoal furnaces that once were active in the area. Norvin Green State Forest (c/o Ringwood Park, RD Box 1304, Ringwood, New Jersey 07456; 201-962-7031) was named after its donor, Norvin H. Green, and contains a number of high hills offering good views. Construction of the Wanaque Reservoir, which is visible from several high points in the area, was started in 1920, and the reservoir was filled by 1949. Many Indian names remain in these parts. Wanaque and Wyanokie mean sassafras, and other Indian terms will be noted in the text of this hike.

The Wyanokie Circular hike offers spectacular views, together with pleasant walking in the woods and the possibility of swimming at several points en route. Partially on private land and partially in the Norvin Green State Forest, the hike uses one of the largest concentrations of trails in New Jersey. These trails were originally laid in the early 1920s by Dr. Will S. Monroe of Montclair and his co-workers in the Green Mountain Club. On his retirement, the property and the maintenance of trails were taken over by the Nature Friends under the name Camp Midvale. The name has now been changed to the Weiss Ecology Center.

The hike starts at the Weiss Ecology Center and, with minor exceptions, follows the Wyanokie Circular Trail marked in red, although from time to time the route is marked with additional colors. Overnight accommodations and swimming are available at moderate charges at the center, and there may be a small daily parking fee during the summer. The Wyanokie area borders the reservoir and it is important not to trespass on the Northern Jersey District Water Supply Commission property.

Norvin Green State Forest is accessible from County Road 511, reached from the north by way of Skyland Drive or from the south from NJ 23. Turn west on West Brook Road about halfway along the Wanaque Reservoir. The road soon crosses the reservoir on a causeway and then parallels the water on the left-hand side. Shortly after passing the end of this inlet of the reservoir, there is a junction with Stonetown Road to the north. Continue on West Brook Road, and after about .5 mile look for Snake Den Road on the left. Drive uphill, bearing left, past private homes to the parking lot on the right-hand side, just before the gate into Weiss Ecology Center.

When leaving the parking area, do not enter the Weiss Ecology Center grounds but walk up Snake Den Road to the left of the center entrance, following the red markers painted on the trees on the right-hand side. Within five minutes, the trail makes a right turn into the woods and, moving downhill on a narrow, woodsy trail, arrives almost immediately at the Weiss Ecology Center swimming pool. This deep pool is fed by the stream, which is crossed right away on large rocks. The trail then climbs steeply up a slab of rock. Ignore the two other trails signed on a tree at the top of this rock slab and pursue the red-marked trail to the right, leading over another section of the swimming pool inlet. The blue markers of the Hewitt–Butler Trail run concurrently with the red markers of the Wyanokie Circular Trail at this point.

Soon a wooden bridge over a stream in the valley to the left is passed, and after climbing up six, widely spaced wooden steps, the trail widens and levels out. The markers now change from paint patches to white rectangles with a red blob in the center, and the blue markers still march along with the red ones. Approximately seven minutes after entering the woods, ignore the indistinct path crossing the main trail and continue the

steady uphill climb. In another ten minutes, the trail turns right and snakes uphill amongst large, rocky outcrops.

The trail continues to climb more steeply over rocks and out to a viewpoint, reached about twenty-five minutes after commencing the hike. Look to the right for the first glimpse of New York City. At this viewpoint, only the tops of the Empire State Building and the World Trade Center are visible. Immediately opposite is Windbeam Mountain, with Bear Mountain to the left and New York State on the horizon. (Windbeam comes from the Indian *wombimish,* meaning "chestnut tree.") In the foreground is the Wanaque Reservoir. A hot-blast charcoal furnace called the Freedom Furnace (alternatively, "Whynockie" or "Ryerson's") made many tons of iron during its operation from ore mined from the Blue Mine, to be passed later in the hike. The old furnace stack stood until 1928 when it was demolished during the construction of the Wanaque Reservoir, the stone being used for constructing of Midvale Dam.

From this viewpoint, continue to follow the red and blue markers, which lead steeply uphill across slabs of rock to another viewpoint at the first of three pine paddies. Pine paddies are rocky outcrops with a concentration of pitch pine, and each one will give an improved view of the same scene. Still following the red markers, the trail leads slightly downhill amongst mountain laurel and sweet fern until the second pine paddy is reached. At the crest of these rocks there is a 360-degree viewpoint, and, looking straight ahead, the third pine paddy can be seen. In season, amongst these rocks is stunted goldenrod, struggling to survive in a windy atmosphere with little soil. The route now descends through similar rocky terrain and, within fifteen minutes, turns right and climbs again through

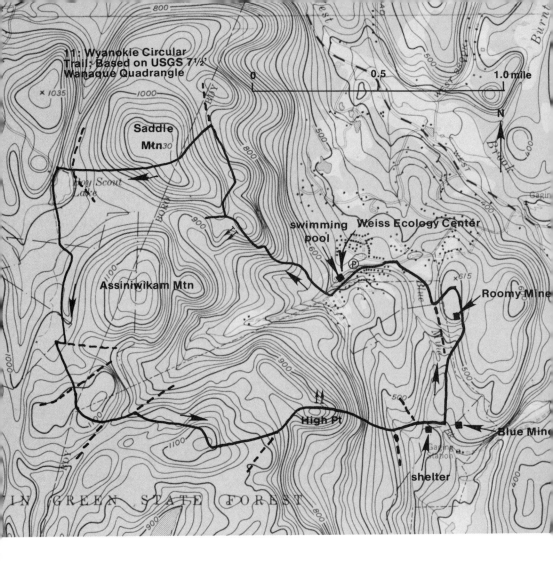

11. Wyanokie Circular Trail; Based on USGS 7½' Wanaque Quadrangle

trees that are slightly thinner. Because more sunlight comes through here, the trail is grassier. The yellow-marked Wyanokie Crest Trail comes in at the left, but the red-marked trail keeps to the right until it reaches the top of the rock outcrop—the third and last pine paddy.

This point is about forty minutes from the Weiss Ecology Center, and from here is the best view yet of the Manhattan skyline. The Wanaque Reservoir is still in the picture, and in that direction as well is Wyanokie High Point. To the right of

High Point is Assini-Wikam Mountain ("Indian rock shelter"). The route later in this hike will skirt the side of Assini-Wikam Mountain and ascend High Point. Fastened to the rock here is a plaque to the memory of Herman Van Dyk, a dedicated hiker of these trails who lived for ninety-one years (1871 to 1962). Scramble around. The plaque can be hard to find.

These rocks have many paint blazes, but there are no junctions here. Retrace your steps just to the bottom of the upper rock where the plaque is situated, find the red marker, and follow the trail downhill to the left. The path is very picturesque, somewhat overgrown, and, although level at first, later descends more steeply to a huge rocky outcrop at the bottom, with many trees surviving in cracks in the rocks. The red markers are still cohabiting with blue markers, and they lead the walker behind and through this enormous outcropping, climbing and switchbacking to its top. Ten minutes after leaving the plaque, the trail emerges at a similar northerly vista of the Stonetown Circular Trail hiking area.

Turning left and descending steeply through tall mountain laurel, the trail proceeds through a stand of spruce trees and rocky outcrops to the valley. Cross two brooks some distance apart, which will probably be dry in summer, and begin to climb again via a switchback to the left. After 100 feet, the blue-marked Hewitt–Butler Trail branches to the right. Be sure to keep left on the red-marked Wyanokie Circular Trail. Now begins the three to four hundred-foot climb up the side of Saddle Mountain, elevation 1,130 feet. The climb here takes ten to fifteen minutes, although the trail does not go over the summit of the mountain.

After this climb the trail descends gently among large rocky outcrops for another ten minutes, at first in a mature forested area and then through an area of young beech trees, until Boy Scout Lake is reached. Just prior to the lake are a well-maintained lean-to in a clearing on the left and a junction with the Mine Trail. Turn right and follow the broad, grassy road to the wide, wooden bridge and cement overflow across the outlet of Boy Scout Lake. Permission to swim in the lake may be obtained from groups using the camp. The yellow-marked Mine Trail is on the right by the cement overflow.

This 150 acres of land is called Camp Wyanokie and is owned by the towns of Caldwell, West Caldwell, North Caldwell, Fairfield, and Roseland. The property was originally owned by the Camp Wyanokie Association, who deeded the property over to the towns about fifteen years ago. A commission comprised of two representatives from each town is responsible for the camp, and a volunteer camp ranger lives a short distance from Boy Scout Lake. The lake covers five acres. There is a dining hall, six lean-tos, two pit toilets, a large, flat area for tents, and tested drinking water. Overnight camping is permitted for a small charge, and applications for a camping permit can be made to Borough Administrators Office, Gould Avenue, North Caldwell, New Jersey 07006; 201-228-4444.

Walk past the dining hall, called the Lion's Den, keeping to the left of the building and up a slight hill to the gravel road. Turn left, and when you see two roads facing you, take the upper (right-hand) road past the water pump. The wide gravel road parallels the lake for a little while, then climbs slightly and passes at least one private home. This part of the trail has been rerouted recently. In a few minutes, look for a white-marked junction turning left on a narrow, flat, slightly overgrown trail through the woods. There is a small stream on the left, and after a few minutes, the trail emerges from the woods onto a woods road. Turn left and follow the red markers.

The next section of the Wyanokie Circular Trail skirts Assini-Wikam Mountain and is bisected by several other trails. It is important to follow the red markers. After a period of level, pleasant walking, the trail becomes much rockier, climbs slightly, and then becomes more grassy as the trees thin out. In season you will find Solomon's seal and Indian pipe. The white-marked Macopin (meaning "wild potato") Trail is soon reached, forming almost a T-junction, at which point you turn right. Almost immediately, another wide junction is reached with one path straight ahead and one going off to the right. Be sure to turn left (following the red markers). After climbing slightly, notice the yellow markers of the Wyanokie Crest Trail crossing the chosen route. The trail is narrower here, with very tall mountain laurel, and within five minutes, it becomes rockier and descends slightly through an area of tall oak trees. At the bottom of the rocky section, a trail turn is signed at the junction with the Otter Hole Trail. Turn left. The green-marked Otter Hole Trail and the red-marked Wyanokie Circular Trail travel together for approximately ten minutes on a wider path.

The next turn is to the right and is indicated by two signs on the trees. Ignore the green trail, which continues straight ahead, labeled the Glen Wild Fire Road, and turn right by the tree carrying a metal plate with "Wyanokie Circular" scratched on it. The Wyanokie Circular Trail is narrower again here with a great deal of mountain laurel, and, as the climb proceeds, the trees become less dense and large slabs of rock appear again. Watch the right-hand side of the trail for a large boulder split cleanly in two. Ten minutes past where the Otter Hole Trail left the Wyanokie Circular and was marked Glen Wild Fire Road, the route crosses a distinct path at right angles. This path is believed to be an inspection path for an old water pipeline that crossed here. A few minutes later, the trail emerges onto a large rock outcrop. This area has been hard hit by gypsy moth caterpillars in recent years. Wild grapes can be gathered in season, and black snakes and grouse have been seen in this section.

Leaving this rocky outcrop, bear left as the trail leads slightly downhill across rock slabs until a stony junction with the Hewitt–Butler Trail marked in blue is reached. The Wyanokie Circular is apparently not much used in this section for the trail is a little indistinct and overgrown. It is well marked, however. At this junction, there is a delightful specimen of a young sassafras tree. Turn left towards High Point, noting that the trail is marked in blue as well as with the red of the Wyanokie Circular Trail. After reaching a wet area, the trail turns and leads to the right over a small stream. At a large, flat boulder, the Hewitt–Butler Trail leaves to the left. Follow the red markers past an enormous boulder with "High Point" written on it in white paint, until the large slabs of rock that form High Point are reached. Views appear during the climb, first on the right and then on the left until at the top a 360-degree view is obtained. Look for familiar objects such as the Manhattan skyline and the Wanaque Reservoir, but, in addition, turn your back to the reservoir and seek two power lines on the horizon with your eyes. If you follow the left-hand one with your eyes to the second ridge over, you can see the pine paddies encountered earlier in the hike.

When the time comes to leave this superb viewpoint, seek the trail in the direction of the reservoir, switchbacking steeply down the rock slabs and entering an area of taller, denser trees, which are very comforting in the heat of a summer day. The descent of over five hundred feet is steep and rocky, but within thirty minutes the beginning of the Lower Trail is discovered on the right, marked with three white paint rectangles. Turn left and cross a stream on large boulders, observing where the Mine Trail (yellow) comes in almost immediately on the left.

Pine paddies on the Wyanokie Circular Trail.

The trail continues to drop approximately four hundred feet through rocky outcrops on a boulder-strewn trail. Keep to the left at the junction of a woods road, and very soon a low-lying area and a grassy clearing is traversed. On the left-hand side of the clearing is the Green Mountain Club shelter. This lean-to is situated in an attractive open area but is in exceptionally poor repair. For some time now, it has been reduced to rocky walls with a corrugated iron roof resting only a few feet above the lean-to floor.

Bear right past the shelter and look for the trail which leaves the open area to the left. After a few minutes, the trail turns left leading to a new bridge over Blue Mine Brook, just to the left of Blue Mine.

Blue Mine (also called London Mine, or Whynockie) is currently filled with water. The ore was mostly used at the Freedom Furnace until 1855. For a short period after Blue Mine's reopening in 1886, the mine produced about three hundred tons of ore per month. Water in the mine was obviously a problem, and the mine was "de-watered" several times. This operation was quite difficult. Mine workers stood on a raft that sank lower as the water was pumped out. Their job was to remove the debris left clinging to the walls of the mine and to shore up the timbers in the sides of the shaft, at the same time keeping their balance on the raft. Even after another de-watering operation in 1905, the mine was not worked again.

From the bridge, walk left along the rocky, eroded path and walk for five minutes to where the yellow Mine Trail leaves the Wyanokie Circular. Follow the Mine Trail right to visit Roomy Mine. Five minutes of climbing will bring you to the mine entrance. Roomy Mine is also called Laurel or Red Mine and was probably opened shortly after 1840. Extensive mining was carried on here through an entrance in the side of the hill above water level. Both underground and surface mining took place at Roomy Mine, and the ore was compact and mostly free from rock. The vein was about four feet thick with a pitch of fifty-eight degrees, dipping sharply to the southeast.

Roomy Mine's passage can still be entered. It is possible to take a flashlight and crawl through the opening at the mine entrance into an open-air section, from which the passageway itself lies straight ahead. Even in dry seasons there is water underfoot, but the passage can be walked for a distance of about 50 feet until it forks and dead-ends. Round dynamite holes can be seen in the roof of the passageway. Exploring Roomy Mine takes about thirty minutes. After leaving the mine, proceed past the entrance on an elevated, rocky path until, within five minutes, the Wyanokie Circular Trail is reached again. The trip to Roomy Mine can be eliminated by ignoring the described detour and continuing straight on the Wyanokie Circular Trail after Blue Mine.

The route now climbs moderately, past a massive boulder on the left, unfortunately covered with graffiti. Walk through an area of spruce trees and the backyard of a private home, keeping to the right along a fence to Snake Den Road. Turn left at the road and walk a minute or so back to the parking lot of the Weiss Ecology Center.

SJG

12

Carris Hill

Total distance: 5 miles
Hiking time: 4 hours
Vertical rise: 580 feet
Rating: Moderately strenuous
Maps: NYNJTC North Jersey Trails #21; HRM #37; USGS
  Wanaque

Although this hike is only five miles long, the rugged terrain and possibly difficult water crossings make for an exciting and challenging day hike. Carris Hill is not the highest point in Norvin Green State Forest but includes a strenuous climb and an arduous descent. Good footwear is necessary, and special care should be taken if this hike is attempted in winter — certain sections are on steep slopes of bare rock that could be difficult to navigate when covered with snow and ice. Post Brook, which is crossed four times, is normally on the dry side and is easily crossed on rocks; however, after a snow melt or heavy rain, Post Brook becomes a raging torrent and can present serious crossing problems.

To reach the trailhead from NJ 23, follow County Road 511 north to Butler. After a series of turns, bear right at the railroad tracks on Main Street, then make a left turn at the T intersection with Riverdale Avenue. From NJ 23 to here is 1.3 miles. Just 0.1 mile after this left turn, bear right on Glen Wild Road. After another 3.3 miles, park at the Otter Hole parking area on the right-hand side of the road. There is space here for about six or seven cars.

For the first part of this hike, follow the blue-marked Butler–Hewitt Trail, an eighteen-mile-long hiking trail that traverses the entire Wyanokie range. Markers (blue dots on a metal strip) are found just before the parking area, heading north into the woods. Amost immediately you will arrive at Otter Hole, a small cascade and falls on Post Brook, popular with the local youth. It is normally possible to cross the brook on rocks, but if this is impractical and dangerous, this hike should be aborted. If you can't get across the brook, try another hike.

Continue following blue markers after leaving Otter Hole to an intersection with the green-marked Otter Hole Trail. Stay on the blue-marked Hewitt–Butler Trail, heading uphill and roughly parallel to Post Brook. After a short distance, the trail begins a long, steady decline. Be alert for a left-hand turn in the trail — the markers direct you away from the woods road you're on to a narrower footpath. The trail is now a little more rugged in places. After about fifteen to twenty minutes, a junction with the yellow-marked Wyanokie Crest Trail will be reached. Bear right here. For a short distance the two trails share the same path. In only a

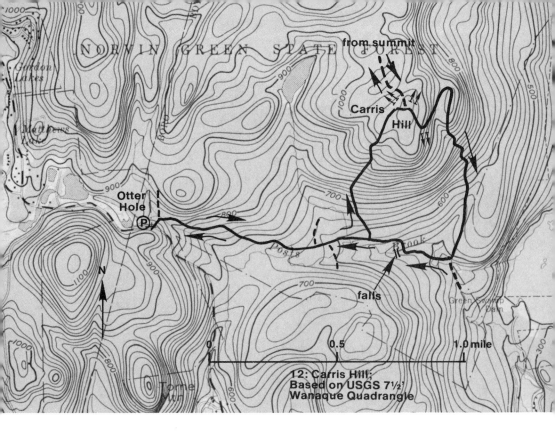

12: Carris Hill;
Based on USGS 7½'
Wanaque Quadrangle

few hundred yards, the Crest Trail swings away to the right. Continue straight ahead, following blue markers along an old lumber road that can be wet in places. Old logs laid crosswise like railroad ties help keep feet dry. To the right, catch glimpses and hear the sounds of falls and cascades as Post Brook now temporarily splits into two streams. Just ahead the trail goes to the edge of the brook and crosses another smaller stream coming in from the left. You are at a junction of running waters, a place where streams merge. Immediately after this stream crossing, the Hewitt–Butler Trail turns left. Straight ahead is the lower trail. This point will be reached again later, on the return trip. The steady uphill climb to the summit of Carris Hill begins here.

At first the trail gains elevation very slowly as it snakes its way through the woods. Soon the path gets increasingly rockier, although there is a temporary reprieve along the bed of an abandoned woods road. The trail then bears to the right, and the climb begins in earnest. The Hewitt–Butler Trail now follows what appears to be a man-made path up the side of the mountain, possibly used for lumbering in the past. Eventually the slope lessens and the footpath meanders through an area characterized by blueberry bushes, moss, occasional glacial erratics, and numerous exposures of bedrock. This terrain is typical of the Precambrian gneiss and granites of the New Jersey highlands. A slight descent into an area that is sometimes wet brings needed relief, but almost immediately the climb resumes. Now gaining elevation, the trail passes through laurel and traverses the first of a series of bare rock outcrops contoured with green moss and tall grasses. The first evergreens (hemlocks) are encountered here, and pitch pines appear, often heavily laden with clumps of pine cones. The trail descends slightly into a dense heath forest before it continues, now fairly gradually, up to bare rock and the first of a few small, false summits. Look behind you. The views of the Torne, Osio Rock, and beyond are steadily improving. After another slight descent into a laurel depression, the trail winds through scrub pine to the true summit, with views to the south, west, and north. There is a real feeling of accomplishment having reached this heavily glaciated summit. Wyanockie High Point is to the north, and from this vantage point it appears as a small cluster of bare rock. To the immediate west are Assiniwikam Mountain, Buck Mountain, and the Torne.

At the summit look for the yellow markers of the Carris Hill Trail, which begins here and heads east. Follow the trail for a few minutes out over the broad, flat summit of Carris Hill to another viewpoint. Here there are pines and a very large glacial erratic on bare rock outcrops. The expansive views are to the south and southeast. To the left of the large boulder, follow yellow markers downhill, off the summit. After only 100 yards, yet another viewpoint is reached, this one overlooking the Wanaque Reservoir and Raymond Dam. From here the trail begins a steep descent. The footing can be difficult until a rock formation, not unlike a wall, is reached. The trail climbs this outcrop and arrives at an even broader view of the reservoir and beyond. Some interesting and unique graffiti is found here. The trail heads south and down, rather steeply, over bare rock. A few cedars line the trail, which winds around a deep and jagged cliff. In sections much care is needed, and careful planning and

Chickahokie Falls.

proper equipment is required in icy or slippery conditions.

Once off the slab, the going is much more manageable, though still quite steep. Continue following yellow markers steadily downhill over rocky ground. A No Trespassing sign indicating the boundary of the reservoir does not apply to hikers who are allowed to use the trails. Eventually a small brook is reached and must be crossed, which might be difficult in times of high water. (If crossing is a problem, keep to the west of the brook and bushwack downstream to Post Brook, about .1 mile from here.) Shortly after this crossing, the yellow-marked Carris Hill Trail terminates at a junction with the Lower Trail, marked in white. Turn right here, following white markers, with the Wanaque Reservoir fence to your left. At a rock outcropping, find a trail junction and turn right, still following white markers. Another crossing of Post Brook is necessary, and if the crossing presents a problem, follow the brook upstream to a rocky area where a large fallen tree can be used as a bridge.

A short distance ahead is Chickahoochie Falls—a twenty-five-foot sluiceway of water, split in two as the water tumbles into a huge plunge pool. These falls are impressive after a rain. Just below the falls, the trail once again crosses Post Brook and climbs the bank—bearing left and following Post Brook closely—revealing other cascades further upstream. In just a few minutes, the junction with the blue-marked Hewitt–Butler Trail encountered earlier (where the climb to Carris Hill began) is reached. Follow the blue markers straight ahead, the way you came. Most of the way back is a gradual uphill climb and can be tiring. After about a half hour of walking, turn left, cross over Otter Hole, and return to your car.

BCS

13

Bearfort Ridge

Total distance: 8 miles
Hiking time: 5.5 hours
Vertical rise: 1,000 feet, total
Rating: Moderately strenuous
Maps: USGS Greenwood Lake (NY/NJ); NYNJTC North Jersey
  Trails #21; WB #21; HRM #21B; DEP Hewitt State Forest

This hike is in Abram S. Hewitt State Forest, administered by the superintendent of Wawayanda State Park (PO Box 198, Highland Lakes, New Jersey 07422; 201-853-4462) as a day-use area; no camping or swimming is permitted. Bearfort Mountain, which this hike traverses, may still even have a few bears—they have been seen in nearby Wawayanda—and it is assumed that this is the derivation of the name.

To find the trailhead from the A&P shopping center in Browns (near Greenwood Lake), continue west .1 mile farther to a fork in the road. Take the right fork (Warwick Turnpike) going uphill. Cross a small concrete bridge, and park on either side of the road just after the bridge. If you go too far, you'll immediately come to another junction (White Road) and a sign for Wawayanda State Park. The trail leaves the north side of the road, just to the right (north) of the bridge. (Road construction in 1988 may result in some changes to this area.)

The beginning of the Bearfort Ridge Trail (BR Trail) is clearly indicated by three white paint blazes, a typical "start of trail" marking. Starting uphill through a

pretty grove of hemlocks and rhododendrons, the trail traverses the slope for a short time before heading gently up and joining a woods road. Following the white markers, proceed left along the woods road and, after a short distance, turn left again, uphill and off the road. The main woods road, occasionally marked with faint, orange paint blazes, continues northward, with some significant junctions, to Surprise Lake.

The trail is very well marked with white paint rectangles (but my opinion of the maintenance quality of the BR Trail may not be objective, since I have been assigned as its official New York–Jersey Trail Conference maintainer). It climbs moderately uphill, with some steep pitches, through a mixed hardwood forest consisting of red, black, and white oaks, some maples, ash, beech, and birch. The forests of this locality were heavily timbered for charcoal production during the area's iron-producing period. This forest is therefore the second, or even third, growth of trees.

After crossing a boggy section in a small hollow, the trail continues ahead along the side of a slope. Except for some road noise from nearby Warwick Turnpike, there is a feeling of isolation in deep woods. As you proceed, gaining elevation, the road noise quickly fades and the real beauty of this area begins to dominate. Passing through some tall and lush rhododendrons—magnificent in June when they bloom—the climb begins to steepen. After climbing through some rocks and along the base of a ledge, there is a worthwhile, south-facing viewpoint off the trail to the right. The steep, barefaced peak across the road is another part of this same mountain in an area owned by the city of Newark (see the Pequannock Watershed hike). Continuing ahead and upwards, you soon reach the first of the pitch pines that dominate the main part of the hike.

As the trail turns right onto the ledge, a scramble up the large rock on the left of the trail yields a fine view. The water in the distance is a small section of Upper Greenwood Lake. This viewpoint is also a good place to take note of the rock formation that composes much of Bearfort Ridge. A collection of white quartz pebbles imbedded in a red "pudding stone," it is considered similar to the Shawangunk conglomerate of the Kittatinny Mountains. These rocks generally make for secure footing, but, as usual, extra care should be taken when they are wet or icy.

Now a little more than a half hour into the hike, return to the trail as it climbs up onto the ledges. The BR Trail now begins a several mile course along the outcroppings, with several dips back into the woods to cross small hollows and streambeds. The elevation is generally 1,300+ feet, and the climb up has been more than 600 feet. The views from this section of the BR Trail are not as sweeping as those just left or those to come, but the charm of the landscape surrounds you. Note the fine array of

mosses along (and occasionally even in) the footway, indicative of the surprisingly light use this tract receives. The boulders strewn along the way are glacial erratics, remaining from the ancient ice sheets as they melted and retreated north. Striations seen on the rock surface can also be attributed to this period. I've always had a special fondness for the pitch pines with their distinctive, thick, shingle bark. To me they are like large Japanese bonsai trees. I admire their intricate shapes and the way they cling to life on the otherwise barren rocks.

One of the nicest spots in all of New Jersey is about half an hour's hike along this ridge-top section. Here, a large section of rock has split away from the base, leaving a deep crevice just to the left of the footway. On the far side of the split is an attractive swamp. This spot has long been a favorite of ours for lunch or "elevens" (our traditional, mid-morning snack break, around 11 A.M.). The separation of rock here possibly commenced as water seeped into cracks and then expanded with repeated freezings. Time and erosion have widened it to more dramatic dimensions.

Continuing ahead, a rather large glacial erratic is passed and, after a while, a stream crossed, with the trail then climbing up through a rock notch. The ridge soon becomes less pronounced, with fewer rock outcroppings and rhododendron and mountain laurel reappearing. As the trail gently rises out of the woods, a symmetrical cedar tree dominates the skyline—the first to be observed. Another 40 yards ahead are three white paint blazes on the top of a small rock bump, indicating the end of the BR Trail, about 2.5 miles (and 1.5 to 2 hours) from the hike's start.

From this spot, the first good view of Surprise Lake is discerned. This lake will be passed later, and the hike route will

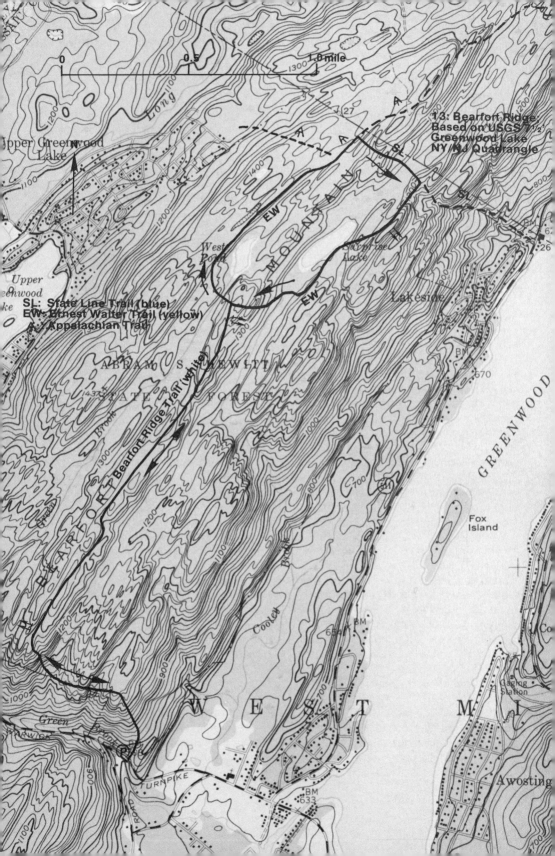

0   0.5   1.0 mile

13: Bearfort Ridge
Based on USGS 7½'
Greenwood Lake
NY/NJ Quadrangle

SL: State Line Trail (blue)
EW: Ernest Walter Trail (yellow)
A: Appalachian Trail

return to this spot. The view is extensive, with only small traces of civilization evident. Off to the right, in the distance, is a section of the new Wanaque Reservoir. From here, the hike begins a loop, beginning and ending on the yellow-blazed Ernest Walter Trail (EW Trail), named for a dedicated hiker and trailblazer.

This trail, and others in the area, is normally well marked. In 1986 and 1987, a vandal systematically and repeatedly painted out the blazes of this trail and portions of others in the area. Volunteers of the New York–Jersey Trail Conference try to keep the trail well marked, but your experience here may depend on which "painter" was on the trail last. If you should find the trail "blacked-out," please inform the Conference (GPO Box 2250, New York City, New York 10116). The trail has not been rerouted. If the yellow paint marks are not evident, follow the black ones. Once you know what to look for, they are really not that difficult to detect, and the loop you now begin past West Pond and Surprise Lake is worth the small, extra effort involved.

The yellow blazes lead both right and left. Proceed left, walking the loop in a clockwise direction. The trail descends 20 feet down a rock face and onto a narrow footpath. Since it crosses against the "grain" on the ridge, the route undulates pleasantly up and down through the woods and outcroppings, soon crossing Green Brook, the outlet stream of West Pond. Shortly afterwards, the first view of the pond is seen. The trail wanders above the shore of the pond but does not actually go down to the water's edge. Take a few minutes to bushwhack down to the shore to appreciate the pond's backcountry charm.

The EW Trail continues along the ridge, then crosses the small outlet of a swamp. The trail bends to the right and leaves the ridge, heading down to a hol-low where one end of the Ernest Walter Trail is reached at a T-junction with the white-blazed Appalachian Trail (see the AT Backpack hike for background information on this national scenic trail).

Follow the white blazes of the AT, climbing to the top of a twenty-foot rock outcropping where the trail veers to the right. Not long after, another view of Surprise Lake is seen before the AT descends to a junction. Here, the State Line Trail, a blue dot (or square) in a white field, departs to the right. Follow the blue blazes (again a target of the infamous "black-outer") downhill off the ridge.

After about fifteen minutes on the State Line Trail, going generally downhill, another junction is encountered. This spot is the other end of the U-shaped Ernest Walter Trail. Some of the yellow markings may be visible through the woods to the right before the junction itself is reached. Make a sharp right turn onto the EW Trail and climb steeply up to a promontory overlooking Greenwood Lake.

Surprise Lake is now about twenty minutes away, but the journey may take longer, for the views on this rise are super and invite lingering. Much of the two-state area of Greenwood Lake is visible. The large island in the middle is Fox Island, and across the lake are the mountains of the privately owned Sterling Forest. Area hikers are supporting a campaign to bring these lands, or at least the elevated parts, into the park systems of the two states. New Jersey has already appropriated funds for two thousand acres. New York conservationists hope for similar action to acquire at least nine thousand acres. If they succeed, the hiking lands of this area will be connected with those of Harriman–Bear Mountain State Park in New York, and, likely, many new trails will be developed.

Leave the ridge and turn right into the woods, passing a pile of shale ruins. The

Overlooking Greenwood Lake.

origin of the ruins is unknown to us (any ideas?). Just before the shore of Surprise Lake is attained, there are a few unmarked side trails, so keep a close watch on those yellow markers. Your impressions of this graceful lake may be determined by how many people are there or by what litter and debris they have left. It is a region of heavy, warm weather use.

Leave the lake, remaining on the EW Trail through a short, muddy section. Shortly, the trail enters a splendid section of large rhododendrons and laurels, forming a junglelike canopy over the trail. Walk carefully down a rocky path to a hollow and then cross Cooley Brook, the outlet of Surprise Lake. The crossing, on some rocks and root islands, may be a challenge after heavy rains but is otherwise not an impediment.

Ascending steeply onto outcroppings, you will soon reach the Bearfort Ridge/ Ernest Walter junction. It was from this point that the loop route began a while ago. From this locale, it is another 2.5 miles out to the parking area. Retracing your steps back along the white BR Trail takes no more than two hours of uninterrupted hiking. You'll be pleasantly surprised at how different the trail looks when you're traveling in the opposite direction.

HNZ

14

Terrace Pond

Total distance: 3.5 miles
Hiking time: 3.5 to 4 hours
Vertical rise: 400 feet
Rating: Moderate
Maps: USGS Wawayanda/Newfoundland, NJ; NYNJTC North
  Jersey Trails #21; WB #21; HRM #36A

This hike is on land once called "The Sussex Woodlands," previously owned by Fred Ferber, an immigrant from Austria during the Depression. Fred Ferber was the founder of the Ferber Corporation, an Englewood company, one of the pioneers in making ballpoint pens in the United States. Two years prior to selling his interest in the company in 1963, Mr. Ferber bought a 6,800-acre timberland tract from the New Jersey Zinc Company with the intention of developing a wilderness nature center primarily for young people. When he relinquished more than half of his original land purchase to the state in 1963, Wawayanda State Park (Box 198, Highland Lakes, New Jersey 07422; 201-853-4462) was created. Fred Ferber was not a lover of state parks as he objected to hunting and to facilities such as restaurants, toilets, and campsites, which are normally part of state parks. His ambition was to keep the remaining acreage as wilderness, untouched by such facilities. Gradually, as over the years Mr. Ferber ran into debt, he sold portions of his land to the state. Bearfort Mountain Ridge, which contains Terrace Pond, was one of the last tracts

to be sold in 1973. Fred Ferber would have been as upset as most hikers are today to see the graffiti on the rock slabs plunging down to the clear water of Terrace Pond and to see the litter left in almost every picturesque spot.

The hike described here uses the Terrace Pond South Trail (marked in yellow), the white trail circling Terrace Pond, Terrace Pond North Trail (marked in blue), and a woods road. The terrain is varied, and all sections are superb. At first the hike is gentle, but in the approach to Terrace Pond, the climax of the hike, there are several ridges reminiscent of a roller coaster to cross, making the hike more strenuous towards the end. Some wet areas have to be negotiated on this hike.

Access to the trails used in this hike is from Clinton Road, which runs north from NJ 23 to Warwick Turnpike. The trailhead is on the east side of Clinton Road, 1.7 miles south of the junction with Warwick Turnpike and 7.3 miles north of NJ 23. There is a parking area just north of the entrance to the Wildcat Environmental Center.

Cross the road from the parking lot and enter the woods on a steep, uphill gradient, following yellow markers. Ignore the blue trail on the left and follow the mossy, yellow-marked trail up and over a small hill, through mountain laurel and white pine. Shortly afterwards, there is a swampy area on the left around which the trail winds, first crossing and then paralleling a small stream. The trail soon moves away from the stream to the right and, still climbing, proceeds through a piney area, passing an interesting, split rock on the left side.

A ridge appears ahead as you climb, and eventually the trail meanders along the valley on the right side of this ridge, winding through white pines and mountain laurel. The trail here is sometimes wet, and there are some blowdowns. Within thirty minutes from the beginning of the hike, the trail turns left to climb this same ridge. This section of the trail is spectacular. It becomes rockier, travels along the side of the hill, with a drop to the right, and follows substantial cliffs on the left, scattered with a large number of huge boulders. A magnificent grove of very tall rhododendrons arches completely over the trail at this point. Red paint marks appear on the trees to your right, probably indicating the boundary between the state park and the Newark Watershed Conservation and Development Corporation property. Some of the trail markers are can tops painted yellow, and others are yellow rectangular markers painted on the trees. Pick your way among boulders and blowdowns until you reach the top of the ridge, where the trail levels out through a more open area until it reaches a whale-shaped rock formation on the left. Look straight ahead for a yellow marker on a tree and walk out to very open terrain through oak trees. Within two minutes from the whale-shaped rock, the trail leads right, over the rubble of an old farm wall. Before crossing the wall, there is a pleasant place to take a break on a large rock to the left. This rock looks down over a tiny, elongated lake. At certain times of the year this area is probably just a marsh, but the rocks to the left make a natural dam to hold back the water.

After crossing a ruined wall, the trail leads through larches to cross the wall again, turning left onto an old woods road. There are many woods roads and old walls in this spot, and within a very short time, the trail makes another left turn onto a woods road where evidence of another ruined wall is seen. The woods road is very wide at this point, and it is not important that the markers are infrequent since the route is obvious. After another wall crossing, be sure to turn right through an area of deciduous trees and mountain laurel.

Another ten minutes brings you to a T-junction. Turn left, descending through a swampy area, and climb back up until another woods road junction is reached, where the trail turns left again. The swampy area on the left here is drained to the valley on the right by two concrete conduits that cross the road. Shortly, the trail turns left off this woods road. Here, by climbing to the top of the rocks to the right of the junction, it is possible to see the Lookout Tower in the Newark Watershed.

After the junction, the trail goes steadily downhill to another swampy area, then climbs again for a short distance. Go straight ahead on the yellow-marked trail, ignoring the one coming in from the left. In this section the markers are again a little indistinct, but the trail is wide and there should be no problem making your way until the trail turns left, loses the appearance of a woods road, and becomes rockier. There are many larger boulders to negotiate in this section. The trail climbs up and down, finally descending and ascending again quite steeply and crossing another wet area.

Pudding stone is found at the crest of this last rise, and there is a view back through the trees of the Newark Watershed area. Look for a very interesting boulder at the north end of this rock outcrop and observe how the harder rock has resulted in spider web markings all over the boulder. Leaving the ridge, the trail bears left between two banks of rocks and descends, with another ridge immediately ahead. Cross the water at the bottom of this gully, turn right, and walk along what appears to be a streambed with a great deal of sphagnum moss. This section is gloomy, with large rocks looming above the trail and with another ridge of rocks closely to the left. Markers are not obvious, but there is no doubt which way to go. After ten minutes in the gully, the still mossy trail drops down to meet the Red Bar Trail. Turning left on the Red Bar Trail eventually brings you to the white trail, but the route is not recommended for this hike as it is difficult to follow.

Continue to follow the yellow trail, which jogs right and immediately left to climb more rocks to another ledge. The way now becomes like a roller coaster, climbing up and down ridges. The trail appears to be infrequently used, for lichen is prominent and slippery when wet. Thirty minutes after the junction with the Red Bar Trail, at the foot of a steep, rocky portion, the Terrace Pond Red Trail joins from the right. The two trails run together through a swampy area with "stepping stone" rocks to negotiate. Look up to the left to see a tall rock pinnacle towering above the already high rock wall. The trail again follows a damp gully, but very shortly the gully flattens out and ends at three yellow markers on a tree to the right, indicating the end of the yellow trail and the commencement of the white.

The white trail completely encircles Terrace Pond. Turning right leads further away from Terrace Pond, and it is sometimes difficult to negotiate the outlet of the pond. For this reason, turn left and follow the narrower white trail, which enables you to look down on another stupendous rhododendron grove in the valley below the trail. The view from here is tremendous when these magnificent shrubs are in bloom. Looking across the rhododendron gully, notice the white pines on the other side of this inlet to Terrace Pond. The white trail at one point has a high-water and a low-water trail, but the way is obvious. Very shortly, the trail descends into the gully and is much wetter, and you can look up to see the rhododendrons, now high above the trail.

After you emerge from the gully and are walking along the base of a large rock slab to the left, a close watch will reveal where the Red Bar Trail (ignored earlier in the hike) joins the white trail. Climbing a short way and backtracking is worth the effort for a panoramic view of Terrace Pond. Cross the next rock area, continuing on the white trail, which climbs to the right, where a good view of Terrace Pond is obtained. The white trail travels along the west side of Terrace Pond, with many beautiful rock slabs and sandy beach areas, until, at the end of the lake, the white trail bears off to the right on its trip around the lake. At this junction, make sure to follow the poorly marked blue trail to the left.

The blue-marked Terrace Pond North Trail travels over ridges and through wet areas consecutively. Be careful to stay on the marked trail until it leads you to a high ridge, which should be climbed for a stupendous view of the Wawayanda Plateau. After refreshing the spirit with the beautiful panorama, continue to follow the blue trail, which passes through woody, wet areas and rock outcrops alternately. Some of the descents, although

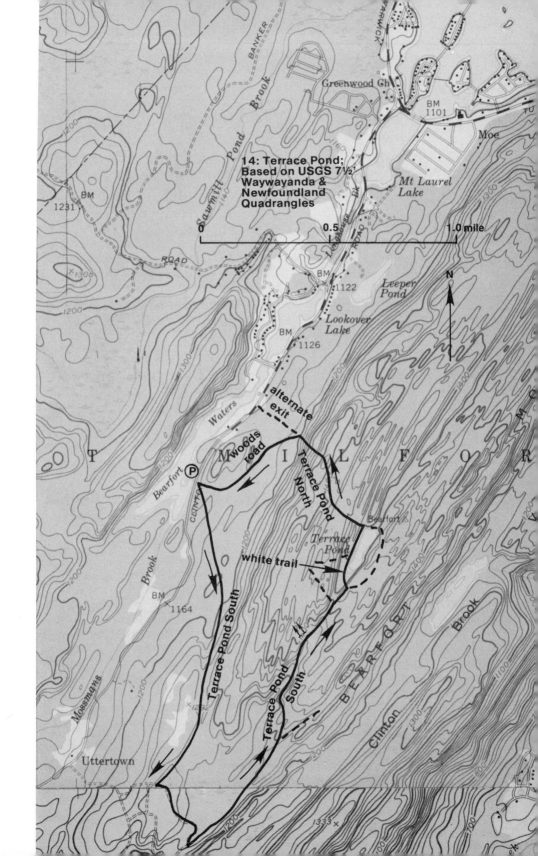

**14: Terrace Pond;
Based on USGS 7½'
Waywayanda &
Newfoundland
Quadrangles**

0   0.5   1.0 mile

N

Glacial erratic.

short, are steep and slippery. The main direction is downhill, until, quite suddenly, the trail comes upon the ugly slash of a pipeline. Turn left and follow the pipeline down, keeping to the left of the gash on the hill and looking for the blue arrows, confirming that you are still on the trail. Ignore the several woods roads to the left and continue until a very distinct, blue-marked woods road is reached just as the pipeline stops going downhill and levels off. If you miss this woods road, follow the pipeline to Clinton Road, turn left, and walk along the road .3 mile to the parking lot. This alternative route should be considered in wet weather.

The blue-marked road is wide, but somewhat damp. Ignore all the other paths and stay with the blue markers. The trail is very low-lying, and as you walk, you will be aware of the ridge to the left down which you have just walked. This section of the trail is very pretty, passing through white pines, thick mountain laurel, and a dense hemlock area with very large trees. There are several streams to be crossed, however, with the trail bending left and right to cross them. The path parallels the road, finally turning right, climbing, and descending to the road immediately opposite the parking area.

SJG

15

Pequannock Watershed

Total distance: 8 miles (9.5 without car shuttle)
Hiking time: 6 hours
Vertical rise: 400 feet
Rating: Moderately strenuous
Maps: NYNJTC North Jersey Trails #21; HRM #36A; Pequan-
nock Watershed Trails Map; USGS Newfoundland

The Pequannock River is fed by the streams, lakes, and reservoirs of this mountainous and particularly scenic section of western Passic County. Owned by the City of Newark, this natural area just south of Wawayanda State Park supplies much of Newark's drinking water. About thirty miles of excellent hiking trails have been cut and blazed in this largely uninhabited area by the Newark Watershed Conservation and Development Corporation (NWCDC), a nonprofit organization, and the land is open for recreational use by permit only (NWCDC, PO Box 319, Newfoundland, NJ 07435; 201-697-2850). All the trails in the watershed are blazed in white. A tree marked with three blazes indicates the beginning or the end of a trail, two blazes indicate a turn, and one blaze is simply the route of the trail. Because there are many junctions and intersections all with the same color blaze, it is necessary to have a map of the area. To obtain a permit and a map for hiking, you must apply in person at the NWCDC headquarters on Echo Lake Road, about one mile north of NJ 23. At the time of this writing, the fee is $6.00 per year and well worth it.

This hike takes you on a grand tour of some of the more scenic and interesting features of the watershed. Though the hike is long, the walking is not difficult, and much of it is along the shores of ponds and reservoirs. Some deep hemlock forests typical of this area are traversed, and there are a few overlooks as well as the Bearfort fire tower from which to survey the area. Part of the hike is on the Bearfort Mountain ridge, with its pink to purple sandstones and conglomerates. This ridge, composed of relatively young sedimentary rock, is a geological anomaly, for it occurs in the midst of the much older, Precambrian highlands formation. Apparently, Bearfort Mountain is the remains of the sand and silt deposits of a long, narrow, inland sea or sound that penetrated the older highlands. Notice the distinct change of bedrock as you hike from Bearfort Mountain to Buckabear Pond, the latter being entirely in the highlands with its typical gray, Precambrian gneiss, a granitic rock.

Of particular interest on this hike are the ruins of Cross Castle or Bearfort House, a large mountain estate built by Richard James Cross about eighty years ago. Cross, a native of England, made a fortune in banking and later erected this fantastic but short-lived mansion. The entire 365-acre estate featured the three-story castle with views in all directions, hot and cold running water, numerous fireplaces, stables, carriage houses, guest cottages, and a boathouse on Hank's Pond. All that is left today are the foundations and walls of stone, which survived the dismantling of the mansion by the City of Newark when it was acquired in 1919.

Also of interest is the Clinton Furnace, one of the very few surviving furnaces used during the region's iron-making era. The furnace, located just off Clinton Road near its intersection with Schoolhouse Road, is still in fairly good shape. Iron smelting furnaces were always built near running water, necessary for the water-wheel-driven bellows. As would be expected, a substantial series of waterfalls is located immediately to the side of Clinton Furnace. Once the furnace was fired up, it would burn for months at a time and was loaded with iron ore from the top. This furnace's location at the base of a sharp drop facilitated this top loading requirement.

This hike can be done as a circuit, which would include an additional mile and a half of road walking, or cars can be parked and a shuttle arranged. The walk on the road is not at all unpleasant and will only add about a half hour to your hike. If you choose to do the extra walking, park at Parking Area 9 (P9) and walk to P1. If not, leave one car at P9 and drive another to P1 to begin the hike.

To find P9 from NJ 23, take Clinton Road north for 1.2 miles and turn left on Schoolhouse Road, a gravel road with good views of Clinton Reservoir. After 1 mile, make a right turn onto Paradise Road and find the small parking area on the right in .1 mile. After parking, walk or drive down Schoolhouse Road the way you came to Clinton Road. At this intersection, directly in front of you, though it may be obscured by foliage in the summer, are the Clinton Furnace and the falls described earlier. Turn left at the intersection and walk or drive .3 mile north on paved Clinton Road to where Van Orden Road (gravel) comes in on the right. This parking area is P1, and you will begin your hike from here.

Begin walking north on the dirt road, which is not marked, heading into the woods. You will pass, but not follow, trails coming in on first the left and then the right. Soon you will see the southern end of Hanks Pond coming up on the right. Stay on this dirt road, bordered with wild azalea and pepperbush, as it swings around the west shore of the pond paralleling the water. After about fifteen or twenty minutes, you should come to the remains of the Cross Castle boathouse on your left, now only a roofless stone building. At the small "paved" clearing with the remains of a fireplace, look for a marked trail heading steeply up the hill—take it to Cross Castle.

At the top of the rise, and with the castle in view, your next turn will be a sharp right onto the marked woods road in front of you, the Fire Tower Ridge Trail. The castle is quite a sight, but it is also abused by beer drinkers—watch out for glass. After inspection, continue by walking north on the Fire Tower Ridge Trail. Follow the white markers, passing the stone water storage tower, which supplied water for the castle, and bear to the right, following the markers where the trail forks. The footing becomes rockier now, and, after a short rise, the trail swings to the right on what is now a footpath over exposed bedrock. White pines, mountain laurel, and an occasional cedar make this section of trail especially sce-

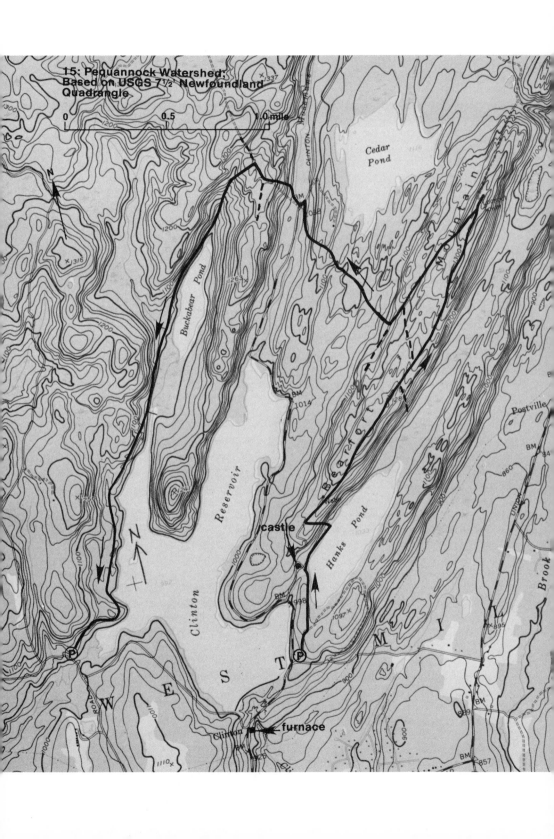

15: Pequannock Watershed;
Based on USGS 7½' Newfoundland
Quadrangle

0   0.5   1.0 mile

Cedar
Pond

×1337

Buckabear Pond

1263

CLINTON

BM
1088

Reservoir

1014

BM

castle

Hanks Pond

1033

Bearfort

Mountain

Postville

BM
84

×1316

×1336

Clinton

Reservoir

998

1097 ×

BM

W   E   S   T   M   I   L   Y

Brook

furnace

Clinton

BM

1110 ×

900

857

BM

BM
895

BM
859

nic. Continue following the white markers (a trail comes in on the right in a rocky area) over slabs of glaciated, conglomerate bedrock and downhill over a small stream and into deeper woods. At the trail junction, which you will soon come upon, bear to the right and slightly uphill in hemlock and laurel. As you rise to the broad summit area of Bearfort Mountain, which contains oaks, laurel, and patches of grass, you'll see that the mountaintop is actually a series of parallel, narrow ridges separated by swamp and wet areas. Some of these ridges are well worth exploring. After less than an hour of walking from Cross Castle (and about 2.5 miles from the start of the hike), you'll come to a clearing, two picnic tables, and the fire tower—a good place for a snack or lunch. Take the time to climb the five flights of steps to the top of the fire tower where you will be rewarded by views of the entire watershed.

From the picnic table area, near a stone fireplace, head west for 100 feet and turn left and south on a footpath, the Fire Tower West Trail. You are now heading south through hemlock and laurel and will soon come out to a viewpoint near a large glacial erratic. Cedar Pond, a natural glacial lake, is below to the north. Continuing, the trail traverses some very beautiful woodland with large pudding stone rock outcrops framed with white pine. Soon a trail will be seen on the left, and soon afterward another, more critical (and obscure) trail junction is reached. Stay to the right here, the way the trail naturally seems to go, and head downhill off the mountain on the Two Brooks Trail.

Soon you will come to a small clearing; follow the white markers through ferns and deep hemlocks and then out to a brook. This brook can be difficult to cross after a thaw or heavy rain. A former bridge was swept away and will hopefully be replaced. Until then, you must cross on rocks. If you look around, you will find trees gnawed by beaver in this area. After crossing the brook, the trail, not well marked here, turns sharply to the right through very tall and dense hemlocks. Continue along the trail over rocks and pine needles and then out to another brook, this one having a log bridge with a wire handhold. After crossing the brook, watch for the trail to turn left and uphill—the markers are not clear here also. After a rise, the trail descends slightly through moss, pine, beech, maple, and especially hemlock, which gets thicker as the trail approaches Mossman's Brook. After a pleasant walk on pine needles through a primeval hemlock forest along the brook, the trail comes out to Clinton Road at P4. This area is very quiet and still. Standing to listen, it is possible to hear needles falling from the hemlock trees sounding like a light rain.

Make a left on Clinton Road and look for white blazes on the right-hand side of the road. After only 100 yards of road walking, follow the white blazes and turn right on a woods road. Another right turn comes up almost immediately as the trail heads temporarily north. In a short distance, the trail swings to the left and heads steeply uphill, this climb being the longest of the hike (a 250-foot climb at most). Notice that the rock in this area is different from that on which you have been walking. Here is the Precambrian gneiss, a much older rock than the purple sedimentary sandstones and conglomerates that make up Bearfort Mountain. When you reach the top of the rise, there should be two trails coming in on the left. Take the second of the two, downhill from the main crest of the rise. You should now be heading southward toward Buckabear Pond.

This trail, the Bearfort Waters/Clinton Trail, heads gradually downhill through

Clinton Reservoir.

blueberry bushes growing abundantly below dying oak trees that have been decimated by gypsy moths. As the trail descends, more ferns appear, and the land gets damper and wetter. You may need to climb over blowdowns in this remote and little-used section of the watershed. Soon the hemlocks begin to predominate again, until the north shore of Buckabear Pond is reached in a swampy area. Cross a little stream and follow the trail, now an old stone and dirt road that runs parallel and above the west shore of the lake. At about the midpoint of the pond, the trail makes a slight jog to the left where it meets a dirt road used by four-wheelers, but then continues heading south in laurel and rhododendron along the west shore of the pond. At the trail junction south of the pond, bear to the right on the Clinton South Trail.

Soon you will see Clinton Reservoir on the left, the largest body of water on this hike. As the trail veers away from the reservoir, it will turn left off the woods road it has been following and head back towards the reservoir on a footpath. The trail now hugs the shoreline with good views of water, islands, and hills and again turns left and downhill where a rocky woods road comes in. In this vicinity, on the right and uphill, are found a number of plaques commemorating the lives of hikers and trail builders of the past. Still following the shoreline, the trail passes a cove, popular with Canada geese that are frequently found foraging there. Just a short walk ahead you will emerge from the woods at Parking Area 9 and your car.

BCS

16

Pyramid Mountain

Total distance: 3 miles
Hiking time: 2.5 hours
Vertical rise: 390 feet
Rating: Easy to moderate
Maps: NYNJTC Boonton-Butler Trails; USGS Boonton

Pyramid Mountain, at 920 feet, is not the highest summit ridge in northern Morris County, but it has much to offer the hiker. It is crossed by trails that can be steep and rugged in places, has several overlooks, and contains a mysterious glacial erratic that may be part of an ancient Indian calendar site. To the west of the mountain ridge is Stony Brook and its wetland. Here is found the gigantic Bear Rock, a granite monolith that towers over the brook and swamp. The land containing these wonders is, at the time of this writing, privately owned, and plans are being made to develop this valuable suburban land. To challenge and halt the potential desecration of this natural and historic area, a grass-roots committee has been formed and continues to be active. Hopefully, the next generation of New Jersey hikers will find this area as it is today, not developed with condos.

The hike begins on the blue Butler–Montville Trail where it crosses NJ 511, about halfway between Boonton and Butler. This point is .8 mile north of the intersection of NJ 511 and Taylortown Road where a high voltage line crosses the road. Parking for a few cars can be found on the west side of the road here,

though additional parking can be found at Mars Park, an industrial park about 100 yards south.

Begin hiking following the blue markers that lead away from the road and head west. The trail crosses a few wet areas on planks and then crosses a brook. Here the trail follows a dirt road for a short distance before it turns off to the right and begins a short, but steep, climb to the shoulder of Pyramid Mountain. The stone steps leading up the hill are said to have been constructed by the utility company many years ago. The climb ends under a high voltage tower, which is also a trail junction. Do not follow the blue markers to the right here or the white markers to the left. Look for and follow white markers that lead straight ahead, via a woods road, along the power line cut or parallel to it.

For the next quarter mile the white markers lead through a combination of woods and field, all dominated, unfortunately, by the power lines. Numerous wildflowers can be found along the route including healall, a member of the mint family, and the closed gentian. As the trail heads downhill where there are no trees, pay close attention to the markings found mostly on rocks. The trail, which may be wet and muddy in places, will turn left off the woods road, cross a brook, then reenter the woods near a high voltage tower.

Now heading north away from the power lines, the white markers follow an old farm lane. On both sides of the path are remnants of former habitation. A foundation is located just to the right where the trail first enters the woods, and rock walls parallel the lane as it penetrates the woods. To the right is Stony Brook. In about a quarter mile from the power lines, you come to Bear Rock.

Standing alone in the woods at the edge of a large swamp, Bear Rock has been used as a boundary marker for at least two hundred years. Even today it marks the borders of the Kinnelon and Montville boroughs. Although it is difficult and even dangerous to scale, some very old surveying markers can be found near its highest points. Bear Rock is a glacial erratic, plucked from the side of Stony Brook Mountain and dragged several hundred feet by the glacial ice sheet that covered the area twelve thousand years ago. To the northwest, about 150 yards away, is a waterfall that cascades over bare rock during the spring and after heavy rains.

From Bear Rock, continue following white markers, which are now concurrent with blue markers, across the brook and along the edge of the Stony Brook Swamp. Along the path are many dwarf ginseng plants, pepperbush, and spicebush. The trail will swing to the left and then to the right, where it begins to climb steeply the ridge of Pyramid Mountain over rocks. The climb, though only about 150 feet of vertical rise, is stiff. Lining the trail are clusters of mountain laurel, which create a tunnel effect in places. As the ridge summit is reached, the trail comes to a T-junction. A left turn here following

16: Pyramid Mountain;
Based on USGS 7½'
Boonton Quadrangle

white markers leads in 200 yards to Tripod Rock.

Tripod Rock, perhaps the most massive perched boulder of its kind in the entire Northeast, is the focal point of what may be an ancient calendar site. The sheer size and bizarre appearance of Tripod Rock, a two hundred-ton boulder standing on three medicine ball-sized rocks, staggers the imagination. If it is simply a chance product of the last ice age, which is what most geologists believe, then it is unique. Others suggest that it was modified by man. Nearby are

Tripod Rock on Pyramid Mountain.

two smaller stones partially perched on exposed bedrock. An observer seated on a lip protruding from a piece of bedrock four feet high will see, through the gap between these two stones, the summer solstice sunset. The alignment constitutes a simple solar observatory. Whether or not it was used by the early inhabitants of the area is an open question.

From Tripod Rock, retrace your steps to the junction and continue heading south along the ridge following blue markers. This section of trail is overshadowed by tall rhododendrons and mountain laurel, a beautiful sight in winter. Just before the trail swings sharply to the left, look for a small side trail on the right. This blue-and-white-marked trail leads west in 100 yards to Lucy's Lookout, named for Lucy Meyer who has led the crusade to save this beautiful area from development. You will have a view

to the south and west over Stony Brook Mountain from this rocky point. Return to the main trail and continue heading south.

After a series of ups and downs, the blue trail leads to the open southern end of the Pyramid Mountain ridge. Here, over bare rock, are very expansive views to the east and south, including a view of the New York skyline when visibility is good. Many years ago a fire tower was located here, but evidence of its former existence is scant today. After taking in the view of woodland, hills, and encroaching suburbia, head steeply downhill on the blue trail to the power line cut and its junction with the white trail. Bear left and downhill here, retracing your steps, and follow the blue markers east to NJ 511 and your car.

BCS

17

Wawayanda State Park

Total distance: 7 miles
Hiking time: 3.5 hours
Vertical rise: 200 feet
Rating: Easy
Maps: USGS Wawayanda; NYNJTC #21; WB #21

Wawayanda State Park (Highland Lakes, New Jersey 07422; 201-853-4462), covering almost ten thousand acres of forest and water, is located along the Passaic and Sussex county boundaries and borders New York State at the northern extremity of the New Jersey highlands. The name "Wawayanda" is the phonetic rendition of the Lenape Indian name said to mean "water on the mountain." In spite of urban development, the feeling in Wawayanda is that of wilderness, and the hike described is delightful in any season. In summer, the walker is protected from the heat of the sun by the leafy canopy of mature trees and is able to cool off in the lake after hiking; in fall, the same trees are a riot of color, although squirrels from above can bombard the unwary with acorns; in winter, these trails are so gentle and wide they are admirably suited for cross-country skiing when the snow is deep enough. Because of the high elevation of the plateau, snow accumulation remains longer in Wawayanda State Park than in other areas. The terrain undulates and winds in a relaxed way, making for very pleasant and companionable walking. This hike uses the Wingdam, Laurel Pond, Cherry, Old

Coal, and Lookout trails, as well as Cherry Ridge Road, and the hike roughly describes a figure eight.

The park office in Wawayanda State Park is accessed from the northern section of Warwick Turnpike, approached from the north from NY 94 and from the south on Clinton Road. The park entrance is on the west side of Warwick Turnpike approximately 1.25 miles north of Upper Greenwood Lake. A good road map is an asset. Just beyond the park entrance, stop at the office to obtain the park map and other literature. The hike actually begins at the boathouse area, the second parking lot after reaching the lake. Out of season parking is free, but in season a small fee is charged. During the summer months, it is advisable to arrive before 10:00 A.M. to be sure of a parking space.

Wawayanda Lake was once two separate bodies of water called Double Pond. The narrow strip of land that divided the two areas of water still partly shows on the west side of Barker Island, now in the center of the lake. In winter, when the lake is frozen solid, it is pleasant to walk across the ice to Barker Island and to observe the ice fishermen.

With Wawayanda Lake on your right-hand side, leave the parking lot, walk towards the left to a wide gravel road, ignoring a woods road coming in, and follow the main road by the side of the lake. The stone dam coming into view at the northeastern end of the lake was built in the middle of the last century by the Thomas Iron Company. On the lake, admire the many yellow pond lilies and white fragrant water lilies and note, as the dam is reached, that there are picnic tables and a disconnected water pump. The hike returns to this point. Here, turn right, cross the dam, walk through the barrier of large boulders, and find, immediately ahead, the beginning of the Wingdam Trail. At this point, you have walked for approximately ten minutes.

The Wingdam Trail, marked in blue,* is a wide gravel road climbing slightly uphill through mature hardwood trees. On the left is an old stone wall, and the road itself is in a dip, ground rising on both sides. After another five minutes, the sound of running water can be heard, and the trail begins to drop towards a wooden bridge spanning a water spill to Laurel Pond. Just before the wooden bridge, and at other times, there are woods roads joining the main trail. At present there are still areas of private property in the park. These properties will become state owned eventually, and most of the side roads are often posted and do not merit much attention.

The "wing dam" on the right-hand side of the wooden bridge was constructed by the Thomas Iron Company, and, together with the dam crossed at the beginning, raises the lake level by about seven and a half feet. The water comes over this dam in a wide, swift fall and rushes on its way to feed Laurel Pond,

*May be changed to yellow in 1988.

out of sight on the left. Wildflowers abound in this lush area at all times of the year.

Soon after the bridge is crossed, Laurel Pond is glimpsed through the trees on the left. The trees become slightly shorter in stature, and rhododendrons begin to appear, hinting of the large stands surrounding this end of Laurel Pond. Soon after passing a large boulder on the right, another woods road comes in on the same side. This one is worth exploring because it leads to an abandoned home and a derelict walkway across a swampy area on a peninsula, from which a small island in the center of Waywanda Lake is visible. The boathouse at the northern end of the lake is partially in view also.

Once back on the main trail, there are other home roads coming in on the left, some of them with the owner's name posted. The route for a while is grassy and less gravelly. Within about thirty minutes from the start of the hike, the trail grows narrower, begins to climb with more boulders underfoot, and looks more like a hiking trail. Here there are a few evergreens as the trail becomes even steeper and more rocky and, instead of continuing across the side of the hill, turns sharply right. In another five minutes, the trail reaches the crest of the hill and emerges into a rocky, grassy area, with a slight view through the trees to the left of a tree-covered ridge across the valley. This clearing is another pleasant place to pause. The highest point in this part of the park is off the trail to the right, 1,375 feet above sea level.

Turn left and follow the marked trail downhill to a grassy woods road and the end of the Wingdam Trail. This woods road is the Laurel Pond Trail, marked in yellow. Turn right. Traveling slightly downhill, the trees are denser again, and the terrain soon develops into level, pleasant walking.

An interesting section is reached after a few minutes. On the right-hand side of the trail there is a large outcrop of big rocks split many times with trees growing in the cracks, and farther to the left, another ridge of such rocks is discernable. Even farther down the trail to the left, watch for a large boulder split completely down the center and fallen apart. This section is a paradise for chipmunks.

The road is wide and distinct and becomes even sandier and smoother. Within fifteen minutes and after passing another woods road on the right, the T-junction with Cherry Ridge Road is reached. Turn left here, but do not expect to find markers. The road is still wide and gravelly and the trail is bordered by mature trees with some evergreens mixed in with the deciduous trees. Notice that in times of heavy rain the road becomes an escape route for excess water. The next, slowly moving stream is crossed within a few minutes on a wooden bridge. Look to the left-hand side of the bridge to see "539" etched in nails, a New Jersey Department of Transportation number.

As expected after a stream crossing, the road climbs away from the stream, becoming wider and stonier. At the top of this short climb, Cherry Ridge Road goes off to the left. Take the Old Coal Trail, straight ahead, marked in red and with a new wooden stake with "Old Coal TR" carved into it. Soon the first white pines make their appearance. Within about five minutes, at a wide, grassy junction, leave the Old Coal Trail and make a right turn onto the Lookout Trail, marked in white. The three white markers traditionally designating the beginning or ending of a trail can be clearly seen.

Within a few minutes, you will come to a very old, large hemlock just to the right of the trail. There are several other an-

cient hemlock in the vicinity, but this particular specimen is at least nine feet in circumference. Gradually the trees begin to thin out, and the trail is more grassy, with young trees, wildflowers in season, and a large number of wild strawberry plants for your summer pleasure.

Through the trees to the right there can be seen a swampy area with dead trees, and across the road there is a metal drainage pipe, evidence of human habitation in Wawayanda.

After ten minutes of leisurely walking from the great hemlock, Lake Lookout comes into view on the left, preceded by a grassy, open space. This spot is a delightful, seldom-visited place. Take time to admire the wildflowers and to sit, quietly admiring the plants and wildlife: numerous dragonflies in summer, frogs and the occasional turtle sunning themselves on the bank, some fine specimens of pickerelweed, and a good supply of cattails.

Leaving Lake Lookout's peaceful environs, continue straight past the lake outlet and into the woods.* The footway is now narrow and a little indistinct but marked clearly with white paint and white metal patches. The trail climbs steeply for a short distance among large boulders wearing hair pieces of fern. Within five minutes from the lake, look for a trail turn at a T-junction. Turn right and follow the road around a sharp, left-hand bend, climbing slightly at the same time and noticing that you are now among mountain laurel instead of the larger rhododendrons seen previously.

The T-junction with Cherry Ridge Road is arrived at within ten minutes, where you turn right and a further ten minutes of flat walking brings the junction of Laurel Pond Trail and Cherry Ridge Road

*Rerouting is planned here during 1988.

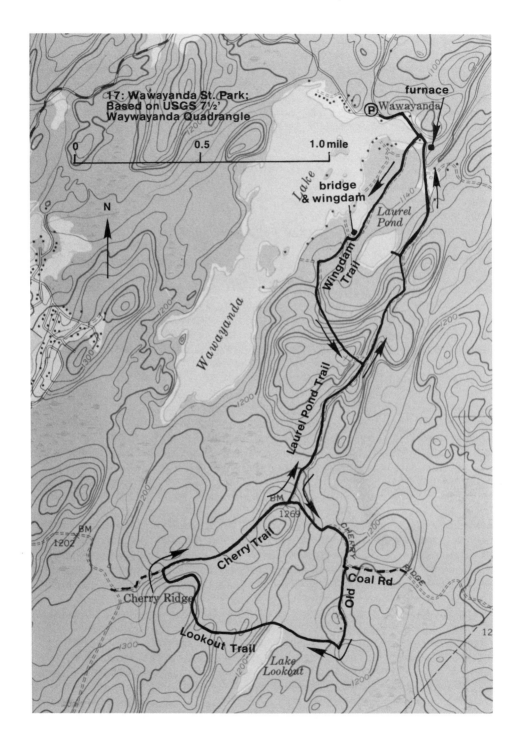

17: Wawayanda St. Park;
Based on USGS 7½'
Waywayanda Quadrangle

N

0   0.5   1.0 mile

furnace

Wawayanda

Lake

bridge
& wingdam

Laurel
Pond

Wingdam Trail

Wawayanda

Laurel Pond Trail

BM
1269

Cherry Trail

CHERRY

BM
1202

Cherry Ridge

Coal Rd

RIDGE

Lookout Trail

Lake
Lookout

into view. This junction should be familiar, since it was encountered previously in the day on the route out. Turn left here and retrace your earlier footsteps. After the Wingdam Trail enters, the ground being covered is new. Stay on the Laurel Pond Trail. The road loses altitude slightly, gradually becoming rockier and narrower with tall rhododendrons concentrated on the left-hand side of the trail.

A visit to the shore of Lake Laurel is worth the short, five-minute detour from the main trail. Shortly after a downhill grade, approximately ten minutes from the junction of the Wingdam Trail, watch for a yellow marker on a tree to the left of the trail. At this point, there is a clear trail to the left that goes slightly downhill, on a narrow path practically overgrown with tall rhododendron bushes, to the top of a rocky outcrop just above Lake Laurel. If the scramble down to the water's edge is a deterrent, bear left and then switchback right to achieve the same result as climbing down the rocks. Laurel Pond is a favorite place for fishermen, and if this first access point is passed, there is a second opportunity to reach the lakeshore a little farther down the main trail. As you are sitting on the lake edge, observe that the inlet to Laurel Pond, passed earlier in the hike, is practically opposite you. The slope of the opposite bank is much more shallow than would be expected from the noise of the water entering Laurel Pond from Lake Wawayanda.

After rejoining the Laurel Pond Trail, the route parallels the lakeshore for a few minutes, then swings away from it to where, within another five minutes, there is evidence that the road was once gated. Here, too, is a yellow-marked tree with the sign "Laurel Pond Trail." Ignore the gated road coming in on the right and walk towards the open, low-lying area ahead. After heavy rain, this part of the trail is often flooded but is usually negotiable without a problem. After crossing the wooden bridge at the outlet from Laurel Pond, the site of the old "Mule Barn" is passed on the left. The barn has only recently been burned down by vandals. It once housed the mules used to haul the raw materials required for producing iron in Wawayanda.

Straight ahead is the old charcoal furnace, and on the right is another wooden bridge leading to a group campsite furnished with picnic tables. Pause at the furnace and, standing with your back to the swiftly running stream, try to imagine the busy scene of yesteryear when Wawayanda was the center of the iron industry in New Jersey. This structure is all that remains of a charcoal blast furnace built by Oliver Ames and his three sons, William, Oaks, and Oliver, Junior. William was in charge, and his initials, W.L.S., and the date 1846 can still be seen on a lintel in the main arch. Iron ore from local mines was smelted here continuously for ten years until 1857 when cheap coal became available in Pennsylvania, making it more economical to transport the ore for smelting to those hotter and more efficient furnaces.

In an average day, seven tons of iron would be produced from this type of furnace and would be poured off twice daily at noon and at midnight. Wawayanda iron was of such superior quality that it was used to manufacture railroad wheels, and, during the Civil War, the Ames factories filled government orders for shovels and swords. During the time of greatest activity, a small village grew up in the vicinity to house the workers and to provide services such as a post office, store, gristmill, and sawmill. Nothing remains now. The building is currently supported by metal framing and protected from vandals by substantial fencing.

Peaceful moment overlooking Laurel Pond in Wawayanda.

After visiting the furnace and reading the bulletin board, retrace your footsteps a little to where a sign on the right reads, "Positively no vehicles beyond this point." Follow this wide, slightly uphill gravel road. It leads past the side of the old furnace and over another old wooden bridge across a mostly dried-up stream. There is an old stone wall to the left and evidence of buildings probably used in conjunction with the furnace. Soon the picnic tables and disconnected pump passed on the way out, at the north-eastern end of Lake Wawayanda, can be recognized. Return by way of the shore-line to the parking lot, on the same path used at the hike's beginning.

SJG

18

Mahlon Dickerson Reservation

Total distance: 3.5 miles
Hiking time: 2.5 hours
Vertical rise: 238 feet
Rating: Easy to moderate
Maps: USGS Franklin; Morris County Park Commission park
   brouchure and map

The Morris County Park Commission, steward of this reservation, believes that only ten percent of its parkland should be developed for intensive recreation (picnic sites, ball fields, and playgrounds), while most of it should be left in its natural state. As a result of this policy, hikers in Morris County have a number of excellent and nearby parks to hike in. The largest county park in Morris County, Mahlon Dickerson Reservation, is more like a state park and contains tent sites, several Adirondack-type shelters, and trailer camping areas. The park covers nearly three thousand acres at the time of this writing and seems to be expanding at a steady pace.

To find the reservation from NJ 15 near Sparta, follow signs to Milton and Weldon Road. After a few miles on Weldon Road, you'll see a sign indicating that you've entered the reservation. The road will swing around to the right, and in roughly another mile, you will come to three entrances, the first two for campers. Take the second entrance on the left, which leads to a large parking area and the trailhead.

The reservation was named for one of

Morris County's great achievers, Mahlon Dickerson (1770–1853). Dickerson, who lived near Dover, had a model life of political service. He never married but was successful in nearly everything else he tried. He mastered several languages and attained distinction as a botanist. He owned and operated the Succasunna iron mines, some of the largest in the county. He was a general in the military, served in the state legislature, and was governor of New Jersey for a short period. He served as a member of Congress between 1817 and 1829 and, during the presidency of Andrew Jackson, served as secretary of the navy. He was said to have been popular with everyone and very consistent in his political faith.

In the reservation are a number of marked trails that are, for the most part, old logging roads, which make for easy walking and a wide path. The park is well suited for cross-country skiing, and, along with the wide path, there are many small ups and downs and a few good-sized hills. Also, because the average elevation in the park is twelve hundred feet, snow remains on the ground longer

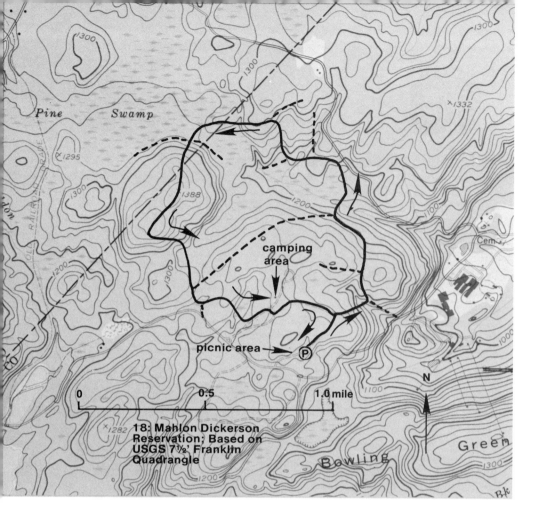

Pine Swamp

camping area

picnic area →

N

0   0.5   1.0 mile

18: Mahlon Dickerson
Reservation; Based on
USGS 7½' Franklin
Quadrangle

Cem.

Green

Bowling

than in many other areas in north Jersey. There are a few cut trails in the trail system, one of which crosses the center of the loop trail we'll be on and which you may wish to explore at another time. Check the directory at the parking area for further trail information (and possible changes) on this relatively new and continuously developing hiking area.

Although this hike does not offer any sweeping views of the countryside, the change in woodland environments more than makes up for this deficiency. Along the route are deciduous forests, rocky scrub growth, damp hemlock groves, laurel thickets, and remote swampland.

The reservation is located on a high plateau in the New Jersey highlands province. The bedrock, which is very close to the surface due to glaciation, is Precambrian gneiss, a granitic rock that contains large amounts of iron. There are a few iron mines, long abandoned, to be found in the reservation. Since the park is large and located in the most remote part of Morris County, wildlife, including the red-tailed hawk, many deer, and an occasional bear, make their homes here.

From the parking area, walk north past the water pump on the wide asphalt path through a picnic area. A ball field will be on your left. The access trail you are on, which should have a few white markers on the trees, leads in .1 mile to a junction with the Pine Swamp Trail, a 3.5-mile loop marked in white that passes through the northern part of the reservation. Make a right turn at the junction and walk downhill and over a small brook. At the next junction, which is the starting point for a blue trail, bear left, following the white markers. After a short climb, the trail veers to the right at an intersection, heads downhill, and then swings to the left through an open forest.

After a short, level stretch, the trail comes to a triangular junction with another trail and turns to the right, down a long hill to a brook. This unnamed brook is one of the principal drainages for the swamp that dominates the interior of the northern portion of the reservation. At the time of this writing, the old wooden bridge over it was falling apart, and it is hoped that a replacement will soon be built. If not, the brook can be easily crossed except in times of severe flooding. Notice that the brook's water is a dark color. Like in the Pine Barrens, the tannins in the roots of hemlocks and other swamp evergreens color the water. After crossing the brook, be alert for a left turn off the main path onto a cut trail through a corner of the swamp.

In this section of trail, mountain laurel and rhododendron dominate, putting on a display of flowers in June and July. The footing is much rockier here, and there can be a few wet areas that may require some stretching. As you reach the end of this part of the swamp, the trail climbs up a few feet to higher ground and connects with a woods road, on which it turns left. Since this part of the trail is near Sparta Mountain Road, you may hear the occasional sound of a motor vehicle.

After about .1 mile, where the white blazes turn to the right, you'll come to a junction with a yellow trail, the Cut-off Trail. Take this trail straight ahead, following yellow markers down to and over a small brook and then through a wet area of hemlocks. You'll come to another junction, where a blue trail begins on the left. Continue following yellow markers, which lead uphill on an old logging road through hemlocks. At the end of this climb, the yellow Cut-off Trail meets again with the white Pine Swamp Trail— you will have saved some walking and not missed any of the remarkable Pine Swamp.

Turn left on the Pine Swamp Trail, following white markers, and enter the area of the Pine Swamp itself. Just ahead on your left, at the edge of a small cliff, look for an area that overlooks the dense foliage of the swamp. This spot is a pleasant place to stop for a rest or to have a snack or lunch. Below you is not a typical swamp of grasses and water, but a pine swamp with tall spruce, hemlock, rhododendron, and laurel.

Continue farther along on the trail, which now heads downhill to the level of the swamp, and get a closer view of this peculiar area. About .2 mile ahead, the trail, which is a woods road and is very dry, comes closest to the main swamp itself. Off to your right you can see how wet the area is and how huge boulders protrude from the ground providing, in their cracks, dryer areas for plants incapable of growing in water or very wet soil. You are now in one of the most remote areas of the reservation. On your right, the swamp extends for perhaps nearly a mile into Sussex County. It is virtually inaccessible, since no paths cross it. You get a feeling of wilderness here, broken only by the calls of birds and an occasional aircraft. In fact, several years ago a small private plane crashed in the swamp in May. It wasn't until November of that year that the wreckage and the bodies were found.

The trail, which travels a high area between two parts of the swamp, continues through hemlocks, crosses a small brook, and then begins a climb, leaving the swamp for good. You'll pass a junction with a blue trail near a resting bench and then climb gradually to the flat, rounded summit of an unnamed hill that, at 1,388 feet, is the highest point in Morris County. There is a resting bench at the summit of this hill, also making it a good spot for a rest. Unfortunately, there are no views from this high point, except through the trees during winter.

From the bench at the summit, the trail, which in this section is used occasionally by maintenance vehicles, swings to the left, then to the right as it descends to lower ground. Follow the trail through a low area and then up a gradual climb. Just before meeting a trail that comes in from the left (the Boulder Trail), a few remnants of iron mining during the last century, mostly pits and rock piles, can be found by exploring the woods to your left and uphill. Just past this junction, the trail turns left at another junction and heads east on a wide footpath. After about a quarter mile, you'll emerge from the woods into the middle of the trailer camping area.

Following white markers, make a left on the paved road and bear right near the rest rooms. Walk through the fence opening on your left, cross the field of grass, and reenter the woods on a trail to your right. In about .2 mile, you'll arrive at the trail junction you began the loop hike on, which is marked by a sign. Make a right here and walk the path through the picnic area and back to your car.

BCS

Hemlock grove.

Allamuchy Mountain State Park

Total distance: 4 miles
Hiking time: 2.5 hours
Vertical rise: 110 feet
Rating: Easy to moderate
Maps: USGS Tranquility; DEP: Allamuchy Mountain State Park

Allamuchy Mountain Park (Hackettstown, NJ 07840; 201-852-3790) is not known to many New Jerseyites. At present, access to the park is unmarked, and the drive to the parking area is over a rough, bumpy dirt road. The effort made to get there is worth it, however, for this park is rarely crowded and offers some excellent, though gentle, hiking. The trails, which are old farm and lumber roads, are graded and excellent for cross-country skiing. Because of its varied habitats, and also due to its privacy, this park maintains a large wildlife population and may be of interest to birders and naturalists.

From exit 19 on I-80, take NJ 517 south towards Hackettstown. You'll have to travel exactly 2 miles south of I-80 to find the access road to the park, which, at the time of this writing, is not marked. The road is found on the left near a brick house. There is also a wooden post in the ground at the corner. Turn left here and drive .6 mile over small hills and many potholes to the park entrance, which is only a parking area and a directory. Keep going for another mile, past a residence and through a gate. About .5 mile past this gate is a second gate and a large field for parking on the left. Park

your car here. During the winter, the rangers often close the first gate. If they do, park just before the first gate and walk the additional half mile.

From the parking area, walk through the gate on the dirt road you have been traveling on. This road swings to the right almost immediately and then begins a long, gradual descent through deciduous forest to Deer Park Pond. The road is marked with white markers on trees and is very easy to follow. Since this trail is the most frequently used one in the park, encounters with others hiking in both directions may be frequent. One of the striking things about this section is the openness of the forest. The forest floor is nearly all ferns, particularly on the right, and above that, nothing but open space until the lowest branches of some very large trees are reached. The effect is remarkably expansive for a New Jersey forest.

As you walk on, a portion of the lake appears through the trees on the left. This body of water is Deer Park Pond, once part of a private estate. Beavers have been introduced to the pond and have established themselves in a few areas. As you get closer to the water, you may spot one of their lodges on the opposite bank. Several years ago, a considerable amount of tree felling was done by the beavers along the northern shore of the pond. An entire section of shoreline was denuded, large trees were downed, and not all of it was used for construction. Along with the beavers, you could expect to see ducks, Canada geese, and possibly osprey, which nest here.

The road with its white markers will bring you down to the pond, over the dam and spillway, and along the eastern shore. There are some lovely areas here, stands of tall hemlocks and pines right on the water, popular with fishermen and walkers. When the park first opened, the public was allowed vehicle access right down to the pond. The amount of litter that accumulated, much of it related to fishing, was staggering. The present half-mile walk to the water has certainly discouraged the worst of this behavior, allowing those willing to exercise access to a much cleaner park.

Near the end of the pond, where there is a clearing down to the water on the left, look for and take a lightly used path heading uphill to the right. There is a gate at the top of the small rise, and from here the walking is downhill through deep forest. This trail is marked with both white and blue markers and is lined with numerous highbush blueberry shrubs that produce very tasty berries during July and August.

After about a quarter mile or so of walking, you'll come to an intersection near a swamp. Because of its isolation, openness, and water, this area is frequented by deer. Make a left here, following white markers. The trail now climbs gradually on a somewhat rockier pathway towards the highest elevation on the hike. Just after the trail levels off and bears sharply to the right, it turns left at an intersection and begins heading in a western direction. Continue following the white markers through a series of turns and along the remains of old rock walls. The highway sounds you hear are those of I-80. The trail will soon turn to the south, parallel to a wire fence.

If you care to, cross under the wire fence (which has an opening through which an unmarked footpath crosses) and out to the rest area and vista on I-80. The footpath is narrow and windy and, in one section, nearly overgrown with bushes, some of which have thorns. The view out to Kittatinny Mountain and the Delaware Water Gap is quite spectacular. On the other hand, it may be easier to visit this spot by car after returning from the hike.

Continuing on white markers, follow the path past a large rock wall and then along the edge of former farmland, which is reverting back to woodland. This spot is another area frequented by deer and home to many birds and small mammals. Numerous wildflowers may be found here, including wild yarrow. This flower, a member of the sunflower family, is recognized by its clumps of small white flowers at the top of a green, leafy stem. The leaves are delicate and pleasantly aromatic. Yarrow has been used by herbalists in the treatment of fevers and for hemorrhages and bleeding from the lungs. A tea made from the leaves and flowers is said to break up a cold if taken regularly right from the beginning of the illness.

As you continue walking south, you'll

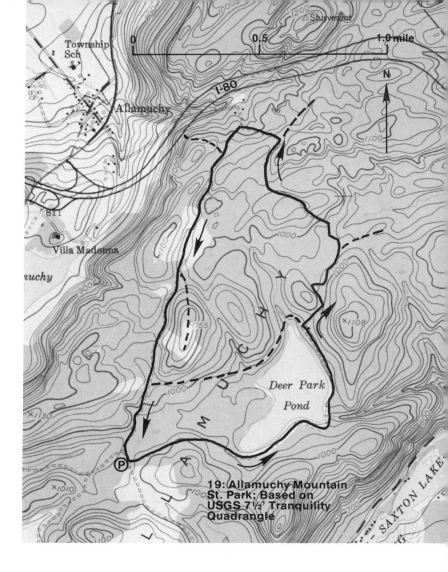

19: Allamuchy Mountain St. Park; Based on USGS 7½' Tranquility Quadrangle

notice a path leading off to the left up what seems to be the open summit of a small hill. Though there are no views, the area is also a field in transition and contains many sun-loving wildflowers. Farther ahead, although you should still follow the white markers, another path, this one marked in red, leads off to the left and downhill. The pond is about a quarter mile down this lane. After crossing this intersection, which is quite open, the white markers will lead you, in about one-third mile, to the gate and your car.

BCS

20

Jenny Jump State Forest

Total distance: 2.5 miles
Hiking time: 1.25 hours
Vertical rise: 250–300 feet
Rating: Easy
Maps: USGS Blairstown; DEP Jenny Jump State Forest

Jenny Jump State Forest is named after a young colonial girl. As the tale goes, Jenny was out picking berries with her father. Some hostile Indians came across the pair and her father yelled out for her to jump from the cliff—if only to save her chastity. Although Jenny was successful in keeping herself pure, the result was her death from the fall . . . or so the tale goes.

To reach Jenny Jump from I-80 exit 12, go 1.1 miles into the town of Hope. Bear left onto County Route 519. After little more than a mile, turn right (near a small pond) at a junction. After going another 1.4 miles uphill, bear right at a fork and then right again after an additional .6 mile. The entrance is .4 mile farther on your left. Most of the route is marked with "Jenny Jump SF" directional signs, but some are rather small. Stop at the park office (Box 150, Hope, New Jersey 07844; 201-459-4366) for a free map, then drive uphill to a comfort station, small parking area, and the start of the hiking trails. There is also a trail sign here. Consider combining this short hike with a picnic lunch. There are lots of tables around.

The route to the trails goes along a woods road somewhat uphill. Paths in this state forest are marked with round paint blazes. Here, white blazes, often intermixed with red, are encountered as the trail turns right and heads up towards the crest of the ridge. A few picnic tables are passed as the path swings left, upwards along the ridge. After about four minutes, a junction is reached with blazes going both ways. The right fork is the Summit Trail upon which you will return. Take the left fork—the Swamp Trail.

The Swamp Trail is wide and proceeds gently through the woods. Continue straight ahead, avoiding a fork to the left. The small gorge off to the right contains some small, wet areas that probably gave the trail its name; however, the going is generally dry and easy. As the trail descends into the lower tract, Campsite #11 is reached. This state forest has many such campsites available to the public for a small fee. Reservations are advisable, we were told. There are also two cabins for rent, with four bunks each and a maximum capacity of six.

Proceed ahead, past the sign to the Summit Connection Trail and onto the paved road. Bear right, going along the road and passing several more camp-

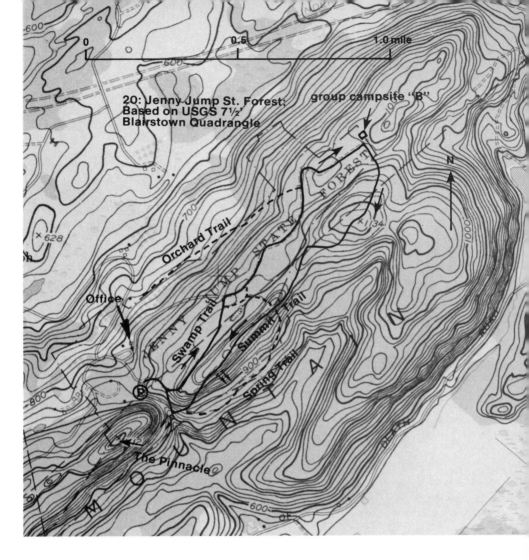

20: Jenny Jump St. Forest:
Based on USGS 7½'
Blairstown Quadrangle

sites, some water faucets, and out-
houses. The road changes to gravel after
passing site #14. Just after passing site
#21, note the large glacial erratic on the
left side of the road. One can only imagine the strength of the ice sheet that
ripped out this monster, then left it here
after melting and retreating north.

Continuing ahead, the road passes a
sign for the Orchard Trail. Keep going
ahead. Just before Group site B, on the
right-hand side of the road, there is a
sign, "No vehicle parking in trail." Turn

right here, proceeding up this woods
road. The park map is wrong at this
point. It shows this junction beyond site
B. It is, in fact, just before it. Here the
trail goes outside the state forest boundary, at least as shown on the current
DEP map.

Back again in the woods, the course
sways gently to the left and back again
through a small grove of hemlock trees.
There are white paint markings on the
trail in this section. Be alert here. The
marked trail makes a sharp right turn off

Jenny Jump State Park.

the woods road and onto a narrower trail, following the white paint markings. There was, at one time, a trail sign here; the post is still visible. If you find yourself on the woods road with no more paint markings, you've likely passed this turn and will need to retrace your steps to find it.

The path becomes narrower and woodsy, much more trail-like and pleasant after the campsite area. It ascends, at first moderately and then more steeply, as it gains the summit ridge of Jenny Jump Mountain. As the terrain begins to level off and approach the top, note the mountain laurel off to the right. You are now on the Summit Trail, the "official" beginning of which was presumably back by Group site B. The path undulates along the ridge, not always on the very top, with some evidence of old yellow blazes. As it approaches the summit and viewpoint, the woodland begins to thin and trees are shorter.

The trail turns slightly left and leads out onto a rock outcropping. Here is our first extensive view—Hackettstown and the surrounding farmland. The DEP map will show that you are on the mountain in the white area, near the scale bar of the map. Proceeding ahead, there is another trail junction, and you are, once again, back inside Jenny Jump State Forest. This intersection is the Spring Trail. A left turn leads down steeply to below the summit ridge; a right leads back to the junction with the Swamp Trail, which we passed earlier at Campsite #11.

Continue ahead. Through trees to the right are some limited views towards Pennsylvania. More people are usually encountered along here. Many take the short hike up from the parking area for the vistas. The hill protruding through the woods ahead is a part of Jenny Jump called the Pinnacle. A microwave tower sits on its top.

As the trail turns right and starts downhill, there is an open area to the left. Walk out to a viewpoint some 30 yards off the trail. This lookout is the best view in the region. To the left is the previously seen vista—the Hackettstown region—ahead, the Pinnacle, and to the right, the Delaware Water Gap and Pennsylvania.

Look for the gap; it's clearly visible—a sharp drop in the crest of the horizon. To the right of that "dip" is New Jersey, to the left, Pennsylvania. Notice, too, the rock surface underfoot. The striations were made by the glaciers during the ice age.

Back on the Summit Trail, proceed downhill through a grove of hemlocks back to the junction where the Swamp Trail originated. Bear left and return to the parking area. Have extra time, more energy? Try a loop out along the Spring Trail following one of the maps.

HNZ

21

Jockey Hollow

Total distance: 4.5 miles
Hiking time: 2–4 hours
Vertical rise: 600–700 feet
Rating: Moderate to easy
Maps: USGS Mendham; HRM #11; NPS Road and Trail Map

At just under one thousand acres, Jockey Hollow is the largest section of the Morristown National Historical Park (Morristown, New Jersey 07960; 201-539-2016), about three miles south of the city of Morristown. The site, operated by the National Park Service, is open year round, but some of the buildings are closed on Thanksgiving, Christmas, and New Years, and possibly on a few weekdays, depending on the year's budget. Call ahead to be sure the buildings are open, for they are well worth the visit.

To reach Jockey Hollow, take I-287 to exit 26B and follow US 202 north about 2 miles to Tempe Wick Road. A left on this road for 1.5 miles will bring you to the park entrance and the main visitors center. The route from the I-287 exit is well marked with National Park Service (NPS) signs.

The whole hike, indeed this whole park, is fine for cross-country skiing as well as hiking. Start your hike with a visit to Wick House, just behind the visitors center. Henry Wick built his house around 1750 and made his living from farming and from his large woodlot. While better off than most, the family was

by no means wealthy. During the winter encampment of 1779–1780, the farm served as both the Wicks' home and as the headquarters of Major General Arthur St. Clair.

The main building has been restored, and there is usually a ranger in attendance in period dress to explain the fascinating history. You will enjoy visiting Wick Farm in the morning. We have been there on a magnificent fall Saturday yet had it all to ourselves for an hour; but it became crowded with other visitors later that afternoon. Be sure to save some time for the visitors center. As well as the usual helpful ranger, there is a book nook, orientation film, and "talking" display of a soldier's hut. Simple trail maps are available for a nickel—splurge!

To start the hike, leave the rear door of the visitors center and proceed to the NPS sign about the Wick Farm. This sign is about 80 yards behind the center at the end of a graveled path. Turn right and proceed along a wide path, flanked by a fence on the left surrounding the orchard. Crossing a paved park road, continue through the opening in a wood "snake" fence. A little farther on, take a few minutes to read the NPS sign on

Hand's Brigade, and then continue straight ahead on the grass-covered woods road that descends slightly.

After about five minutes, a junction marked with signpost #23 is reached. Signs like this one occur throughout the park at almost every trail junction. Each is numbered and has a posted trail map—you'll always know where you are! Turn left and proceed into the woods on the Patriots Path (PP). This mixed-use trail is a partially completed linear park, generally beside the Whippany River from Mendham to East Hanover.

The trail is now a wide woods road, and the walking, easy. Take time to note the surrounding forest. The huge tulip trees are not typical of New Jersey. Since the Park Service took over the area in the 1930s (and probably for some time before that), there has been only inconsequential cutting of timber. The result is an unusually mature forest with a lush understory. For ten to fifteen minutes the route ambles through this forest with slight ups and downs on a generally straight course.

After skirting the side of a hill, the path becomes narrower and more trail-like and arrives at junction #25, making a loop path that will be crossed again as the Patriots Path continues. Cross two streams flowing under wide wooden bridges, the first one with a railing and the second without. Just across the second bridge is sign #27. Continue directly ahead.

You are now about an hour (this time will vary widely) from the start. At sign #29, the Patriots Path turns left. Turn right and continue slightly uphill for ten minutes to signpost #55. At .12 mile ahead is a ranger residence, but our hike route turns sharply left. A few minutes later, sign #71 is reached. Straight ahead would shorten the hike by going directly to sign #73, but, unless you're tired,

make a right as the trail now starts to circle Mount Kemble. The house you might see through the woods is the NPS ranger residence mentioned previously. Quickly coming to #79, stay on the main trail. The sounds now heard are from I-287, for the eastern boundary of the park is close by.

An opening in the woods with a view to the east is shortly reached. The tall buildings in the distance are in Manhattan. The tops of the World Trade Center and the Empire State Building are visible; but the rest of New York City is hidden from view by the Watchung Mountains. This area was the camping grounds of Stark's Brigade—New Hampshire frontiersmen who fought at Bunker Hill, Trenton, and Princeton. Take a few moments to read the signs and plaques. It's a good spot for a break or lunch. The Watchung Mountains are the reason George Washington chose this tract for his winter encampment. Some thirty miles from New York City (and Howe's British troops), they provided a fine natural defense. Lookouts posted on ridge tops could easily spot enemy troop movements towards Morristown or across the plains towards the "capital" of Philadelphia. How easy it is still to imagine this area as a colonial wilderness.

After about five minutes of additional walking, there is a metal gate and post #78. This area is a little confusing and not well shown on the park map. Go past the metal gate onto the gravel road and continue straight on the road for about a minute, avoiding the woods road on the left, which heads into a grassy area. Look for a second woods road on the left, which is signed #76 about 20 yards off the gravel road. At this sign, make a left, through another metal gate and slightly downhill—not ahead on the one that goes behind #76. You'll soon know you made the correct move, for

21: Jockey Hollow;
Based on USGS 7½'
Mendham Quadrangle

sign #73 is reached in just a few minutes.

At junction #73, take the right fork slightly downhill. Soon passing by #15, cross a small stream running through a culvert and begin winding uphill. Ignore the level path branching off to the left, just beyond the culvert. Our path will take you close to the northeast boundary of the park, where private residences can be seen to your right.

Continue straight across the paved Jockey Hollow Road and past the metal gate (#85). The trail will soon become a moderate climb and then a fairly steep one—but the ascent is short. This section is the only one in which most novice skiers may have to take off their skiis.

Another of the many junctions is at the top of the rise (#83). A detour from here of 200 to 300 yards, along the path on the right, leads to one of the few scenic overlooks in Jockey Hollow, with limited views to the north. The main hike, however, makes a *left* turn. Continue, at first on the level path, then undulating somewhat, for some four minutes until signpost #C5 is reached (we have no idea why all the signposts have been just numerical until now), where you make a right over the hill towards the soldiers' huts. Be alert at this point—stay on the main trail. Some NPS informational signs can be seen off the trail. Go over and read them, of course, but return to the trail and avoid several unmarked left turns. Note also the understory in this area. There may be stinging nettles here, which could temporarily annoy those in short pants. The path comes out behind the soldiers' huts, a major tourist attraction.

The NPS has reconstructed four huts as typical examples of those built by Continental troops. The one you come to first was for officers, the twelve-bedded ones for the troops. Some two hundred huts lined this hillside during the winter of 1779–1780, while perhaps as many as a thousand stood in all of Jockey Hollow. Washington ordered all of them to be constructed alike, in neat lines with officers' huts in the rear. The majority were finished by Christmas, and those for the officers in January and February.

Proceed down, across the open field, to the visitors parking area where there are some informative signs explaining the harsh winter spent here. After reading this sign, don't you feel quite comfortable and warm? There is a welcome pump here to replenish your water supply.

From the pump, with your back to the huts, make a left through a grass field with some mature cedar trees. Passing a plaque to commemorate the war dead buried here, you'll come to trail post #C3 at the edge of the woods. The trail

passes through some brush, tall, clinging grape vines, and blackberry bushes. The forest floor is especially lush here, and the trail is level and easy to follow.

After about ten minutes, observe a narrower path paralleling you on the left. Look down. The stone construction with the slate top is a spring house. The route described here circles above it and comes to a sign for Wick House. Continue straight ahead, gently upwards. Here again are some especially tall trees and a lush forest floor. Perhaps you'll be lucky, as were we, to have a deer pause calmly in front of you. The trail soon ends on the paved road just below the Wick House barn—horse usually in residence. It will be easy to guide yourself back to the visitors center and the parking area.

The amount of time spent on this hike depends, of course, on the time you spend at some of the many historic areas. You could even combine the hike with a visit to Washington's Headquarters and Fort Nonsense in Morristown, also part of the NPS Historical Park. Do you have time left for another visit to the ranger? You've covered a lot of turf and are sure to have some questions.

HNZ

Jockey Hollow.

22

Hacklebarney State Park

Total distance: 3 miles
Hiking time: 1.5 hours
Vertical rise: 200 feet
Rating: Easy
Maps: USGS Chester/Gladstone; DEP park map

Hacklebarney State Park (RD 2, Long Valley, New Jersey 07853; 201-879-5677) hours vary with the season, but information can be easily obtained by calling ahead. Dogs are permitted provided they are leashed. The park covers 574 acres and contains two feeder streams for the beautiful Black River in its glacial gorge. The river is stocked annually, and trout fishing is a popular pastime. No swimming is available in the park, and, as the fall foliage is spectacular, autumn is the most popular season in Hacklebarney. The original thirty-two acres was donated in 1924, and there are two possible anecdotes to account for the name Hacklebarney. One theory is that the name is a combination of the two Indian words *haki* meaning "ground" and *bonihen*, "to put wood on the fire," thus developing into "Hackiboni" and, thence, to Hacklebarney. The other conjecture is that employees at the local iron mine constantly heckled a quick-tempered foreman named Barney Tracey and that, over time, "to heckle Barney" evolved into Hacklebarney. Supposition apart, Hacklebarney State Park is in a delightful section of New Jersey and is amply supplied with picnic tables, charcoal grills, and

water fountains (unfortunately, only a few of the latter are working). The hiking trail described here has no particular name and is infrequently marked with painted metal signs (green footprint on a yellow background); however, the route is easy to follow.

There are discrepancies on the relevant topographical maps. The name "Hacklebarney State Park" is printed incorrectly on the Chester map and should read "Morris County Park." The Black River is wrongly labeled "Lamington River." The latter difference in name is the result of a name change, and the river throughout this hike description is correctly referred to as the Black River.

To access Hacklebarney State Park from the north, take exit 27A from I-80 onto US 206 south to the town of Chester. To reach Hacklebarney State Park from the south, exit from I-287 at the Bedminster exit for US 202 and US 206 and drive north to the town of Chester. Turn west on NJ 24 in Chester at the traffic light. There is a small, brown sign at this junction indicating the turn for Hacklebarney State Park. Approximately 1 mile from the traffic light, pass the old Cooper gristmill, cross a bridge, and turn

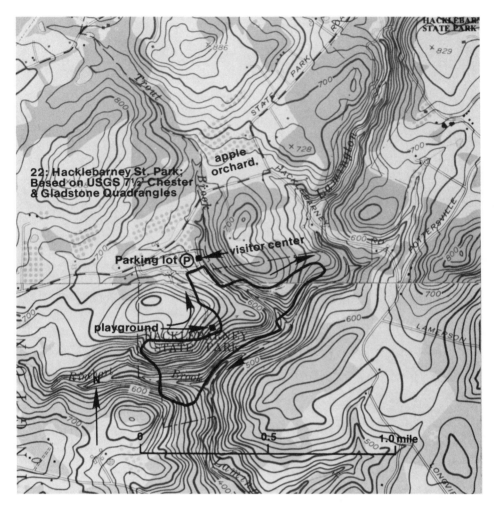

22: Hacklebarney St. Park;
Based on USGS 7½' Chester
& Gladstone Quadrangles

left at the green sign. Immediately there is another sharp left turn onto a road through a pleasant residential area paralleling the Black River. After another 2 miles, the road splits where there is an apple orchard and farm store on the corner. Turn right onto paved State Park Road and travel for .75 mile until a brown, wood sign on the left indicates the entrance to the park.

The visitors center at Hacklebarney is small but adequate. After obtaining the park map there, begin by turning imme-diately left from the building towards the comfort station on the right-hand side at the bottom of the first slope. The warning against poison ivy should be noted at the commencement of the trail. The woods road is wide and descends gently until, within a few minutes, a flight of stone steps crossing and at right angles to the trail is reached. There is also a water fountain here. The steps lead down to a wooden bridge over Trout Brook and into picnic areas. This hike, however, con-tinues straight ahead until the woods

Fishing the Black River, Hacklebarney.

road forks. Do not go uphill to the right but take the left fork on the trail to the waterfalls.

Cross the wooden bridge over Trout Brook and continue uphill through an area strewn with boulders, looking back occasionally for fine views of the waterfalls in this section of Trout Brook. Stay on the woods road until a sign is reached indicating that the trail straight ahead is closed. This closed section, running close to the Black River, is blocked by dangerous blowdowns and will not be reopened until these obstacles have been removed. Make the sharp right turn and parallel the river until a short descent brings you to another wooden bridge crossing Trout Brook. After crossing the bridge, turn immediately left onto a rocky

trail down towards the Black River. You will see another wooden bridge to the left, formerly providing access to the closed river trail, and another comfort station is available.

Colored with tannin, the river chatters its way along, and the trail stays close to its banks on very rocky terrain. Pick your way carefully along the side of the river until the "three pools" area is reached. Here there are some fine places supplied with picnic tables. The attractive water scenery and the coolness of the gorge make this spot an excellent site for lunch.

The trail is not marked after the three pools and is indistinct. There is no problem following the route, though, for it stays close to the river bank. Just where the river widens and becomes calmer, there is a short climb and descent over a small ridge to a wooden bridge over another picturesque tributary cascading down to the river. After crossing Rinehart Brook and a wooden plank over a smaller stream, the trail turns uphill, away from the Black River, until it arrives at a T-junction with a substantial woods road. Turn right here. Rinehart Brook is in the gorge to the right, and, when the leaves are off the trees, waterfalls can be seen from the trail, which climbs and then gradually descends towards another wooden bridge. Turn right over the bridge and then immediately left.

The trail parallels Rinehart Brook for a short distance, but then climbs away from the stream, switchbacks right, and continues to climb away from the water. On the left, partway up the hill, is a wooden sign. One directional arrow indicates the way back to Rinehart Brook, the other, forward to the (discontinued) playground. During your walk you will have seen at least one other area of evergreen trees that has obviously been planted, probably by the Civilian Conservation Corps during the 1930s, and the trail now passes through another such grove of spruce and white pine. Another woods road parallels and eventually merges with the road you are on, both leading to the old playground where there are still benches, a large open space, and two superb cedar trees.

At the end of the playground is a crossroad. Turn left and pass first through the abandoned swings and then, very shortly on the right, the concrete reservoir containing the park water supply. The road is wide, and the walking is easy with some views of the New Jersey countryside to the right. Ignore any other side roads until a grassy area is reached and the road to the parking lot becomes visible. It is possible to go through the fence at this point and walk back to the parking lot on the paved road, but the more pleasant route is to turn right, crossing two open areas, until the parking lot can be seen on the left.

SJG

23

Ken Lockwood Gorge

Total distance: 4 miles
Hiking time: 2 hours
Vertical rise: 100 feet
Rating: Easy
Map: USGS High Bridge/Califon

The South Branch of the Raritan River roars through the Ken Lockwood Gorge in the New Jersey highlands, creating a trout fisherman's paradise. It is truly a wild and scenic river through the few miles of the gorge, particularly in the spring. There are big rapids, huge boulders in the water, calm pools, and tall hemlocks dominating the banks. The hike in this gorge is simply a walk along the eastern bank of the river on a dirt road. Because this hike is in a wildlife management area, you should expect a different environment than that found in a park or state forest. The dirt road is open to vehicles and, if you happen to be there on a beautiful spring weekend, expect a crowd. We suggest that you visit the gorge on a weekday or during the winter. This place is really for fishermen, but they'll share it with you.

Access to the Ken Lockwood Gorge is via NJ 513 from Clinton. After passing the entrance to Vorhees State Park, which is just north of High Bridge, look for a right turn in 1.6 miles. Turn right, cross the single-lane bridge, and immediately turn right again at the crossroads

After passing through a residential area, the paved road will turn to dirt for two miles before it becomes paved again. These two miles of dirt road follow the river through the gorge on public land and constitute the trail for our hike. Park in one of the spaces alongside the road as soon as you enter this section. You are now in the Ken Lockwood Gorge Wildlife Management Area and should see a number of posted signs indicating this.

Begin your hike on this dirt road by walking downstream with the river on your right. Be advised that there may be occasional vehicular traffic on this road. Pay particular attention when rounding a bend with little visibility. As you walk along, you'll come to a number of scenic views of the rapidly moving water. The water is clean, clear, and noisy, and there are many places where one can stop for a while, sit on a large rock (as do the bullfrogs found here), and take in some sun.

The South Branch of the Raritan River is a stocked trout stream and is very popular with New Jersey fishermen during trout season, which is in April and May. Fishing is permitted twenty-four hours a day, and the catch is limited to six per day during season and four per day otherwise. No baits or lures are allowed, all fish must be caught with dry flies. The wildlife management area restricts camping, picnicking, swimming, and alcoholic beverages.

After walking a short distance, notice that the river temporarily splits into two channels, creating an island densely forested with hemlock trees. There is a coolness here, even on hot days, due to the deep shade and temperature of the water itself. The river drops swiftly in rapids in this particularly picturesque section.

If you look to your left, high up on the bank, you may notice a flat, cleared area that has been paralleling the road. This is a railroad bed that, just ahead, crosses the river on a high trestle. The railroad serviced the mines of Highbridge, the sources of iron ore for the iron industry that for many years thrived in north Jersey. One of the interesting contrasts of this hike is the difference in vegetation on the two banks. The side that you are walking on has been cleared to build the road (and, for part of the distance, for the railway), and the regrowth has been mostly deciduous trees and other plants common to the highlands. Here is flowering dogwood, wild begonia, buttercups, and plenty of poison ivy. The opposite, untouched shore is deep and dark, and also very steep—the reason the road was built on the east bank.

A memorial to Kenneth F. Lockwood is located on your left a short distance past the trestle and just before a small stone bridge. A plaque, dedicated by Trout Unlimited of New Jersey, set into a huge piece of granite reads, "To Ken, sportsman and conservationist."

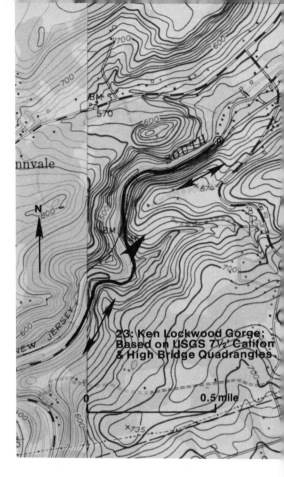

23: Ken Lockwood Gorge; Based on USGS 7½' Califon & High Bridge Quadrangles

When mists and shadows rob pool and run of shape and substance, when the voice of the wood thrush stills and the dog trout shakes its lethargy, we will remember stalwart gentle master of the anglers art half submerged in the smother unerringly shooting that long line, watchfully mending the drift nevermore will your skilled hands tempt the patriarch of the flood . . . farewell old timer.

A little farther ahead, cross a stone bridge over a small brook that cascades down the eastern side of the gorge to join the South Branch. Here, where there are a few large boulders reaching out

South Branch of the Raritan River in Lockwood Gorge.

into the water, the river makes a sharp bend. After crossing the bridge, the forest, now undisturbed by the railroad bed that has crossed to the opposite shore, shelters the road. The road swings away from the river temporarily, but soon rejoins it. A little farther, and the river begins to drop below the road in a section filled with many rapids. After having walked nearly 2 miles, you will reach the paved road again. Turn around and walk back to your car, this time viewing the river from a different perspective.

BCS

Piedmont Province

24

Palisades Hike — #1

Total distance: 7 miles
Hiking time: 4 hours
Vertical rise: 400 feet
Rating: Easy
Maps: USGS Central Park (NY/NJ); WB #4; HRM #24; Park
   map (Palisades Interstate Park Commission)

Originally funded by gift money, the Palisades Interstate Park Commission was created in 1900, mainly to curb the opening of quarries supplying traprock for the concrete used in building roads and skyscrapers. Most of the 2,472 park acres are in New Jersey, and the average width of the parkland between the Hudson River and the cliff top is less than an eighth of a mile. Apart from the talus slopes at the base, the cliffs are well wooded and feature a wide variety of trees and shrubs, some of them remaining from former estate gardens. The highest clear cliff is 520 vertical feet.

Numerous old woods trails complement the two main trails that run the length of the Palisades. The hike described here utilizes parts of the Shore Path, marked in white, and the Long Path, marked in blue. Enjoyment of the Shore Path is enhanced by the sound of the water lapping on the shore, and on both the upper and lower levels there are many superb views of the river and its boating activity. Binoculars are useful on this trip. If a longer expedition is desired, this hike could be linked with another

hike described in this book called Palisades #2.

The hike begins at the Palisades Interstate Park Commission's Administration Building. On the weekend you may park in the large lot to the north of the building, but during the week, parking may be limited so check inside with the police department. Access to the Administration Building of the Palisades Interstate Park Commission (Alpine, New Jersey 07620; 201-768-1360) is east of exit #2 on the Palisades Parkway, approximately 7 miles north of the George Washington Bridge.

Walk south at the wooden sign near the road with "New Jersey Headquarters Palisades Park Commission" and the blue Long Path marker on it. After a very short road walk, turn left downhill away from the road on a wide path with frequent water bars and a seasonal stream running on the left. After passing the stone tunnel on the right, the trail runs steadily downhill in a gentle zigzag, passing a large rock with the painted words "Top of the Palisades Shore Trail." Passing a steam covered with concrete on the right, the trail bends left and reaches a T-junction and the first view of the Hudson River. This junction is with the Shore Path, confirmed by a signpost and the white blazes. Turn left at the junction and pass over a stream with a waterfall on the left. There are several exploratory side trips in this area, the first one being two flights of forty-six and twelve steps to the left of the trail, leading through a gate in a wire fence to two small, rock-constructed buildings. Side trips to the river bank include one on the right that leads to a small rocky beach with views of the supporting pillars of the George Washington Bridge and of Yonkers, immediately across the river.

At the rock signpost, continue to follow the Shore Path, which on the left-hand side is now supported from erosion by large boulders. The trail now runs closer to the water's edge, and the route at this point is very attractive. The trail is wide and grassy, protected on the water side by large rocks and affording excellent river views. Opposite Excelsior Dock, thirty steps to the left lead to the Excelsior Flats Picnic Area, which is supplied with picnic tables, fireplaces, and an outhouse. At this point beware of poison ivy, which is widespread in the area.

During the next stretch of the trail there are many signs of human activity. Several streams run under cemented rock covers, and there are two painted-over signs on rocks indicating the way up steps to where buildings once existed. Very soon you'll see many attractive lunch sites, each with a natural rock table and chairs. This area is known as Twombley's Landing and is named after the former owner who donated this section to the park. Twombley's Landing is believed to have been an Indian campsite due to the layers of oyster shells found here. Because of the prevalence of giardia llamblia and other pollutants, it is *not* recommended that you use the water

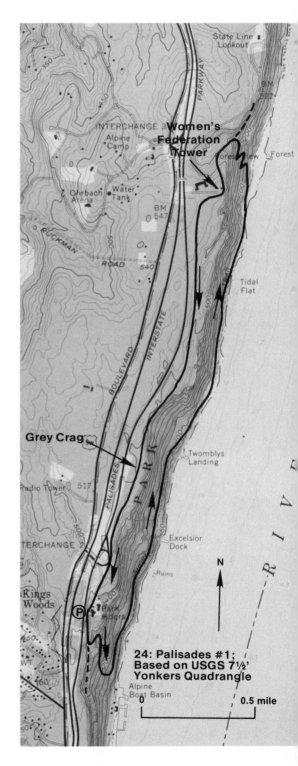

24: Palisades #1; Based on USGS 7½' Yonkers Quadrangle

0   0.5 mile

Women's Federation Building.

from the two places labeled "Drinking Water." There is also one cookout fireplace provided at Twombley's.

Moving slightly uphill, the path is again edged on the left by rocks, and very shortly afterwards comes the first view of the cliffs. These outcrops are the two bastions of Ruckman's Point, and it is interesting to know that in a little while you will be looking down from there to the Shore Path. Watch the cliffs to the north at this point to get a good view of Indian Head and, at river level, observe the Tappan Zee Bridge in the distance.

Shortly after this point, take the steep trail on the left. (Here it is possible to extend the hike by walking straight ahead, following Palisades hike #2.) These cemented rock steps climb in a switchback, marked blue on white by the Scout organization, to a trail junction with a stream on the right and a boulder with trail directions painted in white. Ignore the routes to the State Line and to the River Trail and bear left on the trail to US 9W, climbing uphill on more steps and following both the blue blazes and the Scout blue and white blazes. The stone lookout memorial of the New Jersey Federation of Women's Clubs is at the top of this climb amongst mature trees. The building, commonly called "The Women's Federation Building," was erected in 1919 in memory of the work performed for the preservation of Palisades Cliffs. Stand awhile and admire the view of the river.

Shortly after passing this building, the blue on white Scout trail turns right at a junction. Proceed straight ahead on the Long Path, marked in blue, on a wide two-track trail until the Palisades Parkway is sighted in the distance, at which point the trail veers left. The trail is soon joined by another woods road from the right. Here there is a broken wall at the cliff edge. This site is Ruckman Point. On the cliff edge there is a carving on the rock face dated June, 1981, and the Shore Path is visible below.

The now grassy trail with smooth rock outcrops goes slightly downhill to a boggy area with a stream and corrugated trail construction. The damper, rockier section continues until a larger stream is crossed over a substantial wooden bridge. Shortly after the bridge, watch for a small footpath to the left leading over a steel girder/cement bridge to a very secluded lookout called Grey Crag. This section of the cliff is separated from the main cliff and gives a tremendous feeling of isolation. Again, watch for poison ivy.

Tall maples mark the next section of the trail, and the path runs very close to the Parkway until it finally emerges into a grassy area, which is crossed to reach the Administration Building parking lot and your car.

SJG

Palisades Hike — #2

Total distance: 3 miles
Hiking time: 2 hours
Vertical rise: 400 feet
Rating: Easy
Map: USGS Yonkers; WB #4; HRM #24; Park map (Palisades
Interstate Park Commission)

This circular hike is a short loop on the Palisades (Palisades Interstate Park Commission, Alpine, New Jersey 07620; 201-768-1360), but it could be lengthened by joining it with Palisades hike #1, already described. The terrain is varied, and the Hudson River is viewed from the cliffs as well as from water level. The shorter walk is useful if time is limited, but since the cliff area and lookout are easily accessible by car, an early start is recommended to avoid the crowds at the parking lot.

The hike begins at the parking lot at the State Line Lookout, also known as Point Lookout. The State Line Lookout is reached from Palisades Interstate Parkway. Follow the sign just north of exit #3, which is approximately 10 miles north from the George Washington Bridge and 1 mile south of the New York/New Jersey border. Walk south towards the river from the parking lot and turn right down the old road for a couple of minutes, passing through a barrier of large rocks and onto the road you have just driven. Continue walking on this road, noting that there are blue markers on the left rock wall and on the trees behind the wall. Just af-

ter the road bears right, there is a large tree on the left with a prominent blue marker. Turn left into the woods here, taking note of the sign warning that the cliffs and steep slopes are dangerous and that for safety you should stay on the marked trails.

The path heads directly towards the river on a wide, slightly rocky trail, until it bears right to parallel the water. A better view of the river bank is seen to the left of the trail just before beginning the descent. Faint blue markers will be discernable. The trail turns left and leads downhill towards the river on small flights of stone steps, which can be very slippery when wet or icy. The sound of running water will soon be heard, and the waterfall itself will come into view, tumbling down the cliff to the right, crossing the trail, and continuing on its way to the river. Just prior to the stream crossing, the trail is marked for a turn, indicating that you should not go up the flight of rock steps immediately ahead. Painted signs on a large rock on the far side of the stream indicate that these steps lead back to US 9W and that the trail marked with blue and white rectangles down which you will continue is the River Trail.

The steps continue down to the river, twisting and turning but always descending, imitating the stream that was just crossed. There are few markers on this section of trail, but the way to go is obvious and the switchbacks are marked at each turn. The trail, alternately a dirt path and steps, is vulnerable to erosion, and blowdowns are found from time to time, which accentuates the problem of trail damage. The sound of running water gradually fades. It is interesting from here to look up at the towering cliffs of the Palisades and to observe the cracks that will eventually widen, bringing more boulders crashing down. Just before reaching river level, the trail passes between two large boulders after which there is a side trail on the left leading to a picnic table. After twenty-five minutes of descent, the end (or the beginning) of the trail is indicated by a blue and white marker on a boulder at the junction of the trail near the water's edge.

At the river, turn left (north) on a wide, grassy trail bordering the water. The quietness of this section is accentuated by the sounds of trains and other activities from across the river. Honeysuckle grows in profusion, and the impression of being below water level is accentuated by the large stands of cattails by the water's edge. The area has a large number of sweet gum trees, and in the spring, the paulownia tree, a native of China, is a profusion of purple blossom. Numbers of wood and stone picnic tables are set out on both sides of the trail and make pleasant places to rest on a warm day.

The stream crossed on the way down reappears shortly after beginning the walk along the west bank of the Hudson. At certain times of year, or after heavy rain, this low-lying section is very wet, and the stream, rushing down the cliffs on the left, makes the trail its course.

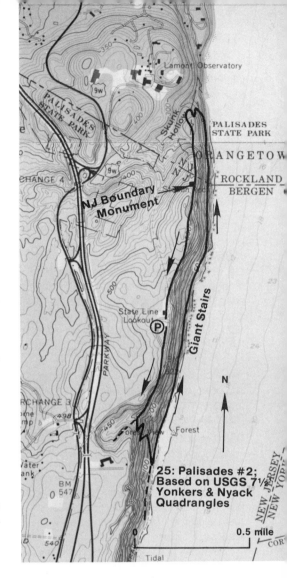

25: Palisades #2; Based on USGS 7½' Yonkers & Nyack Quadrangles

0   0.5 mile

Very shortly, the strip of land between the water and the cliffs becomes narrower. The trail makes its way closer to the river and then takes a sharp left turn up through the boulder field called "The Giant Stairs." Rocks form naturally steep stairs. Extra care is needed if these rocks are wet, and if they are icy, turn back. Follow the white markers carefully as they lead the adventurer up and away from the water before turning to parallel the river once more. The trail gains elevation very fast here, and it is interesting to look back and see that the river bank is now composed of large rocks. Ten minutes of climbing will bring you the reward of a short section of easy walking on a flat trail. The one or two red markers and unofficial, white-painted numbers seen on the rocks in this section should be ignored. The markers to be followed are frequent and will either be white rectangles or white half-moons on their backs.

Clambering across the boulders with the cliffs above and the river below is the most exciting part of this hike. All too soon the trail is back amongst trees again, still quite high above the river and right at the base of the cliffs. This point in the trail is immediately below the State Line Lookout.

Watch the right-hand side of the trail for three white dots and an arrow pointing towards the river. Follow the steps down to find a level, grassy area with a rock barricade on the riverside, and take a break to watch the river traffic. The hike to this point has taken approximately 1.25 hours. It appears there was once a fully maintained trail lower than the one now in use. An exploration of the faint trail down river from this rest area will lead back to the original trail.

The footway rolls along easily. There is considerable rock-hopping, but the path is well defined, climbing, at first, until a corner is turned and an attractive bay comes into view before the next boulder field. Two more boulder fields are crossed, separated by sections amongst trees, before the trail makes its way back to the river's edge and a small beach. The size of this beach varies with the tide. Shells can be collected here, but, unfortunately, garbage is also washed up.

With your back to the water and lining up with the longest part of the peninsula, look at the foot of the trees for what must be a boundary marker, for it resembles other New York/New Jersey boundary markers. The rectangular, concrete marker protrudes about six inches above the ground and is marked on the top in quarters. On the top nearest to land appears RO NJ, and on the lower side, nearest to the Hudson River, 1872 is engraved. To date, no one to whom we have spoken has been able to explain why the NJ appears on the north side of the marker nor the meaning of RO, unless it is Rockland/Orange for the adjoining counties.

After leaving the little beach, the trail, marked clearly with white markers, follows the shoreline and within fifteen minutes moves closer to the water on large boulders, two or three of them exceptionally large but unfortunately spoiled by graffiti. The trail is very near the water's edge, and here is an attractive spot at which to linger. Very soon afterwards, the trail turns left up through the woods and begins a steep climb, sometimes on a leafy, dirt surface and sometimes on wood or stone steps, until it reaches the cliff top about forty-five minutes after leaving the boundary marker. There is a lot of white paint here, but amongst the superfluous markers there are three indicating the end of the white trail. Turn left on the Long Path up a flight of stone steps. The blue markers are a little indistinct here. Climb the stone stairs and ignore any side trails until you arrive at a section close to and parallel with the edge of the cliff, finally emerging after a short distance onto a rock slab with a tremendous view both up and down river. The Tappan Zee Bridge to the north can be seen clearly, but the view of the city is obstructed by a bend in the river. The marking of the trail is still unclear, but the two or three stone steps near the edge of the Palisades is the correct route.

Watch for the pinnacles of rock on the left. A flight of concrete-reinforced, wooden steps leads through a gate in a wire fence. Turn immediately right and walk up the stone stairs paralleling the fence to the New Jersey Boundary Monument. The fading inscription lists the date (1882) and the names of the commissioners and the surveyor and states, "488 ft. west from Station Rock"—the large boulder passed down by the river.

Turn your back on the monument, bear right, and return to the path. At the bottom of the steps, turn immediately left and head in a southerly direction towards your parked car. The trail is wide and in winter is used for cross-country skiing. The trail climbs but is only faintly marked, so stay to the left and avoid the wide road coming in from the right. The walk is pleasant, and although it parallels the river, this fact is not noticed as the trail is some way in from the cliff edge. This area is crisscrossed with trails, any one of which leads back to the parking lot to the south. At one time, the picnic area was supplied with stone fireplaces, remains of which appear from time to time as stone rectangles. It is pleasant to walk for a few minutes in an area bordered by rock walls between the cliff edge and the paved road and to sit on a stone slab seat facing the river. In a few minutes, the cafeteria and parking lot can be seen to the right. The cafeteria, a franchise, is not always open, even in summer, and the hours of operation are unpredictable.

Immediately opposite the restaurant is a sign for Point Lookout. The elevation here is 532 feet. Immediately opposite the Hudson River is Westchester County, New York; Long Island Sound; and Long Island, New York. In addition to this sign, there is a metal plaque commemorating the construction in 1926 of the section of state highway that leads to the Palisades Interstate Park and listing the names of the commissioners and the engineer. Two or three telescopes are in place for viewing the scenery.

SJG

View of the Hudson River from the shoreline.

26

South Mountain Reservation

Total distance: 8.5 miles
Hiking time: 6 hours
Vertical rise: 500 feet
Rating: Moderate
Maps: USGS Caldwell/Roselle; HRM #6; Essex County Park
    Commission South Mountain Reservation map

South Mountain Reservation has a lot to offer in the middle of such a built-up area. The 2,048-acre track contains a substantial river, many streams and cascades, a twenty-five-foot waterfall, and nineteen miles of trails through gentle woodland. At certain junctions, the bustle of the world is encountered, but the trails are mostly free from traffic noise. The first and second of the three Watchung ridges of New Jersey form the eastern and western boundaries of the reservation. The name "Watchung" is a legacy from the Lenape Indians, to whom the ridges were the "high hills."

The Lenape Trail Committee, funded by the Sierra Club, has proposed a hiking and biking trail system for Essex County, which is now being implemented. The name "Lenape" was chosen for the trail in honor of the state's original inhabitants and preeminent foot travelers. The route will use three aqueducts belonging to Newark and will obviously take advantage of existing parkland, but it does need to be routed on some sidewalks and over some private land. At the northern end, it was anticipated that the Lenape Trail would link with the Patriot's Path.

The distance covered in this hike is nearly nine miles, but since there are no difficult climbs, the hike is useful for developing a good walking pace and to increase hiking stamina. The woods and rhododendron groves make this an excellent spring hike, although the trail near the Rahway River is sometimes wet. The groves of rhododendron, wild azalea, and mountain laurel were deliberately planted, together with white pine and hemlock, when the land was acquired by the Essex County Park Commission at the beginning of the twentieth century in an effort to eradicate the previous damage done by logging and paper mills. The cost of the rhododendrons planted in 1910 was forty-three cents each—a little different from the price of a rhododendron today. Watch for the tame herds of deer as you walk. In addition to this hike, Mayapple Hill at the northern end of the park is another area of South Mountain Reservation that warrants explorations, as well as Turtleback Rock, also in the northeastern part of the park.

Public transportation can be used easily to reach South Mountain Reservation, for Millburn Station is opposite the trailhead at Locust Grove parking lot. If driving, leave I-280 at exit 10 (Northfield Avenue) to Mount Pleasant Avenue. Turn south, following Gregory Avenue, Wyoming Avenue, South Wyoming Avenue, Sagamore Road, and Glen Road, and turn right into Locust Grove parking lot at the wooden sign.

There is no park office at which to obtain a map of the South Mountain Reservation. Maps are available by writing to or stopping at the Essex County Environmental Center, 621 Eagle Rock Avenue, Roseland, New Jersey 07068. The office is open seven days a week from 9:00 A.M. until 4:30 P.M. The hike described here forms a figure eight. It begins at the Locust Grove parking lot, using the yellow-marked Lenape Trail out to the Oakdale Trail, marked in red, and returning on a different part of the Lenape Trail and the Cascade Trail, once marked in purple and now in white.

Walk away from Glen Road towards the woods, pass an outhouse on the left, and cross the junction of three or four wide woods roads. Ignore all these roads, including the one to the left with the sign "No motor vehicles," and walk to the right up a wide, rocky path, checking the route by finding the faint yellow markers. Close to the picnic area, there is a small, brick housing for a spring, which runs year round and is considered safe for drinking. Pass the rain shelter and picnic tables and go to the far end of the open area, where the trail enters the woods on the left. The path climbs on a narrower, rocky trail. Within a few minutes, ignore the wide road to the left and continue on the yellow-marked trail as it turns right and moves across the side of the hill. During the climb, you will pass below and circle around a large concrete structure, part of the old waterworks system used to supply East Orange with water from the valley. At the top of the rise, the trail turns left and par-

allels the paved road on the right, until it eventually emerges onto that road. At this point, the first, large rhododendrons are to be seen. Turn left onto the paved road, which now is closed to motorized traffic, and walk by the side of the stone wall towards Washington Rock, located opposite a disused parking lot on the right-hand side.

The climb will have taken approximately ten minutes from the parking lot, and a pause should be made to admire the view to the left. Looking down and over the old water-holding area, the panorama includes New York City, Newark Airport, I-280, and, looking straight ahead, I-78 in the valley of the Watchung Reservation, with the Bell Telephone tower on the ridge to the right.

The plaque on Washington Rock describes the events of 1780, which George Washington watched from this point. It describes British efforts to destroy the American supply base at Morristown, the burning of Connecticut Farms, now called Union, and other military efforts. The plaque records that, after the British efforts failed, they were forced to retire and "quit New Jersey soil for ever." History tells us that, at the time of the Revolution, all the suitable trees in New Jersey had been cut for shipbuilding and housing, giving good visibility to observe the movements of the British in the valley. A sentry was posted at Washington's Rock, and as soon as he became aware of troop movements in the valley below, a bonfire was lit to alert the soldiers at Jockey Hollow.

Look for the yellow marker on the tree to the left, just at the end of the wall. Leave the commemorative rock and walk downhill to an area of man-made steps and a decorative building block viewpoint. There was once a roof over this shelter, but it was not replaced when the original building fell into disrepair.

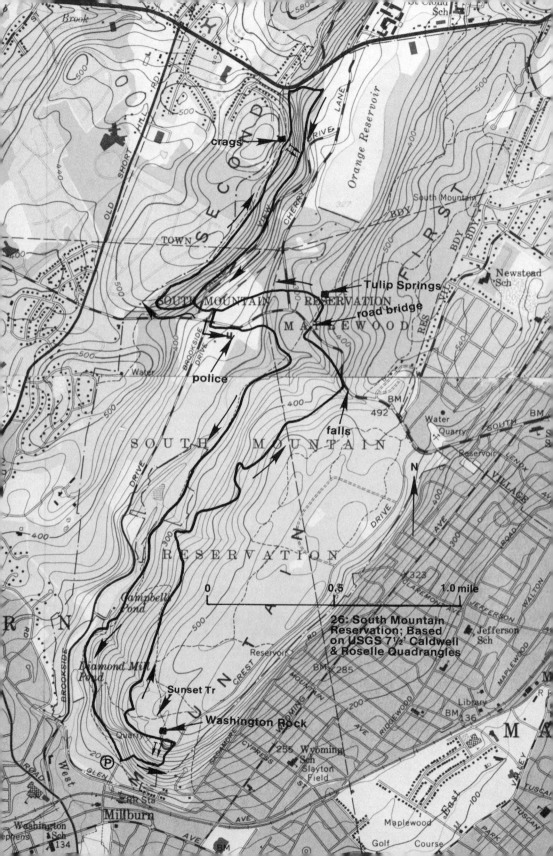

crags

Orange Reservoir

Tulip Springs

road bridge

police

falls

N

26: South Mountain
Reservation; Based
on USGS 7½' Caldwell
& Roselle Quadrangles

0   0.5   1.0 mile

Campbell
Pond

Diamond Mill
Pond

Sunset Tr

Washington Rock

Millburn

The Essex Park Commission was established in 1895 and, drawing on Frederick Law Olmsted's ideas and in consultation with his firm, created twenty-three parks and three reservations within the county. Olmsted was also the creator of New York City's Central Park. Although the concept of South Mountain Reservation was Olmsted's, the smaller items such as bridges, trails, and steps were, in fact, built by the Civilian Conservation Corps in 1934.

Continuing downhill, the trail passes over several blowdowns, a rocky lookout on the left, a small stream, and, also on the left, a large rock with a chain-linked fence behind it. The rock is an example of traprock, and the fencing protects the walker from a traprock quarry. The first and second Watchung ridges are intrusions (or extrusions) of lava similar to those of the Palisades. As these layers rose from west to east and were glaciated, the top layer of the Watchungs cooled more quickly than the lower layers that formed the Palisades. Because the layers in South Mountain Reservation cooled more quickly, the hexagonal columns that formed are considerably smaller than those on the Palisades.

Proceed downhill on a wider path until Sunset Trail is crossed. Our trail travels along the side of the hill in a slightly downhill direction until Maple Falls Cascade is seen on the left-hand side, about a mile into the hike. Cross the stream and climb away from the brook until the trail levels out and crosses several small streams and Pringry Road. The yellow-marked trail moves ahead on similar terrain, passing Lilliput Knob. This unusual rock is called a turtleback rock for obvious reasons. It was formed when the traprock fractured into small hexagonal blocks. The cracks were filled with minerals, and, when erosion wore away the

traprock faster than the minerals, the result was a patterned rock similar to the back of a turtle. There are several examples of this type of rock throughout South Mountain Reservation, one on the northeastern side of the park actually called Turtleback Rock. It is believed that the word "traprock" developed from a Dutch word, "trappen," meaning steps, indicating that the square hunks of rock were useful for step construction. Cross Bear Lane, ignore the two trails entering from the right at Mines Point, and proceed straight ahead to Ball's Bluff. A roof used to be supported by the columns seen here, which are all that remain of the shelter erected by the Civilian Conservation Corps in 1934.

Descend the short grade, leaving Ball's Bluff on the left, bear left, cross Bluff's Trail, and walk downhill by the side of another small stream. Go straight ahead at the next wide woods road crossing and, within two or three minutes and at the next T-junction, turn left and walk steeply downhill through large rhododendrons and hemlocks to Hemlock Falls. There are picnic tables by the falls, and for the energetic there is a way to the top of the falls.

Cross the stone bridge, leaving the falls on the right, and at the end of the bridge turn left. At first, the trail is on a wide path, but soon after passing another pretty falls on the right and another substantial stone bridge to the left, which now leads nowhere, the footway becomes narrower and reaches a triangle intersection. This intersection is with River Trail. To the left can be seen a stone bridge. Turn right and then, shortly afterwards, make a left turn just before a metal barricade. Where the path turns left, stop to admire the enormous oak tree.

Pass the white trail coming in on the left and cross the road bridge over

South Orange Avenue. Ignore the trail just by the bridge and stay on the wide track ahead, until the trail turns sharply left through a magnificent stand of pines. The trail going downhill parallels the main road and emerges into the Tulip Springs Picnic Area. About three miles of the hike will have been completed at this point. In the summer, this parking lot is crowded with many bus loads of picnickers. Cross straight over the main road, following the markers straight ahead to a cement bridge over the Rahway River. Pick your way uphill over the rocks to another picnic area with grills and to another rain shelter, turning left at the top. At the end of the parking lot, there is a brick drainage chute to the left and a "No parking beyond this sign" notice. Look for the faint yellow marker and turn right to cross the open space.

Look ahead for the yellow markers leading across the open area and follow them to the traffic light at the intersection of Brookside Drive, Cherry Lane, and South Orange Avenue. There is a turn signal and an arrow on a telephone pole at the intersection. Cross Cherry Lane and walk uphill, passing a small stone building on the right. (If it is necessary to shorten the hike, cross South Orange Avenue, turn left toward the police station, and proceed with the hike from there.) Until about 1950, this whole open space was a fenced-in deer paddock. Food could be purchased at the small house and fed to the deer.

The yellow-marked trail reenters the woods just to the left of the paved car circle, protected by a guard rail, and almost immediately joins a red trail. The red and yellow trails form a circular path through a narrow, wooded area to the north of Valley View Drive (the park road). The red trail, called the Oakdale Trail, travels along the foot of the ridge, and the yellow-marked trail parallels the

bridle path, West Ridge Trail, at a higher elevation.

Climb uphill, paralleling South Orange Avenue for a short while. Red and yellow markers mingle at this point. Ignore the trail to the left and follow the markers to the right, turning away from the main road. Over to the right it is possible to see Tulip Springs parking lot, and, farther along the now level path, the city of Orange reservoir can be glimpsed through the trees.

The Crags rain shelter is reached 1.5 miles from the crossing at the traffic light. Originally intended as a viewpoint, the trees are now too thick to allow much visibility. Just at the Crags, the markers split. The yellow ones turn left onto the bridle path close to private homes. They approach a bridge over Northfield Avenue and turn right. The red markers go straight ahead from the Crags, and the trail joins the yellow trail just after the latter makes a right turn to avoid crossing the bridge over the road. It is immaterial whether the red-marked route or the yellow-marked one is followed, for they both lead to the same place. After the red and yellow routes join again, it is necessary to follow red markers, which are not plentiful along here.

After the right turn, the trail parallels the main road for a short distance and then makes an S-bend downhill through the woods. As soon as a field is seen ahead, watch for the right turn onto a narrower trail and, shortly afterwards, look up to the right to see the Crags above. There is a red-marked spur trail leading left to the comfort station and parking lot at Oakdale Picnic Area. Proceed ahead through tall rhododendron groves. The trail parallels the park road until it reaches the paved circle and the point at which the hike entered this loop. Turn left at this point to emerge onto the open space, and retrace your footsteps

Hemlock Falls, South Mountain Reservation.

downhill to the traffic light. Cross straight ahead over Cherry Lane, right across South Orange Avenue, then turn left. (If the hike was shortened, the description should be picked up here.) At this point, the hike is not on any trail. The route parallels South Orange Avenue on the left and passes a grove of white pines on the right. Walk in front of the park buildings, now housing a police station in the courtyard, and continue straight to find the left of two gravel roads leading downhill to the Rahway River. The police station marks about 6 miles of the hike. The white trail enters from the left and turns towards the river, using the wide road you are already walking down.

At the river bank, leave the wide woods road and turn right to parallel the river on a narrower, white-marked trail. The path climbs away from the river and travels across the side of the hill, soon reaching the site of an old incinerator, now used as a garbage dump. Because water erosion wiped out the original trail and left a gully, a right turn uphill is made just past the incinerator.

The trail bends right to cross a small tributary and bears back to the left after the crossing, emerging onto a crossroad with a sign "Well No. 4" marked in green. Turn left to cross the Rahway River again on a bridge. Before reaching River Road straight ahead, the trail turns right into the woods, passing the pumping station on the opposite bank and paralleling the river. This trail is sometimes wet in spring, but can be negotiated by moving uphill slightly to the left of the trail.

Immediately after passing a second pumping station on the opposite bank, the trail passes a protective piece of chain-linked fencing around pumping equipment and emerges onto a road opposite a fire hydrant. Walk straight ahead, bearing slightly to the right, and note the cement dam across a ford on the main river. To the right of the trail is a blue metal marker with a "3" marked in orange. The white markers are not plentiful, but the trail passes a low-lying, flat area on the right and another cement spillway. Brookside Road and the location of Painters Point can be seen across the river to the right, just at the site of another concrete dam.

The trail makes a few detours up to the River Trail to utilize the bridges over streams, crosses another woods road, and enters a prolific rhododendron grove just as Campbell's Pond comes into view. Throughout this whole valley there is evidence of pumping stations now using electricity for fuel. The trail passes close to the buildings and chimney of the old, steam-driven pumping station. The large boilers housed in this building provided steam for pumping water to a reservoir on the hills, using water from Campbell's Pond. Campbell's Pond is very shallow and is probably not more than a foot in depth.

The white-marked trail continues in a southerly direction, using the bridges on the River Trail when necessary. It is interesting to look at the dams across the Rahway River. Some are derelict, with water seeping through the structures, and one in particular is sealed with a gate from the far side but unprotected from the trail side. The trail crosses Sunset Trail, and, just as the end of Diamond Lake Pond is reached, the traffic light at Glen Avenue and Brookside Drive can be seen. The trail navigates the side of a small hill, and the library and parking lot for Millburn Station become visible to the right.

SJG

27

Watchung Reservation

Total distance: 6 miles
Hiking time: 4 hours
Vertical rise: 500 feet
Rating: Moderate
Maps: USGS Chatham/Roselle; Union County Department of
　Parks and Recreation park map

Watchung Reservation is a two thousand-acre patch of wooded land straddling the first and second Watchung ridges in central New Jersey. Along with South Mountain Reservation and Eagle Rock Reservation to the north, Watchung Reservation has preserved what was for many years a long wall of mountain wilderness overlooking the flat plains that lead toward New York City and the Atlantic Ocean. General George Washington used the long Watchung Ridge as a natural fortification against the British during the Revolutionary War. He planted a number of lookouts along the ridge and kept his troops safely to the west in Loantaka and Jockey Hollow. Much earlier, the Watchung Ridge formed the eastern rim of the basin that contained glacial Lake Passaic, a thirty-by-ten-mile lake of which the Great Swamp is but a remnant.

Although it sits in the middle of suburbia, Watchung Reservation is large enough for a good workout and also contains a number of interesting features, most of which will be seen on this hike. Recently, the construction of I-78 on the boundary of the reservation has made

access easier for many hikers not from the immediate area.

To reach Watchung Reservation from I-78, take exit 43 to Diamond Hill Road. Once off the exit, turn around so that you are heading east on Diamond Hill Road. In less than a mile, turn left onto NJ 527, then bear to the right where the road forks and head into the reservation on Sky Top Drive. Pass through a residential area and arrive at a large parking area where the road swings, after about a mile, to the right. Park here, near the Trailside Museum and planetarium. Maps are available in the museum, and the trailhead is on the left side of the paved road that passes the museum.

From the trailhead, marked with some posts and painted maps on plywood, begin your hike on the Sierra Trail. The Sierra Trail is marked by white Xs painted on trees. In addition, a green trail begins here and runs concurrently with the Sierra Trail for a short distance. As you cross the brook on a very well-made bridge, note the exposure of bedrock in the streambed. These rocks are basalt, or traprock, which has been quarried extensively throughout the Watchung Mountains. Once over the brook, bear right following the white X markers. Pay very close attention to the markers in this section. There are numerous paths, and it is easy to lose the correct trail. The trail heads gradually downhill after this turn and then bears to the left through an area that is sometimes wet. Watch closely for markers as the trail makes a subtle jog to the right.

The Sierra Trail takes you along the rim of a small glen quite beautiful in any season. On the left, the brook is eroding the red shales that overlay the basalt. Exposed basaltic bedrock is soon encountered, and then hemlocks appear as the glen widens. In this section, a blue-marked trail coincides with the white trail for a while.

After descending through the hemlocks in this beautiful section of the reservation, cross the brook, still following white markers, and begin to climb. Below, Blue Brook makes an oxbow bend as it snakes through the drainage between ridges. As you climb, watch the markers carefully. There is a steep climb at one point, which then levels off in a pleasant mixture of deciduous trees and hemlocks. Farther along, the Sierra Trail comes to another, smaller glen with some fairly large boulders and even a grassy area. This spot is good for a break and perhaps some exploration. Deer are plentiful in this reservation—perhaps you've spotted one already.

Following white markers, cross the brook and climb the opposite bank. After this small climb, the trail levels off and, as it swings to the right, passes a residential area. Next, cross a gravel road, head back into the woods, and begin another long, gradual loss of elevation. There are no hemlocks here, and the ground is higher and dryer. Notice on the descent that where the trail has been deeply eroded there are some exposures

of shale and sandstone, hardened mud, and silt deposited during the Triassic period. Later, volcanic magma intruded into these shales, forming the erosion-resistant, basaltic Watchung Mountains. At the bottom of the descent, the trail comes to a dirt road and turns left. Tall cedars line the west side of this road, which was once a driveway. Within a few hundred feet, the trail turns left and cuts back into the woods in a pine plantation, heading uphill once more.

Look carefully for the markers here; the trail jogs slightly to the right and then heads straight through a row of tall pines. This is a peaceful environment. Little patches of sunlight decorate the uniform brown carpet of pine needles. These pines were planted in the 1930s as part of a Civilian Conservation Corps project, and though some are not as tall as others, all the trees are the same age. If you are lucky, you might spot one of the owls that nest here. Too soon the trail emerges from the pines, swings to the left, and then, after crossing a small bridge, enters a picnic area with a shelter. The trail leads through this cleared area on a gravel service road, crosses Sky Top Drive, and reenters the woods on a dirt road.

At the first intersection, bear right and begin a long, nearly level walk on a dirt road that parallels Sky Top Drive. Along with the familiar white Xs that mark the Sierra Trail, cross-country ski markers of green and white will be apparent. Several intersections will be crossed before a section arrives that is very close to the actual summit of the first Watchung Mountain. Bushwack to the left to obtain a glimpse of civilization through the trees. From here the trail begins to head downhill, and, after another ten minutes of walking, you will come to a small overlook to the south and west. Here the effects of quarrying in the Watchung Hills

27: Watchung Reservation;
Based on USGS 7½' Chatham
& Roselle Quadrangles

can be seen and often heard during the week when the quarries are operating. Traprock, the popular term for basalt gravel, has been used for years to pave New Jersey's roads and highways.

At the overlook, the trail swings to the left and heads down the mountain. Now the sounds of civilization are more apparent. The trail makes a sharp right at the bottom, just before a house, and may not be marked very well. This section of trail is washed out in places and tends to be clogged with leaves and branches washed down by the rains. Soon Green Brook is seen on the left and, beyond that, New Providence Road. Green Brook is a stocked trout stream and attracts many fishermen. As the trail heads north along the bank of the brook, it becomes rockier. The trail, the brook, and the road all pass together through a gap in the long wall of the Watchungs.

Above on the right, some outcroppings of basalt can be seen. Look closely at the rock and observe the way it forms hexagonal columns much like the Palisades of the Hudson, only on a smaller scale. The remains of some former structures will be reached next. Nobody is sure about the history of the old mill that once stood at this site, using the power of the brook to cut wood and grind flour. The brook drops quite a few feet in a short distance here and once was diverted to turn a mill wheel. Look around to find where the water was channeled away from the brook and over to the mill. The trail, which is not well marked here, swings to the right and steeply uphill after leaving the ruins of the mill.

At the top of the climb, another rock outcrop offers more views to the south and west. I-78 is clearly visible. During the late 1970s and early 1980s, many conservation-minded people tried to prevent the construction of I-78, which planners had routed through the western and northern section of the reservation. It was a major regional issue that was finally settled by replacing the land used for the highway, which totaled about seventy acres, with land from a nearly adjacent rock quarry. With the deal came $3.6 million for the upkeep and development of the reservation. The highway was also built low in the ground and is flanked by walls that muffle the sound somewhat. In one place, a "cut and cover" structure, a 220-foot-wide bridge with soil and plants, allows animals to cross the highway safely; we were told that it didn't take the large deer population long to find the way across.

From this overlook, the trail turns right and heads back towards the woods into a grove of old hemlocks. Now following a woods road, the trail bears to the left heading gradually downhill. Just before reaching Sky Top Drive again, the markers lead to a short cut on the left, ending at the paved road near a bridge at Seeleys Pond. Head towards the bridge on the left.

Cross the bridge and immediately bear right to find the trail that heads back into the woods. This point is at the edge of the reservation, and suburbia is just across the street. Continue following the trail, which soon becomes a footpath in some fairly dense vegetation. In places the trail is crowded by wild roses. Violets and spring beauties are found along it, where an occasional spring keeps the ground moist. Watch for poison ivy in this section, both as a vine on trees and as a bush.

After a few minutes, a quiet spot where some large hemlocks dominate the land between two small brooks will be reached. The trail, which may not be clearly marked here, crosses the second brook and makes a left on a badly eroded path. Almost immediately, at a small clearing, the trail swings sharply to the right and heads back into the woods, crossing several small streams that run only in the spring or after a rain. As the trail gradually gains elevation, it also becomes wider and more badly eroded.

Continue on this eroded path, heading gradually uphill. At the right turn just before the trail passes a hemlock grove on the right, look right to find a partially exposed conglomerate boulder. This stone, which technically is Shawangunk conglomerate, is not native to the area—it was dragged here by the glacier for a distance of at least twenty miles.

Suddenly there will be a large building facing you, and Deserted Village, also known as Feltsville and Glenside Park, is entered. From 1845 to 1860, David Felt

A pine plantation at the Watchung Reservation.

owned and operated a paper mill on Blue Brook. Feltsville was a factory town then, but when the mill closed, it became Glenside Park, a Victorian retreat with lawn tennis and pure water. Some say there is a salt brook and a magnesium spring in the vicinity that may have been the reasons for making the area a mini-resort between 1882 and 1916. Today the entire area is within the boundaries of the reservation, but the houses are rented.

After passing the last two houses (one with a wooden tower attached to it), the trail bears right, turning off the road and onto a dirt road. The trail immediately turns again to the right and onto a foot-path. In a few hundred yards, there is a small Revolutionary War cemetery where members of the Willcock's family, the descendants of the original settler Peter Willcox, are buried. William Willcox was a "judge and advocate of the Revolutionary War," and he died in 1800. Joseph Badgley was a private in the First New Jersey Regiment and died in 1785. John

Willcocks Sr. died on November 22 in 1776. He was in the Light Horse Company of the New Jersey militia.

Leaving the gravesites, continue along the footpath, following the white markers as the trail snakes through the woods at a nearly constant elevation. Soon the trail begins to descend and then meets a woods road. At this point, leave the white Sierra Trail, turning right and crossing over the bridge and Blue Brook. Where the road swings to the left, bear right onto a footpath that leads to a log bridge and blue markers. Do not cross the bridge but follow the blue markers up-stream, keeping the brook on your right. After a short distance, the blue markers change to orange markers. Do not cross the log bridge, and keep the brook to your right. After a few more minutes, a gate and a paved road is reached. Bear right here and walk uphill, finding the museum and then the parking area on your left.

BCS

Great Swamp

Total distance: 4–5 miles
Hiking time: 2–3 hours
Vertical rise: None
Rating: Easy
Maps: USGS Chatham; Great Swamp NWR (US Dept. of the
Interior, Fish and Wildlife Service)

The Great Swamp National Wildlife Refuge (NWR) (RD 1, Box 152, Basking Ridge, New Jersey 07920; 201-647-1222) was established in 1960 following a successful battle to defeat a proposed jetport. It was this controversy that enabled a local committee of the North American Wildlife Foundation to raise more than $1 million to purchase three thousand acres that now form the heart of the 6,818-acre refuge. In 1968, the eastern half of the NWR was designated by Congress as a wilderness tract. The hike described here is within this wilderness, where only foot travel is permitted.

For a maximum chance to see wildlife, a small group of hikers is advised. The trails are easy to follow but not well marked. They are also often very wet. In fact, this may be the wettest hike you ever take! In spring or fall, waterproof footwear is a must. In winter, much of the surface may be frozen but icy. Even in summer, wear sneakers and wool socks and have a change ready in the car for your return. Once you've decided you're going to get your feet wet anyway, you can just begin enjoying the area. Of course, stay on the trails for safety.

The Great Swamp is a relic of postglacial Lake Passaic, an immense lake some thirty miles long and ten miles wide. The lake existed some five thousand years ago. It formed when the terminal moraine of the glacier blocked the exit of the Passaic River through Short Hills and a bowl behind the Watchungs filled with water. The water eventually drained out at first near Far Hills, then near Great Notch, and, finally, at the present-day falls near Paterson.

To reach the wildlife refuge from exit 26A of I-287 near Basking Ridge, take Maple Avenue south through the town of Basking Ridge to Lord Stirling Road, a distance of about 2.5 miles. Make a left onto Lord Stirling Road, which becomes White Bridge Road after passing the junction with Carlton Road. Pleasant Plains and New Vernon/Long Hill roads are also passed before you dead-end at a large parking area, just under 3 miles from Maple Avenue.

En route to the parking area, you'll pass roads to some places of interest. Along White Bridge Road, the refuge office is located a short distance left (north) up Pleasant Plains Road. It is open weekdays from 8:00 A.M. to 4:30 P.M. Maps and fliers are available there. A wildlife observation center is located about a mile left (north) up Long Hill Road. Here is an information kiosk, blinds for wildlife observation, short trails, and rest rooms. Also in the area, on Lord Stirling Road near Maple Avenue, is the Environmental Education Center operated by the Somerset County Park Commission. The center, with more than eight miles of trail, has a program of courses and field trips (201-766-2489).

After parking, proceed to the trailhead at a wood gate. Park officials have posted a copy of their hiking map here, but some of the trails shown are not passable. Our trail goes along an old woods road through the high grass and swings gently right onto a more gravelly surface. There are occasional splashes of orange paint as a guide. Almost immediately, one begins to notice an abundance of bird sounds. Since the hike is short, there is lots of time to stop, look, and listen, for this area is not the typical woodland environment of most New Jersey hikes.

After twenty minutes or so, pass a blue trail going right. Mark this junction in your memory since a side trip down this fork is recommended later. Continue straight ahead. Ten more minutes brings you to a crossing over a still stream on a recently constructed, boardwalk-style bridge. On the far side, the grass closes in and makes the trail narrower. A few minutes later, there is another junction with a narrow trail going to the right. There is a post here with no sign. Open water has turned this side trail into a quick dead end, but it's worth a jog down to get a good, open view of the swampland. The drier the season, the farther in it is possible to walk. This path is likely the southern fork of the yellow trail on the park map. A trip down the other end is avail-

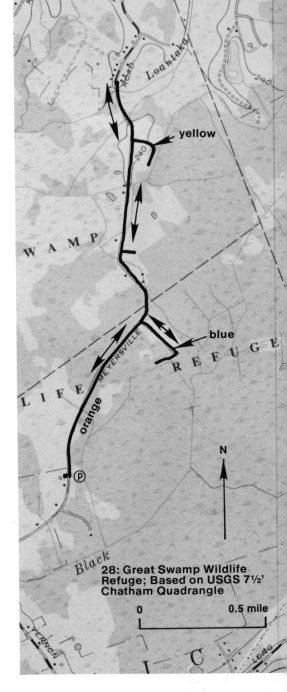

28: Great Swamp Wildlife Refuge; Based on USGS 7½' Chatham Quadrangle

0   0.5 mile

able as an option later in the hike.

Poison ivy is present in the area, as well as ticks carrying Lyme disease (see

Introduction). The trail continues ahead, passing some unusual open water. Crossing over a second boardwalk bridge with views of the surrounding flatland, the route arrives at the end of the trail at a NWR parking area at the end of Meyersville Road, about 1.5 miles from the beginning of the hike. Although you could have left a car here, the drive between the two areas is rather circuitous and, since the hike is so short, not recommended.

Start back the same way. After about seven minutes, the start of the yellow trail is reached, heading towards the left in a grassy field. If you should pass this junction, you'll come to the more northerly of the boardwalk bridges previously crossed. Turn around and backtrack to the intersection, 275 paces back. This yellow trail is worth the short, half-hour detour. It leads through hardwoods with fine ground cover and some open water. The area has a distinct feeling of the jungle, with many different birds adding the "right" sounds. A few minutes in, the trail splits. Take the more prominent right fork, confirmed by some yellow paint blazes. After a short distance (270 average paces), the trail again divides. One with a double yellow blaze goes off to the right. Follow the single yellow blaze straight ahead.

About fifteen minutes into this side trip, look for an enormous beech tree on the left (just after you've spent five minutes walking through various stands of laurel).

This point is really the end of the open route. Though you can go ahead a few more minutes, the trail makes a sharp right into open water and becomes impassable. Retrace your steps to the main trail.

Resuming the hike back towards the car, notice a long row of large conifers on the right. Before the wildlife refuge was created, people lived along this road. This planting was associated with one of those houses. The main trail is, in fact, the route of Meyersville Road before it was closed by park authorities.

Twenty minutes more walking takes you back to the blue trail junction passed near the start of the hike. Turn left down this spur, the beginning of which shows evidence of once being paved. It soon becomes a grassy route, skirts the edge of a field, and reenters the woods. Some seven minutes in, the trail begins to go along a wide area of stagnant water. This location is the shore of Black Brook. Find some dry ground (if you can), sit, and enjoy the peace of this wild domain before retracing your steps to the main trail and back to your car.

For those interested in a wilder, off-trail experience in the Great Swamp, the administration offers ranger-led, monthly hikes through the depths of the preserve. Call ahead for information, for advance sign-up is required.

HNZ

The Great Swamp.

Lord Stirling Park

Total distance: 3.5 miles
Hiking time: 2 hours
Vertical rise: Minimal
Rating: Easy
Maps: USGS Bernardsville; Somerset County Park Commission
trail map

The Somerset County Park Commission operates the Environmental Education Center, located at the edge of the Great Swamp. The Great Swamp is what remains of the former Lake Passaic, a huge (ten-by-thirty-mile) glacial lake created during the previous Wisconsin Ice Age, which shaped much of north Jersey's topography twelve thousand years ago. The lake was formed by melt water from the retreating glacial ice sheet, blocked by the long wall of basalt that is the Watchungs. Today, all that remains of the lake is an extensive series of wetlands along the course of the Passaic River.

The four hundred acres of the Environmental Education Center at Lord Stirling Park adjoin the holdings of the Department of the Interior (the Great Swamp National Wildlife Refuge) and, farther north, the Morris County Park Commission. Combined, these contiguous parks and refuges make north Jersey's largest protected wetland. Within this area are a number of diverse plant communities and habitats of special appeal to naturalists and birders. About nine miles of eight-foot-wide trails and boardwalks and two

observation towers permit exploration of this southernmost section of the Great Swamp, a true relic of the ice age.

Lord Stirling Park (190 Lord Stirling Road, Basking Ridge, NJ 07920; 201-766-2489) derives its name from William Alexander, who was the Lord of Stirling. He served as a general in the Continental Army and was the owner of vast land holdings. The area that is now the park is only a very small portion of the original estate.

To find the Environmental Education Center from I-287, take exit 26A to North Maple Avenue. The road veers to the left at the town of Basking Ridge and becomes South Maple Avenue. After a total of 2.5 miles from I-287, make a left onto Lord Stirling Road and go 1 mile to the Environmental Education Center on the left. Before beginning your hike, stop in at the center, sign your name in the register, and buy a map of the park for twenty-five cents, well worth the price.

To start the hike, follow the trail that begins to the right of the building and heads out along the north side of Brant Pond, a man-made lake. There is a split-rail fence along this route also. The trail

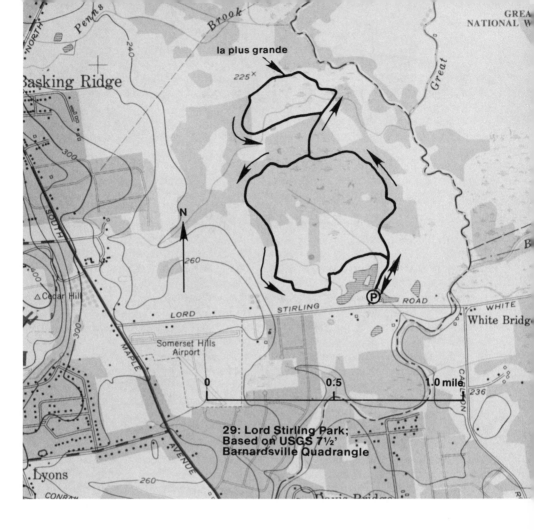

29: Lord Stirling Park;
Based on USGS 7½'
Barnardsville Quadrangle

is marked with both red and yellow markers painted on metal stakes. This area was once a sheep farm. Notice the yellow markers turning off to the right at the end of the pond, and continue straight ahead following red markers. An intersection is soon reached, and the red trail bears to the right over a small bridge. Stay on the red trail, which is eight feet wide and generally quite dry considering that it travels through a very wet area. An occasional bench along this trail provides the walker with a convenient resting place hard to come by in this swampy, rockless environment.

This section of trail passes through a wet forest of white oak, beech, and shagbark hickory. Notice that the roots of the trees are very close to the surface due to the overabundance of water. Some tree roots are actually seen above the surface of the ground, spreading out in all directions. The instability of this situation is evidenced by the number of fallen trees in the woods. After about fifteen minutes of walking, a junction with a boardwalk will be reached. Keep to the left here, staying on the red trail. At the next junction, near the frame of an old automobile, turn right on an unmarked trail that soon becomes a series of boardwalks. The woods now become wetter, pin oaks predominating among hummocks of sedge.

After just a few minutes, a triangular intersection appears. Make a mental note of this junction. There are no markers here, and the intersection will need to be recognized on the way back. From here, walk a loop almost entirely on boardwalk, bearing to the left at every intersection. After passing two more intersections and bearing left at each one, you will be led by the boardwalk into the heart of a fresh-water swamp named "la plus grande," an open section of the Great Swamp. All around are cattails, buttonbush, swamp rose, and sedges. The birds are active here, even in winter. Sparrows flit from bush to bush, and you may even see a pair of cardinals.

It may be hard to imagine, but if it weren't for the efforts of some very concerned residents, this wilderness could have been an international jetport. In the 1960s, plans for the construction of such a jetport in the Great Swamp were halted by a grass-roots effort of concerned citizens. Marcellus Hartley Dodge managed to get the cooperation of many local and national figures and took on the Port Authority itself. In the end, 6,100 individuals contributed toward the purchase of the original three thousand acres, which were then donated to the Department of the Interior.

After leaving the open area, the trail re-enters the woods and alternates between boardwalk and some very wet and muddy sections of trail. Deer are abundant here, and the red-tailed hawk is frequently spotted. After a few more minutes of boardwalk hiking, look for the triangular junction on which you began this second loop, and when it is located, bear to the right, returning to the red-marked circular trail.

Bear right at the red trail, passing another junction where the red trail swings to the right. It is here that the markers for the cross-country ski trail (green metal posts with a circle and wavy line symbol) are found. Look around and notice a number of hollows in the ground here. These sites are where trees were removed during the early 1900s when lumbering began to alter the natural appearance of the woods. Another section of boardwalk, which skirts a very wet and open area full of dead trees, is soon reached, and farther on, a bridge over a small running brook will be crossed. Notice the straight ditches of water in this section. These trenches are the remains of man-made attempts to drain the land when it was being farmed as late as the 1950s.

The trail bears left at a field and begins to swing back to the Environmental Center. These abandoned farm fields were once used for sheep grazing. Here the land is in transition, reverting back to its natural wooded condition. The red markers lead over another bridge passing over another drainage ditch constructed by farmers of the past. Soon the center will be seen. Before reaching it, the trail swings around the ponds, past a large bird blind, before connecting with the yellow trail. Return to the center along the same path on which the hike started.

BCS

"La plus grande" fresh-water swamp.

30

Round Valley Recreation Area

Total distance: 10 miles
Hiking time: 5 hours
Vertical rise: Approximately 400 feet
Rating: Moderate
Maps: USGS Califon/Flemington; DEP park map

Round Valley Recreation Area (RD #1, Lebanon/Stanton Road, Lebanon, NJ 08833; 201-236-6355) is in a natural, horseshoe-shaped basin surrounded on three sides by Cushetunk Mountain. The reservoir covers more than 2,300 acres, with an average depth of approximately 70 feet. These statistics make Round Valley Reservoir one of the largest and deepest lakes in New Jersey. The reservoir holds 55 billion gallons of water, and fishing, swimming, and boating are permitted. The land for the reservoir was purchased through a water bond act in the 1950s. Houses were moved out during the mid-1960s, and the reservoir was full by the end of the decade. In 1972 the campground was opened, and the day-use area was added in 1976. The park is open year round, but a fee is charged from Memorial Day weekend through Labor Day.

Hiking is limited to one long trail circling the lake, at first through open terrain and then through densely wooded areas. It is recommended that this hike be walked "out of season," when the wilderness camping area is not being heavily utilized. Permission to walk back on the main access road through the wil-

derness camping area from the sandy beach should be sought from the visitors center before beginning the hike. During the summer months, a special permit is required to use the camping territory, and day visitors are not permitted in the area; but sometimes, during the off-season the ranger will allow day visitors to walk back on the campsite service road. If such permission is not obtained, the return route from the sandy beach must be the same as the outward route.

Round Valley Recreation Area is accessed from US 22, 8 miles east of Clinton and 4 miles from Whitehouse. US 22 can be reached either from I-78 using exit 20A from the north or from I-287 from the east. Half a mile west of Lebanon, there is a sign to the park. Turn onto the park access road and travel for 2 miles. The park access road merges with County Road 629 later. Pass the road to the boat launch and, after approximately 1 mile, turn left into the Round Valley entrance.

Parking is not allowed at the visitors center, but it is essential that visitors register there first to obtain a car parking permit. It is also advisable to check the park closing time. From the visitors center, drive through the gate and take the first right to the boat launching parking lot. Away from the lake front is a trail-head sign—a horseshoe and a footprint. The trail is used both as a horse trail and a hiking trail, although there is little evidence of horse-riding use.

The trail is uphill at first, through a flat, grassy area with white pine on the right-hand side and an open hill with many dogwood trees to the left. The area is a dogwood lover's delight especially in spring and fall when these trees are their most colorful. Momentarily, the trail is close to the road, but almost immediately a sign indicates that the trail turns and proceeds uphill on the left-hand, wide, grassy road. Look down towards the left to admire the broad sweep of the reservoir and to enjoy the boating and fishing activity usually evident on the water.

At the top of the hill, the visitors center can be seen to the right, and the trail descends towards the lake. Here again there are a large number of dogwood trees. The trail becomes narrower, paralleling the lake and rolling gently up and down until it goes under a power line, maintenance of which requires the usual massacre of surrounding shrubbery. After approximately twenty minutes, a fence protects the walker from NJ 629. Here the path is quite level and curves in and out amongst a variety of small trees and shrubs before beginning to climb. Pass through a chain-linked fence and cross the private, gravel access road to the dam. There are horseshoe and footprint markers at this point, which indicate that the trail turns left into the woods and that the private, woods road to the right should be ignored. After a short distance in the woods, the trail emerges into the open again, with the chain-linked fence protection to the dam on the left and the power line to the right.

After descending quite steeply, you will get a superb view of rural New Jersey ahead. The old trail continues downhill, but where a new piece of chain-linked fencing has been installed at right angles, turn sharply left through the gap in the old fence and proceed downhill on a steep, soil slope towards another section of chain-linked fence protection from NJ 629. The reservoir dam rises behind a second fence to the left, and it is common to see deer congregated here on the slope, particularly at dawn or dusk. This section is grassy and open, and the route is between the two fences. Cross a second dam access road at the bottom of the hill, keep to the upper side of the bushes and ditch near the main road, and cross a stream on concrete stepping stones close to the left fence. Watercress grows in abundance in the stream. If the water is too high to cross over easily, the stream can be avoided altogether by going out to the main road, walking over the bridge, and climbing back over the guard rail on the other side of the stream.

Climb up the muddy, eroded bank on the other side of the stream, noting the trail signs at the top, and walk along the side of the chain-linked fence on a newly cut section of trail. Take care here not to trip on the stobs. Cross another official vehicle entry point to the dam and walk straight ahead. There is a preponderance of chain-linked fencing in this section, and the trail moves gradually away from the dam and into the woods. Turn right at the next T-junction and walk straight ahead at the next crossroads, following the horseshoe signs. The direction of travel to this point has been southerly, but the next bend towards the left changes the direction to an easterly one.

To the left and halfway up the hill, there is an oddly shaped building foundation. Eighty-seven acres in Round Valley is not administered by the state of

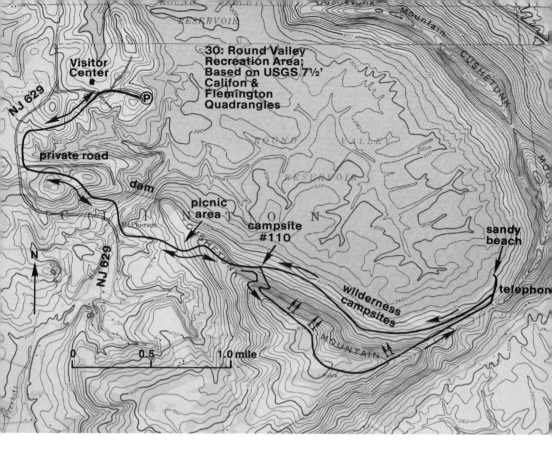

30: Round Valley
Recreation Area;
Based on USGS 7½'
Califon &
Flemington
Quadrangles

New Jersey but, under the original purchase agreement, is leased to a nonprofit organization for group use. This pseudo-building is part of their facility. Shortly after passing this building, a red arrow indicates a ninety-degree turn to the left, and the trail leads slightly uphill and straight ahead to a picnic area. The walk so far has taken approximately 1 to 1.5 hours, so the large, open, grassy area is a natural place for a rest stop. The route to the picnic area goes past the next turn in the trail, but the view of the reservoir to the right and the ridge of hills to the left at the open picnic site is worth the few extra yards walk. There are comfort stations at the picnic site, as well as a flagpost and grills.

After the break, retrace your footsteps as far as the turn now on the left, passed previously, and climb up through tall, mature maple and oak trees. At the top of the hill, watch carefully for the correct route, which turns left and goes downhill. There is another wide road going right and uphill that should be ignored. The trail leading downhill is a wide, dirt road under a canopy of dense trees.

Red squirrels and the eastern chipmunk inhabit the dense woodland at Round Valley and are frequent visitors to the campsites. Squirrel antics are always entertaining. Red squirrels nest either in holes in tree trunks, or, in an area with few trunk cavities or small trees, their nests are constructed from twigs, fibers, lichens, and moss, molded into a ball with a well-protected inner chamber, and located at the top of a tree. The chipmunk lives in an underground burrow with a two-inch entrance or sometimes in rock or brush piles. Both these mammals cache food for the winter months and are, therefore, especially active in the autumn.

At the foot of the hill, there are two wooden signs indicating that the wilderness campsite area has been reached and listing the regulations for the area. The reservoir can be glimpsed through the trees to the left; the trail is marked with the same horseshoe sign and turns right in an uphill direction. The climb is steep, on a rockier trail becoming narrower during the elevation gain, switchbacking, and traversing the side of the hill. A T-junction is reached, with the number six on a tree immediately facing the end of this section of trail and with a footprint sign on a tree to the left. Turn left here. The trail continues to climb after this left turn. Up to this point, the walk will have taken approximately thirty min-

utes from the picnic area and two hours from the hike commencement. The reservoir can be seen periodically through the trees to the left.

The trail continues to climb, until, at the top of the ridge, it levels out and follows the ridge line of Cushetunk Mountain right on the boundary line between private land and reservation property. Wooden seats are provided at intervals along this section of the trail. At the next T-junction, there is no sign to indicate the route. Turn left again, being aware that the trail will be going slightly downhill. The trees are still dense, and the sharp-eyed will catch a glimpse of a private home to the right of the trail. One of the high points on the ridge to the right of the trail is called Pickle Point.

Follow the horseshoe signs wherever they appear, and where the main trail seems to turn left, go straight ahead through the fence. The path is level, and,

Round Valley reservoir.

after a few minutes, keep your eyes open for the horseshoe sign and bear left. The trail is very rocky in this section. There is a blowdown across the trail, and for a short distance, there is a chain-linked fence on the right. The trail moves away from the fencing quite quickly, continuing downhill. Avoid the path coming in from the left, but take the one that parallels Round Valley Road on the right. When the gravel-covered Round Valley Road is reached, turn left and walk downhill towards the water. Some maintenance buildings, a signboard, an outhouse, and a telephone soon come into view. Turn left off the road past the signboard and down to the sandy beach with its all-encompassing view of the reservoir.

If permission has been granted for you to return through the campsite area, walk straight inland away from the water and turn right on the gravel road. (The road by which you arrived at the beach is on the left.) Otherwise, the return route must be the same as the outgoing route just described.

For novice backpackers and for hikers wishing to test their abilities or new equipment, Round Valley Recreation Area is the ideal camping situation. The campsites are widely spaced and provide the feeling of isolation expected in a wilderness area. All the sites are well hidden from the access road and plentifully supplied with comfort stations and water. There is the remnant of an old stone wall near the sandy beach, and various paths between the sites give access to the water from the service road. Amongst the tall trees, there is an abundance of tulip trees. Part way along the wilderness campsite area, a trail marked with a footprint leads back to the outward bound trail, and walking for an hour will bring you back to the junction point where the campsite area was originally accessed. From here, it is only necessary to retrace your footsteps to the parking lot where the car was parked.

SJG

31

Bull's Island to Prallsville Mill

Total distance: 3 miles (or 6 miles using one car)
Hiking time: 2 hours (or 3.5 hours)
Vertical rise: Minimal
Rating: Easy to moderate
Map: USGS Lumberville/Stockton

The twenty-two-mile-long feeder to the main Delaware and Raritan Canal is part of Delaware and Raritan Canal State Park. The towpath in this section was utilized by the Belvidere and Delaware Railroad and is surfaced today with fine stone chips. From Bull's Island to Stockton, at the Prallsville Mill, the railroad bed is located on the east bank of the Delaware River. At Stockton, it swings over the canal to the towpath, which separates the canal from the river. Bull's Island is the only developed section of the state park and invites exploration. The Prallsville Mill, three miles to the south, is a restored historical area scenically located on the canal and overlooking the Delaware River.

From the junction with US 202, take NJ 29 north for 6 miles to the Bull's Island section of Delaware and Raritan Canal State Park (RD1, Box 8, Belle Mead, NJ 08502). The park, which offers car and tent camping, is located on a densely wooded flood plain of the Delaware. As you enter the park, which will be on the left, pass the ranger's house and park in the large day-use parking area. Directly in front of the parking area is a suspension bridge for pedestrians

that crosses the Delaware and allows access to Pennsylvania. The views of the river from this bridge are outstanding.

Bull's Island is an artificial island, created by the construction of the canal. Richard Bull, one of the original owners, gave his name to the island and also to Bull's Creek, displaced by the canal, which separated it from the mainland. In 1832 work on the Delaware and Raritan Canal was started, and by 1834 the Delaware River Dam, which is used to divert water from the river to the canal, was completed. Here, the Delaware River water enters the canal and begins its long journey south to Trenton. This section, known as the canal feeder, was not only a source of water for the main canal but was also a navigation channel that competed with the Delaware Canal on the Pennsylvania side of the river. The feeder meets the main canal at Trenton, where the canal turns north and, following first the Millstone and then the Raritan rivers, terminates at New Brunswick. Along the way, the water level is maintained by a series of locks.

To begin the hike, leave the parking area and follow the entrance road back over the canal. Just before reaching NJ

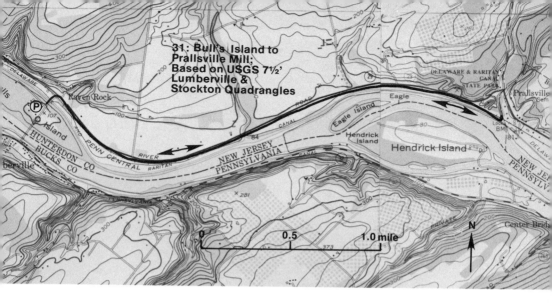

29 (which it will parallel) find the abandoned Belvidere and Delaware Railroad bed, now a seventeen-mile, multipurpose trail, suitable for walkers, joggers, and even bicycle riders. Pass around the gate and begin the three-mile walk to the Prallsville Mill.

As you walk south along the railroad bed, the woods will be to the right and NJ 29 on the left. After only a half mile of walking, the canal will be seen far below. Throughout most of Delaware and Raritan Canal State Park the actual towpath, which lies between the canal and the river, is used as the recreational path. In this section, the towpath is cut by unbridged overflow points that present major obstacles for the walker. The railroad bed, covered with a fine gravel, therefore serves as the main path until the first lock is reached at the mill. Occasional piles of old railroad ties lie along the route, which is quite straight and, of course, very flat.

On the way to the mill, the walkway takes one through a mixture of sun and shade, field and woods. Wildflowers include wild carrot, yarrow, common chicory, goldenrod, mullein, staghorn sumac, morning glories, snapdragons and black-eyed Susans. Wild bergamot, from which a tea can be made that acts as a nerve and stomach tonic, is found along the way also. The large number of blooming flowers attracts swarms of butterflies and bumblebees. At about the halfway point, cross over an inlet leading to the canal on a high bridge. Here, about fifty feet or more above the canal, a break in the towpath out to the Delaware is seen.

Farther along, the path becomes more shaded and crowded in with honeysuckle and other vines. A rock embankment, which separates the path from the road, appears. The stone, the Stockton Formation, is better known as brownstone and is quarried locally. This stone has been used in the construction of many historic buildings in New Jersey including some at Princeton and Rutgers universities. Brownstone is a sandstone, formed during Triassic times, that has been exposed by the cutting action of the river. In the area are a few igneous intrusions of darker traprock, similar to those that formed the Watchungs and Cushetunk Mountain. In fact, the name Raven Rock is derived from such an intrusion.

Ahead on the path, a bridge over a brook flowing into the canal is particularly picturesque. On a clear summer day one can look over an expanse of water to wooded islands, banks of purple loose-strife, and the mighty Delaware River. Ahead are the first locks on the feeder canal, and to the left are the buildings of the Prallsville Mill.

The Prallsville Mill, located just north of Stockton, is named after John Prall who, though not the original owner, bought the property in 1794. He enlarged the original gristmill and sawmill operation by adding a stone building used to mill linseed oil and plaster. In 1874 the original grist-mill burned, ignited by a spark from a passing steam engine on the B & D Railroad, but the mill was rebuilt on the old foundations three years later. After milling came to an end in the late 1940s, the entire complex of seven buildings was acquired by the state and gradually re-stored by the Delaware River Mill Society, which leases the site. What makes the Prallsville Mill unique is that it is the only historic multiple milling operation remaining in the state.

Today, the displays at the restored mill include an industrial herb garden, an exact scale model of the mill built by the last mill owner, and a craft shop, along with the restored buildings themselves. Near the old sawmill is a picnic table, a good place to have lunch or a snack after the walk from Bull's Island.

After visiting the mill, head back to Bull's Island the way you came—or leave from here if you have arranged a car shuttle.

BCS

The Delaware River and feeder canal.

32

Washington Crossing to Scudders Falls

Total distance: 6 miles
Hiking time: 3 hours
Vertical rise: 100 feet
Rating: Moderate
Maps: USGS Pennington; DEP: Washington Crossing State
Park

Washington Crossing State Park (RR1, Box 337, Titusville, NJ 08560; 609-737-0623) is #13 on the state's historical site listing, and signs for it displaying this number are found as you approach the site from any direction. From I-95, take exit 3B and follow signs to County Road 546 west. The well-marked entrance to the park will be found a few miles ahead on the right. Enter the park following signs to the visitor's center and park in the large lot just to the north of the center.

From the parking area, walk to the visitor's center, which contains a large collection of Revolutionary War artifacts, maps and descriptive brouchures, and a short slide presentation on the history and offerings of the park. Get a feeling for the momentous event that justified the creation of this park. The importance of what happened here in 1776 cannot be overestimated. This was the site of probably the single, most important offensive in Washington's military career. At the very least, it kept him and the country alive during the early days of the American Revolution.

Since declaring Independence, the

Continental Army, led by Washington, had not scored a point against the British. Washington and his men had tried to stop the British invasion of Long Island (Brooklyn) but were driven back to Manhattan and then to New Jersey. Denied adequate troops and supplies to meet the threat, Washington had no recourse but to retreat across the middle of New Jersey, across the Delaware, and into Pennsylvania. Although the situation appeared to be cause for extreme depression, Washington took a risk and won, and in the process stirred hope for the revolutionary cause.

On the night of December 25, 1776, he ordered three divisions of troops to attack the Hessian garrison at Trenton. The plan called for each division to cross the Delaware at different points and then converge on the enemy by surprise. Washington himself and 2,400 men crossed the river in ferryboats at the site of the present-day park. After a difficult crossing in the ice-choked river, he and his men marched south to Trenton, caught the Hessians by surprise, and won the victory. The other two divisions never made the crossing that night due to river ice. Washington immediately followed up the victory with a successful attack on the British at Princeton. Having pushed back the enemy halfway to New York, he took shelter for the remainder of the winter behind the long curving natural wall of the Watchungs in central Jersey. These two battles marked one of the major turning points in the war, and they kept Washington in place as commander in chief.

After your visit at the center, walk over to "Continental Lane," the grassy walking path found about 100 yards due west (in front) of the center. You'll find it between a long line of trees and other plantings just across the paved road. Turn left onto the lane and head towards the Delaware River. Continental Lane is a very pleasant, tree-lined walkway between park service roads. Ash, oak, white pines and cedars line the path on either side. After a few minutes of walking, you'll come to a few colonial buildings. To your right is an old barn that now houses rest rooms and a flag museum. In front of you is the Ferry House, fronted with an herb garden. You may wish to explore these buildings now, or perhaps on your return. At the terminus of Continental Lane, bear left for just a few feet on the paved road and turn right onto a paved path heading south. This path will lead you past a walled-in overlook (overlooking NJ 29 and the Delaware) and out to a pedestrian walking bridge over the highway. This area is part of the memorial arboretum, and the varied plant life here may be of interest. Take the pedestrian walking bridge over NJ 29, make a left, crossing the road leading to the bridge, and head south (through the gate) on the canal feeder towpath. En route you'll pass two stone markers commemorating the crossing.

The towpath, which was used for a time as a bed for the Delaware and

32: Washington Crossing to Scudders Falls; Based on USGS 7½' Pennington Quadrangle

0   0.5 mile

N

Belvidere Railroad, is very flat and is surfaced by a very fine, though loose, gravel. The path gets much use from joggers and bicycle riders as well as walkers. To the right, and quite a drop below, is the Delaware River. To the left is the feeder canal, and beyond that, NJ 29. It is unfortunate that the highway is so close, but that is an unavoidable reality in such a densely populated area. This section of towpath is very exposed to sunlight and, during hot summer days, it may be advisable to hike in the late afternoon when the shade of the taller trees on the west bank covers the entire path.

As you walk along the towpath, you'll see vegetation very different from that of the highland mountains or the Pine Barrens. The plants, weeds actually, are more typical of highways, urban vacant lots, and other places that receive much sunlight. Don't be put off by this fact, some of the most valuable medicinal herbs are found in such environments. For example, you'll see thistle, with its prickly leaves and round flower heads, used for fevers (it produces sweating). The common mullein, the tall, spikelike plant commonly seen along the roadside, is also found here; a tea made from its leaves and flowers is used for lung complaints and asthma. As for flowers, you'll find purple gentians, black eyed-Susans, goldenrod, and wild carrot, better known as Queen Anne's Lace. Poison ivy is in abundance here as well, though it doesn't encroach upon the path. Pokeweed, edible as a young shoot but poisonous fully matured, is found here also. You'll find the staghorn sumac with its red berry clusters that, when soaked in cold water, make a lemonade-like drink. At the edge of the dense woods that separates the towpath from the river are flowering dogwoods and even a few catalpa trees with their large heart-shaped leaves and long, beanlike pods.

Where the canal curves to the east slightly, notice the outcroppings of red Brunswick shale, also known as brownstone, on the opposite bank. This rock is the primary bedrock throughout all of central New Jersey, except for the igneous intrusions that make up the Watchungs, Cushetunk Mountain, and Rocky Hill. A little farther ahead, Jacob's Creek passes under the canal and empties into the Delaware. There's a nice view of this wild and rocky confluence from the towpath, which stands fifty feet above it. Blue Herons may be seen wading in the shallows, where they are safe from intruders. Don't be surprised if you see deer hoofprints on the towpath; they've got a dense woods to hide in during the day.

After passing a flood control structure, which allows the canal to drain into the river if necessary, you'll see a bridge across the canal ahead of you. Bear right here and head downhill on the paved road. Take one of the pathways to your left down to the river, and you'll come out near Scudder's Falls, a class II set of rapids on the Delaware. At the time of this writing, the best path to the falls was directly opposite an abandoned house (which could conceivably be removed, along with a few others, by the state in the future).

Scudder's Falls was named for the Scudder family whose eighteenth-century farmstead and mill were once located in the area. One well-known member of the family was Amos Scudder, one of Washington's scouts at the Battle of Trenton. John Hart, one of the signers of the Declaration of Independence from New Jersey, was married to a Scudder. Unfortunately, nothing is left of the orginal house today, and the several cottages in the vicinity are being torn down or renovated by the state, which owns the land.

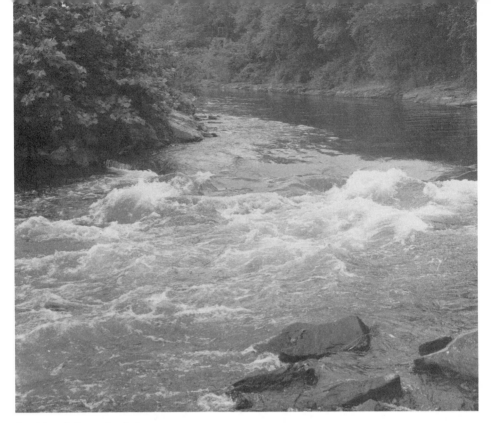

Scudders Falls on the Delaware.

Notice the huge sections of concrete on the island just across from the falls. A structure located here once utilized the immense power of the water, which drops several feet in a short distance. The area, though heavily used by fishermen and party goers, is still pleasant and very interesting, making it a good spot for lunch. You can sit on some of the big rocks near the river's edge, listen to the roar of the rapids and gaze out towards Pennsylvania, far off on the other side.

After watching the rapids, return to the towpath and begin your 2.4-mile walk back to Washington Crossing State Park. The benches placed about every quarter mile can provide a welcome rest should you need one. Before taking the pedestrian walkway over NJ 29, you may wish to take a look at the Nelson House, just below it towards the river. There is a portion of the original tavern here at the ferry dock. The building contains a large collection of period pieces, a flag collection, and, adjacent to the building, a reconstruction of one of the original ferryboats that took Washington and his men across the frozen river on that cold December night.

From the Nelson House, take the pedestrian bridge across the highway and bear left through the walled overlook. Continue retracing your steps toward the Ferry House and flag museum to find Continental Lane that, in .3 mile, will bring you to the visitor's center and parking area.

BCS

33

Delaware and Raritan Canal Towpath — Kingston to Griggstown

Total distance: 5 miles (or 10 miles using one car)
Hiking time: 2.5 hours (or 5 hours)
Vertical rise: Minimal
Rating: Easy to moderate
Maps: USGS Monmouth Junction/Rocky Hill/Heightstown; DEP:
   Delaware and Raritan Canal State Park

From its opening in 1834 to its closing 100 years later, the Delaware and Raritan Canal served as a major transportation link between Philadelphia and New York. From the northernmost point of navigation on the Delaware River at Bordentown to the head of navigation on the Raritan River at New Brunswick, the canal totaled forty-four miles. A water supply for the canal was created by digging a twenty-two-mile long feeder canal to divert water from the Delaware River at Raven Rock to the main canal at Trenton. Both main and feeder canals had towpaths, walkways for the mules that pulled the barges along. Today, sixty-six miles of canal and towpath are used by hikers, joggers, canoers and nature lovers. The linear Delaware and Raritan Canal State Park (RD 1, Box 8, Belle Mead, NJ 08502) is a green corridor through the center of the nation's most densely populated state, and even though it is never far from suburbia, it offers the hiker many miles of uninterrupted walking.

The Delaware and Raritan Canal State Park has many access points. For this hike, a large parking area located on the south side of NJ 27 in Kingston (where it passes over the canal and river) near a canoe rental area is used. If you wish to hike the full 10 miles, park your car here and begin hiking. A car shuttle is necessary for a one-way hike of 5 miles. To leave a second car at the northern end of the hike, take Laurel Avenue in the center of Kingston north for 1.6 miles to a T intersection and then bear left for .5 mile. Make a right onto Canal Road (do not cross the bridge) and drive 3.4 miles to Griggstown Causeway Road. Make a left here and park at the large parking area about .2 mile ahead on the left. Return via the same route to the Kingston parking area in the other car.

To begin the hike, take the paved path on the west side of the parking area through the tunnel which passes underneath the highway, allowing safe access to the towpath. As you emerge from the tunnel, the Millstone River will be to the left and the canal to the right. This area is the Millstone River flood plain, the densely vegetated, though muddy, strip of land lying between the river and the canal. The path, which swings to the right and towards the canal towpath, is marked with occasional metal markers containing the head of a "patriot."

Once on the towpath, walk north on what is a well-used multipurpose recreational trail. The path is wide enough for a vehicle (though they are not allowed) and is used mostly by hikers, runners, bikers, horseback riders, and fishermen. Throughout the hike, the canal will be on the right and the river below you on the left. A word of caution: posion ivy abounds along the towpath. Frequently it is found as a vine climbing trees. Although the walkway is wide enough to avoid any contact with the plant, be sure you know how to identify it if you care to approach either the canal or the river more closely.

For much of its length, the canal is paralleled by roads, though most of these are secondary country roads. In the section covered on this hike a road follows the river for a while but then veers away, and with it the sounds of cars. A feeling of isolation is experienced through this stretch. All kinds of wildflowers grow along the towpath here including yarrow, wild carrot, pokeweed, and lobelia. In the water, in places, are clusters of arrowroot, a favorite food of the American Indians. The trees that line the towpath are mostly oak and maple with some horse chestnut, ash and sumac. The large blue heron is also a frequent sight along the canal.

After a mile and a half of walking, the large Kingston Trap Rock Quarry, which borders the east bank of the canal, will come into view. This basalt quarry is one of the largest in the area and supplies crushed basalt, called traprock, to road builders. The rock is quarried from what was once a large igneous intrusion, similar to and contemporary with the Watchungs and the Palisades. If you are hiking

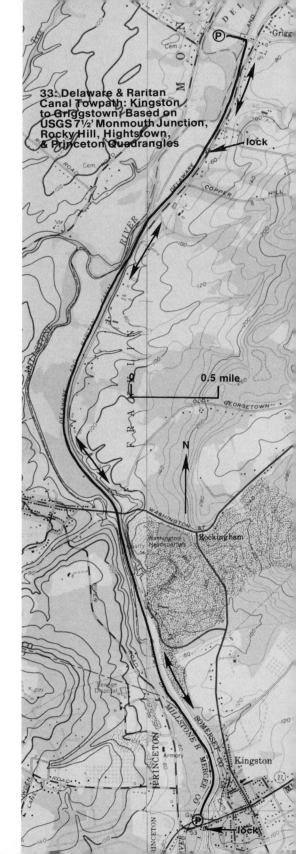

33. Delaware & Raritan Canal Towpath: Kingston to Griggstown. Based on USGS 7½' Monmouth Junction, Rocky Hill, Hightstown, & Princeton Quadrangles

0.5 mile

Milepost 24 along the Delaware and Raritan Canal.

during the week, the solitude may be spoiled by the activities of this large operation.

Look for a square concrete pillar with a tapered top, not unlike a fat, three foot high obelisk. This is a canal milepost, actually a replacement for the original stone markers. Notice that the number 23 is facing south and that on the other side, facing north, is the number 21. These figures indicate the number of miles from New Brunswick and Trenton, respectively. Adding the two gives the total mileage between these points. The markers, at least the ones that have survived, are found at every mile along the towpath.

After about forty minutes and just under 2 miles of walking, you reach paved Rocky Hill Road. Cross the road and continue past the small dock back onto the towpath. From here to Griggstown, Canal Road, a small country road, parallels the canal. A number of old homes are located in this area, some of them well over two hundred years old. In fact, George Washington himself gave his farewell address to the Continental Army in 1783 from a house originally located not far from the canal. Washington was said to have enjoyed his three-month stay in this house on his way from Newburgh to Mt. Vernon. It was there that he came to know of his great popularity, and history reports that he did much official entertaining. For a few months, this area was the social capital of the new nation. The house where Washington stayed, now called Rockingham, was relocated twice as the quarrying operation expanded. It is now about three-fourths of a mile from its original location.

Ahead on the towpath, pass mile marker 22/22, the half-way point between New Brunswick and Trenton. Beyond this marker come to a small wooden bridge over the canal, a good spot for a rest or snack. Farther ahead, on the left at milepost 23, is one end of the Silver Maple Trail, a bridle trail that explores the Millstone River flood plain. Just beyond the trailhead, notice that the towpath is lower than usual. This area is a spillway which allows a swollen canal to shed water into the flood plain of the river. At the end of this section are stones placed to prevent erosion of the towpath. Just ahead is the Griggstown lock.

Canal locks on the Delaware and Raritan, which measure 220 by 25 feet, allowed boats to change water levels. Though seven locks were necessary in the six-mile stretch of canal from Bordentown to Trenton, only seven more were needed for the remaining thirty-eight miles, a low route which follows the river valleys of the Millstone and Raritan. The house behind the lock is one of the old locktender houses found near every lock. Alongside the lock are some round concrete posts, which were used to secure boats making the passage. One wonders what the activities of boats entering and exiting the lock were like a hundred years ago.

Returning to the towpath, find the other end of the Silver Maple Trail nearby. Some may wish to walk a short distance on this trail to the banks of the Millstone River. A large, shagbark hickory tree grows on this well watered spot.

Milepost 20/24 is found at a point where the canal and the river are very close to each other, though the river runs well below the level of the canal. Just ahead is the paved Griggstown Causeway and several historic buildings. The long structure, built about 1800, is the Griggstown Barracks, used to shelter the men who built and worked the canal. The bridgetender's house and his station, from which he could telegraph and receive news of approaching boats, are here also, both built around 1831. If a car has been left here, turn left and walk along the road to the parking area. If one hasn't, turn around and walk the 5 miles back to Kingston.

BCS

34

Delaware and Raritan Canal – Weston to East Millstone

Total distance: 4.2 miles
Hiking time: 2 hours
Vertical rise: Minimal
Rating: Easy
Map: USGS Bound Brook

To reach this section of the Delaware and Raritan Canal towpath from I-287, take exit 7, Weston Canal Road. When you reach the end of the exit ramp, turn left on Weston Canal Road, following signs to Manville. In 1.7 miles, pass Ten Mile Lock and the locktender's house on the right and, after that, the religious community of Zarepath. In 3 miles, the road will swing around and cross the canal. Park on the left at the first parking area just after the canal crossing. Additional parking can be found a few hundred feet ahead on the right.

Walk back to the canal and turn right on the towpath heading south. On the other side of the canal, on the left, is the old bridgetender's house built circa 1831. Originally, a swing bridge spanned the canal here. If hiking in summer or early fall, notice the duckweed, the miniature lily pad plant that floats in clusters on the water. This plant tends to accumulate, sometimes covering the entire canal surface ten or fifteen miles before New Brunswick, the terminus of the waterway. The towpath, which receives an equal amount of sun and shade, is quite grassy here, though the actual walkway is worn to the dirt. The trees, mostly oak and maple, form an intermittent canopy over the towpath. Poison ivy is, unfortunately, abundant. On the other side of the canal is Weston Causeway Road, a country road with light traffic. On your right is the large Millstone River flood plain.

After a few minutes of walking, notice that the Millstone flood plain, undoubtedly very fertile, is being used as a cornfield. At about the same point where the cornfield ends, Weston Canal Road turns away from the canal, and the towpath enters one of its very few sections not paralleled by a road. For the next 1.5 miles the walking through this quiet and somewhat wild area, rare in densely populated central New Jersey, becomes very pleasant.

As the sounds of civilization fade out, the towpath takes on a wilder look. The Millstone River itself swings close to the canal, but twenty feet below it. The sounds of insects, fish jumping, and the hurried scrambling of turtles startled by your intrusion fill the void left by the

The Delaware and Raritan Canal -- Weston to Millstone.

sounds of traffic. If you are lucky, a great blue heron may wing its way down the canal. The only evidence of civilization is the boat dock for a day camp on the opposite bank of the canal.

A century ago the canal was the scene of intense commerical activity. Hard coal was the most important item shipped on the canal, accounting for eighty percent of its total tonnage. The barges used on the canal were of the "hinge-boat" variety and measured about ninety feet by ten feet and drew about five feet of water. Long strings of these barges loaded with coal were pulled by steam tugs, while other barges and boats were towed by mules. Towing charges varied according to the service used. Steam tugs charged a flat rate of $22.22, plus an extra $11.11 per barge for the trip to New York City. Mules and horses were available from barns at Bordentown, Griggstown, and New Brunswick.

The open season on the canal was about 250 days a year, from early April to mid December. Canal hours were from 6 A.M. to 6 P.M. daily, and the speed limit for barges was set at 4 miles per hour. When steam tugs began to be used on the canal, the wash began to undermine the banks in places. A stone lining called "rip rap" was installed and can still be seen today in many places.

Just before a spillway, come to milepost 31/13. Ahead, on the opposite bank, is a section of Colonial Park that is cleared and also has a small dock. Next, pass over a culvert through which Spooky Brook runs, going under the canal on its way to the Millstone.

In another half mile, and all too soon, the quiet and privacy of this section of towpath comes to an end. Ahead is a bridge and a parking area off Amwell Road in East Millstone. If interested, cross over the canal on Amwell Road and take a short walk into East Millstone,

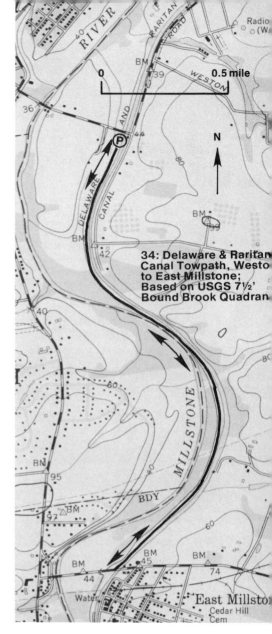

34: Delaware & Raritan Canal Towpath, Weston to East Millstone; Based on USGS 7½' Bound Brook Quadran.

a small town that has changed very little over the years. The first road on the right leads to a small general store, the second, to a deli that has a few outside tables. After lunch, or without it, return to your car via the way you came.

BCS

Coastal Plain

35

Cheesequake State Park

Total distance: 3.5 miles
Hiking time: 2.5 hours
Vertical rise: Approximately 200 feet
Rating: Easy to moderate
Maps: USGS South Amboy; DEP: Cheesequake State Park

Located in the transition zone between New Jersey's distinctive northern and southern plant communities, Cheese-quake State Park (Matawan, NJ 07747; 201-566-2161) may be of particular appeal to those interested in botany. There are a variety of habitats throughout the park, including salt- and fresh-water marshes, northeastern hardwood forests, Pine Barrens, and a cedar swamp. The park is located near Raritan Bay and was occupied as early as six thousand years ago by Indians who hunted and fished there. The name "Cheesequake" was taken from a word in the language of the Lenni-Lenape Indians, who lived in New Jersey when the colonists first arrived.

There are three marked trails in the park, mostly footpaths, that are marked yellow, red, and green. The markings are large colored circles painted on square boards that have been attached to trees. There are also numerous, unmarked side trails, also mostly footpaths, that could be misleading. Our hike will be on the long-est of the three trails, the green trail, which begins after you walk a section of the red and yellow trails. The footpaths, and in some cases sand roads, that the trail follows are soft and bouncy in

places, covered by pine needles. There are many wet sections that have been covered by boardwalks or bridges, and in a few places are found rough stairs made of railroad ties. Rugged footwear is not required. Because of the proximity to swamps and marshes, it may be best to visit the park during the fall when insect populations, and also human populations, are at their lowest.

To reach the park from the Garden State Parkway, take exit 120 and turn right (east) at the end of the ramp. Turn right at the gas station onto Cliffwood Avenue and turn right again at the T intersection onto Gordon Avenue, which will take you in 1 mile to the park entrance. Pass the park office and park at the parking area on the left, about .2 mile ahead. A directory and map of the trails, and also a fountain, are found here at the trailhead. There may be a parking fee during high-use periods.

Begin your hike at the trailhead, just to the left of the directory. At the first fork, bear to the left where the sign indicates that the green and red trails part with the yellow trail. Immediately cross a small brook on the first of many wooden bridges. After crossing the brook, climb a

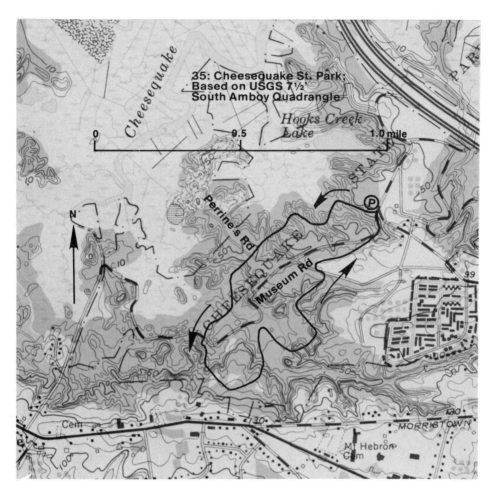

35: Cheesequake St. Park: Based on USGS 7½' South Amboy Quadrangle

small rise through some sweet pepper-bush, perhaps the most common plant seen along the trail. Pepperbush is re-lated to mountain laurel and blueberry, also common in the park. During the spring, wild honeysuckle is in bloom here and in other sections of the trail. After leveling off, the trail passes a protected wet area on the right filled with tall ferns. Ahead is a view through the trees to the salt marsh below. The trail, still primarily marked with red, bears to the left here and heads downhill, crossing a muddy area. After crossing a few bridges, arrive

at the base of an incline on which large wooden steps, made from railroad ties, have been attached. Whether you use them or not, they are certainly unusual. At the top of the rise a resting bench is also found.

From the bench, the trail bears to the left passing through a large stand of low-bush and highbush blueberries growing amongst some large pines, more typical of the Pine Barrens of southern New Jer-sey, mixed with the usual hardwoods of northern New Jersey. In this dry section are some large clusters of mountain laurel that bloom in June. After crossing a large bridge over a small brook, the trail comes out to a sand road (Perrine's Road) near a bench. It is here that the green trail becomes independent of the red trail. Turn right here, not on the sand road but on the green trail to the right of the bench.

Along this level section are many small sassafrass trees, some chokecherry, beech, maple, chestnut oak, and white oak. Through the trees on the right, the now closed Sayreville landfill can be seen about two miles away. Bear left at the junction and head downhill. At the bottom of the drop, the trail passes close to the tall sedges, rushes, and grasses of the salt-water marsh, which forms the western boundary of the park. After a short climb, come to a long boardwalk running over a fresh-water swamp, heavily overgrown with arrowwood, elderberry, and buttonbush. In the middle of the walkway are two benches surrounding a red maple. This quiet area, rich in plant and animal life, is a change from the woods and brush environments traversed so far.

At the end of the boardwalk, bear right at the junction and out to another boardwalk, this one in a cedar swamp. Here is an even more cool and dark environment than the fresh-water swamp passed through a few minutes ago. The eastern white cedars, which grow out of black clay, dominate, shutting out light for other plants. The extreme moisture and the decomposing leaves make the soil very acidic, preserving any cedar logs that become buried. In some similar areas of New Jersey, old cedar logs in good condition have been mined from the dense acidic soil. Great horned owls are known to frequent this swamp.

After leaving the swamp, keep to the right and follow the trail carefully through a muddy area. Come out to another sand road (Museum Road), which the trail crosses, and enter a woods dominated by huge white pines. Because of their height and straightness, these trees were used by shipbuilders during colonial times, and particularly during the Revolution, for masts. Overharvesting of the original white pines eventually forced the lumbering industry out of the state. These trees are estimated to be between 100 and 150 years old and are used as nesting sites for owls and hawks. The trail through this section is narrow and crowded in by pepperbush, mountain laurel, and rhododendron.

After climbing an interesting ladder/stairway on the trail, the highest elevation on the hike is reached. The woods are dry here and composed of mostly oak, which provides food for the gypsy moth that has left evidence, in the form of standing dead trees, of its appetite. On the floor of the forest are large quantities of false Solomon's seal. At the junction, the trail bears to the left, leading to a stand of pitch pines typical of the Pine Barrens of south Jersey. Pitch pine grows in dry, sandy soil (as well as on rocky outcrops as it does in north Jersey) and can survive with few nutrients.

From this high area, the trail gradually descends, passing a concrete and brick structure and bearing right at a junction near a large wet area, a flood plain. The trail is sandy here as it passes through a forest of hardwoods. On the forest floor are numerous wildflowers such as the wild lily of the valley and the pink lady's slipper, both of which bloom in the spring. One can find violets, starflowers, and jack-in-the-pulpit here as well. Ahead, where the trail veers to the left, is a section that is frequently flooded and covered with mud. Only plants that can survive frequent inundations survive here. Farther along, the trail swings around a small, stagnant pond that attracts wildlife.

Cheesequake State Park.

More boardwalk keeps the hiker dry and clean in this section of black mud, clear brooks, and wet swamps. At the time of this writing, the trail was being rerouted in places. Pay close attention to markings. After a rise, the trail comes to a sand road (Perrine's Road) near a bench.

Turn left on the road, following markers past a camping area used by the scouts. Just ahead, the trail swings back into the woods, as marked by a post, and once again merges with the red trail. There are many unmarked side trails in this section that head off to the left. Stay on the main trail, which follows the edge of the cleared area, until markers indicate a left turn leading downhill and onto Museum Road. Bear right here and follow the road, which in .2 mile leads to the trailhead and your car.

BCS

36

Hartshorne Woods

Total distance: 4 miles
Hiking time: 2.5 hours
Vertical rise: 300 feet
Rating: Easy to moderate
Maps: USGS Sandy Hook; Monmouth County Park System trail
  guide

Hartshorne Woods Park (Monmouth County Park System, Newman Springs Road, Lincroft, NJ 07738; 201-842-4000), named for its original owner, Richard Hartshorne, who purchased the tract from the Indians in the 1670s, contains several miles of marked and unmarked trails. The area, which rises 245 feet above the Navesink River Bay, which it overlooks, is surprisingly hilly for central New Jersey. The forest, which totally covers the 475 acres of the park, is primarily a dry, upland, deciduous forest composed of oak, hickory, beech, and maple; however, the many ups and downs of the trails lead one through a variety of very healthy plant communities.

From eastbound NJ 36 in Atlantic Highlands, follow signs to "Scenic Road," a right-hand turn off the highway. Take Navesink Avenue .5 mile to the parking area for the Hartshorne Woods, located on the left-hand side of the road. There is parking for about twenty cars here. A directory, which includes a large topographical map showing contours at ten-foot intervals, and a box of free hiking maps are located in the woods about twenty yards from the parking area.

As you will notice from the directory or from the map, there are three, color-coded, marked trails in the park. The hike described here utilizes the red trail for nearly its entire length and also most of the green trail. The trails are marked at intervals with colored metal tags nailed high on the trees. Many trail junctions are marked with diagonally cut and colored posts, and many turns are indicated by tags with arrows pointing in the direction of the turn. You will need to pay close attention to the markings since there are numerous intersections and turns in this small, but very walkable, park.

Begin the hike by turning left on the red trail just past the directory, following a wide, sandy, and sparsely marked park service road. The road, the first part of which has been recently enlarged, climbs a few hills before gradually becoming narrower and more of a pathway. In sunny areas along the road is poison ivy and a few common wildflowers, including the Asian dayflower and goldenrod. White snakeroot, which when eaten by cows poisons the milk, and the white wood aster, a member of the sunflower family whose leaves are edible as greens

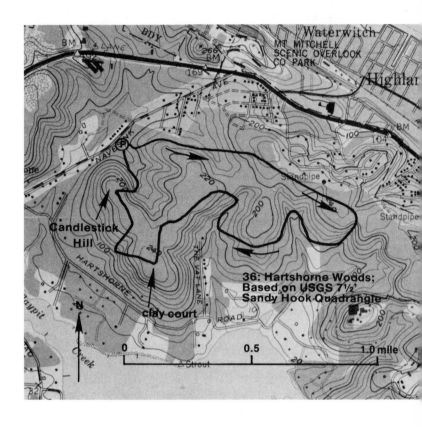

36: Hartshorne Woods;
Based on USGS 7½'
Sandy Hook Quadrangle

earlier in the year, are also found in abundance.

After about twenty minutes of walking, turn right, still following red markings, off the main service road and onto a descending footpath. This turn occurs as you are walking downhill where a number of utility poles have been placed on the ground to stabilize the trail. Here the trail is a sandy path through a predominately pine forest. After this section, the trail turns right at a junction and follows a path through a damp woods filled with an understory of jewelweed. Jewelweed is a soft-stemmed plant that grows to a height of around four feet. Its orange, sack-shaped flower hangs from the stem and explodes on touch at the end of the season in October. For this reason, the plant is also known as touch-me-not. Look for a turn to the left where the trail is littered with rocks and begins to climb uphill.

From this turn, the red markers lead you on a footpath through a magnificent forest. Monster hickory and tulip trees grow here, some of which are three feet in diameter. Smaller sassafras trees are found scattered about, and in the understory are jack-in-the-pulpits. After crossing a low area, the path parallels an old split-rail fence, passes a boundary marker, and meets a service road on which it bears right. The red markers now lead past a log cabin and back into the woods. On the right, towering over the mountain laurel and ferns that form the sparse understory here, is a large holly

Sweet pepperbush.

tree. At a Y-junction, the red trail bears left, climbs a small hill, and then turns left again on a wider path.

Ahead, arrive at an intersection with the green trail. From here, about seventy-five minutes or more into the hike, leave the red trail for good and finish the hike following green markers. By now you will have noticed that the trail has climbed into a much dryer forest. This next section of the hike is on high ground in oak forest spotted with mountain laurel.

Bear left on the green trail, a meandering footpath that does not seem to receive as much use as the red trail. At a junction not so well marked, the green trail turns right, passes another boundary marker, and, after a short distance, turns left. Here the trail climbs gradually and moves deeper into the flat summit of an elevated peninsula of land. You'll notice chunks of conglomerate rock (sand fused with pebbles) along the trail here and for the next half mile. This resistant rock has acted as a protective cap over softer sediments, creating highlands among sea level plains. Ahead, at the end of this neck of land, is a mountain laurel thicket and some limited views out over the water of the Navesink River. This area, the high point of the hike at 248 feet, is called the Clay Court Overlook.

From the point of land, follow the green trail, which is not marked very well, down the hill over rocks, sand, and gravel. Come to another path, turn left on it for about 50 feet, then make a right and continue the descent. After another right turn, the green trail begins a steady and steep climb of over 100 feet. For this part of the state, this elevation gain comes as a real surprise. At the top of the rise there will be a left turn onto a wider path and then a junction with the yellow trail. Stay on the green (the yellow quickly turns left) on a path that climbs to a sparse, high area called Candlestick Hill. Like the Clay Court Overlook, the views are best in the winter. A few white birches and a scraggly pine are found at this high (233 feet) elevation.

From the northeastern end of the overlook area, the trail, not well marked, descends steeply down the hill. It bears left on a moss-lined, gravel road and continues downhill. At the bottom of the hill, come to a major trail junction and, on the right about 100 yards ahead, the parking area.

BCS

37

Gateway National Recreation Area—Sandy Hook Unit

Total distance: 4 miles with car shuttle; 8 miles without
Hiking time: 3 hours
Vertical rise: Minimal
Rating: Easy
Maps: USGS Sandy Hook; NPS map

The Sandy Hook Unit (Highlands, New Jersey 07732; 201-872-0115), adopted in the 1970s, is the only New Jersey Unit in the Gateway National Recreation Area of the National Park Service. Sandy Hook is heavily used so this hike is not recommended during the summer months when the parking lots are closed as soon as they are full, possibly as early as 10:00 A.M. on a hot summer day.

Sandy Hook is a narrow, sandy spit seven miles long, extending into the Atlantic Ocean and lower New York Bay. It is a barrier beach with the ocean on one side and a bay on the other. The beaches migrate because of littoral drift, that is, the sand is slowly moved in the same direction as the near shore current. Every time a wave hits the beach, some sand is picked up and redeposited as the wave ebbs. At Sandy Hook, the littoral drift is from south to north, therefore the beaches at the Hook's northern tip are increasing in size and the ones to the south are decreasing. When the Sandy Hook lighthouse was built in 1764, it stood near the northern tip of the spit, but now, as you will see during your walk, it is a mile and a half south of the

tip. There is some concern that Sandy Hook will again become an island, as it has been several times in the past. In addition to the Hook's island history, this sandy spit has twice before been attached to the mainland at Atlantic Highlands.

Sandy Hook is a major bird migration route, and three hundred species of birds have been seen in the area, attracted by the wide variety of environments, ranging from fresh to salt water and from beach to grassland and forest. The osprey and the great blue heron nest here during the warmer months, and the area has a wintering population of robins. Just north of Spermaceti Cove on the bay side is the oldest known stand of hollies. Some of the holly trunks measure five inches, indicating three hundred years of growth, but the area is closed to the public except for occasional conducted tours.

There is a great deal of history associated with Sandy Hook. In 1524, Giovanni Verrazano supposedly landed on the spit, and Henry Hudson also stopped here. Some of Captain Kidd's treasure is reputedly buried beneath a great pine tree on the Hook, though this booty still remains undiscovered. Other events will be described as the hike narration continues.

To get to Sandy Hook, at exit 117 from the Garden State Parkway take NJ 36 east, following the signs to the villages of Atlantic Highlands, Highlands, and thence to Sandy Hook. For avid beach walkers, only one car is required for this hike, which should be left at the visitors center; then, after exploring Fort Hancock, footsteps can be retraced either along the beach or along the main road back to the center. Alternatively, a car can be left at one of the northern parking lots for use at the end of the described hike.

During the summer months there is a parking fee, but again, the low-use months, from late fall to early spring, are the preferred months for your visit. The visitors center is approximately 2 miles into the spit. A stop should be made to look around the museum with its fish tank and slide program, shown on request. You should also ask for the trail guide to the Old Dune Trail.

The visitors center, in a building dating from 1894, is housed at Spermaceti Cove, an early site of the first eight lifesaving stations built on the Jersey coastline. Many lives were being lost at sea from shipwrecks, therefore these lifesaving stations were established. One of the worst sea disasters occurred in January, 1837. One hundred and seventeen people died and whole families were found frozen in the rigging when, within sight of Sandy Hook, the American ship *Mexico,* full of English and Irish immigrants, was unable to sustain its anchorage in a tremendous gale and snowstorm and was swept aground off Long Island. The method of rescue used by these stations was the Lyle gun, which fired a line to a ship in distress; then, with the line estab-lished, crew and passengers were pulled ashore. Regular practice sessions were held by the crew of the Lyle gun.

Walk away from the visitors center, towards the bay side of Sandy Hook, and find the beginning of the Old Dune Trail on the right. This trail is only one mile in length and ends within sight of the visitors center. Constantly bear in mind that the area is always under bombardment by salt and wind, that plants have adapted to this harsh environment, but that the area can be easily destroyed by careless walking across the dunes. Please remain on the marked trail.

Poison ivy is prevalent in the area, but there are signs to remind you of this fact. Study the guide and stop at the numbered signs to read and learn about the area. Just after the bulldozed section and just before the trail crosses a paved road, there is a large bank of honeysuckle on the left and, scattered throughout the area, large clumps of rhodora. Unfortunately, some of the posted sign numbers are missing (in particular number seven and number eight). Just after the impressive holly forest there is a wooden seat on the left and a tree in the middle of the trail. Take the loop that begins at this point on the left until this side trail rejoins the main trail. The signpost is still standing just before the bench, but the numbered sign is not there.

Shortly, the trail becomes wider, and because of the increased breeze, you will realize that you are walking towards the ocean. The trail turns left and snakes through the dunes to an area where trees left as upright skeletons testify to the damage salty winds cause. At the next T-junction, turn left through a chain-linked fence into an open area. (Turning right will lead to a parking lot.) In the open area, beach heather and prickly pear eke out a precarious existence. To discourage competition for scarce re-

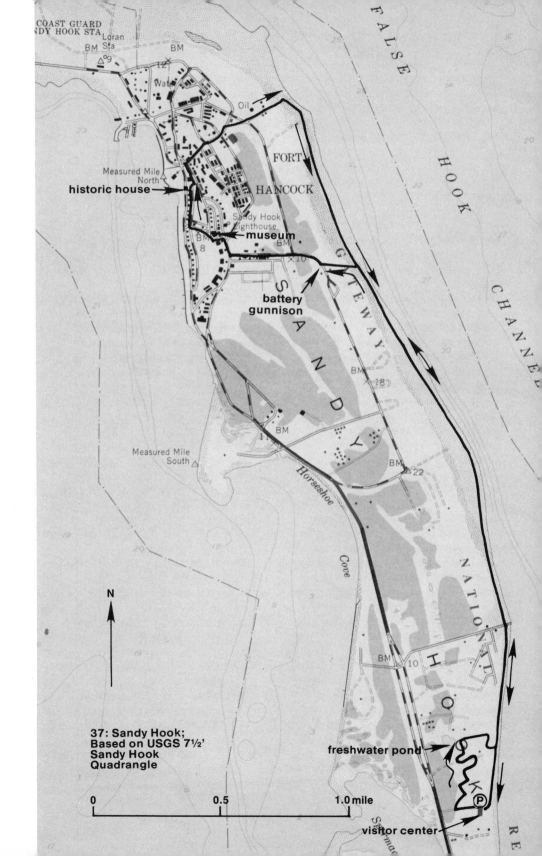

COAST GUARD
SANDY HOOK STA.
Loran
BM Sta
BM

Water

Oil

Measured Mile
North

historic house →

FORT

HANCOCK

Sandy Hook
Lighthouse

→ **museum**

**battery
gunnison**

BM

S
A
N
D
Y

G
A
T
E
W
A
Y

FALSE

HOOK

CHANNEL

Measured Mile
South

Horseshoe

Cove

N

NATIONAL

H
O

freshwater pond →

visitor center ─

37: Sandy Hook;
Based on USGS 7½'
Sandy Hook
Quadrangle

0   0.5   1.0 mile

sources from other plant life, the roots of these two plants secrete a poison that inhibits the growth of neighboring plants. That this strategy is successful is apparent by the concentrated areas of beach heather. Another botanical oddity to be found on Sandy Hook is an import called dusty miller, whose furry leaves catch dew on their velvety surface.

The trail widens and reaches a wooden viewing stand on the left. Go to the top of the small flight of steps for an unusual sight of a fresh-water pond surrounded by a salty area. It is possible to get closer to the pond, supported on the left by a man-made stone wall, by walking for a few yards in a marshy area through tall phragmites down to the water's edge. Look closely along the shore, for a blue heron may be seen here.

Shortly after leaving the tranquil, fresh-water pond with its teeming wildlife, the remains of a Nike missile area is reached. This site was placed on Sandy Hook to guard New York against air attack, for the missiles could intercept and destroy aircraft long before they could pose much of a threat. As concepts of defence changed, the missiles were removed in 1974, and at the end of that year, the military installation at Sandy Hook, called Fort Hancock, was officially discontinued. The site is protected by a chain-linked fence, and since garbage is the only thing to be seen behind the fence, walking down the path to the actual area is not suggested. The trail now becomes narrower, curves around another open area—hopefully you will resist the temptation to cut across—and turns left towards the sea, going up a small rise to the beach.

Dunes normally form two ridges, both roughly parallel to the ocean: the first, a primary dune nearest to the ocean, and, behind, a secondary dune. A different feeling is obtained when walking close to the dunes than from walking close to the water. The sand is much firmer where it is damp, offering easier walking, and the breeze is stronger.

At the end of the Old Dune Trail, turn left and enjoy walking northwards along the shore. There is a great deal of activity to watch, adding zest to your walk— from kites flying to the shore fishermen with their catch of bluefish. Above all, there is the fresh sea breeze, the constant panorama of ocean-going vessels on the horizon, and the interesting items washed up on the sand, from jellyfish, to shells, to flotsam.

The beach is narrow at first, becoming wider, and within approximately thirty minutes you get the first glimpse of Sandy Hook lighthouse. As you progress north, the backdrop of New York City becomes clearer, and the Verrazano Narrows Bridge comes into sight. The walk can be extended by proceeding as far north as you wish before turning inland to Fort Hancock.

Just after a mast is seen in the sand dunes and garbage cans become noticeable, a small snack bar with umbrella rental is seen at the top of the beach. Walk away from the water, passing a paling fence protecting the dunes, and onto a wide road leading to a boardwalk with comfort stations on the right.

Take a few minutes to visit Battery Gunnison, erected in 1904, on the left. The six-inch guns at Battery Gunnison were intended to track and destroy small warships that were too fast for Fort Hancock's huge coastal artillery. There are two separate gun emplacements, accessible by two small flights of cement stairs, and an improved view of the ocean is obtained from this small elevation.

Leave Battery Gunnison and turn north on Gunnison Road past the sign that says North Beach. Sandy Hook lighthouse is visible to the right. Cross Atlan-

Windswept sand dunes at Sandy Hook.

tic Road and walk straight ahead past various parking areas. At the T-junction with NJ 36, the bay can be seen through the houses of Fort Hancock. A left turn leads to the exit from Sandy Hook, and a right will lead to the lighthouse. Pass the Marine Academy of Science and Technology, deserted houses, all numbered, and, at number 76, bear right for the best view yet of the lighthouse.

Sandy Hook lighthouse is the oldest operating lighthouse in the United States. Money to purchase the four acres of property and to build the lighthouse and the lightkeeper's house was raised by two lotteries authorized by the New York Assembly. This action was set in motion by New York merchants anxious to protect their shipping on the treacherous coast. Maintenance of the lighthouse was paid for by levying a twenty-two-cent-per-ton fee on all ships using the New York Bay.

The white octagonal tower was often the first beacon to be seen by travelers to New York, for until 1907, the Sandy Hook channel was the only passageway for large ships entering New York Harbor. Built in 1764, it was one of twelve lighthouses built by the first thirteen American colonies. It was occupied for a short time by British troops during the American Revolution and was fought over by British and rebel soldiers. The tower, visible nineteen miles at sea, is 103 feet tall and still in use, though now unmanned and automatic.

Exploring Fort Hancock will take time. There are deserted batteries, a museum, and an historic house that all hold great interest for history lovers. Fort Hancock was established during the 1890s; but its buildings now stand empty and deteriorating, and there are apparently no plans for its rehabilitation. At the end of your exploration, it is necessary either to exit from Fort Hancock at North Beach and retrace the route south along the beach or to return by car in the vehicle already placed at Fort Hancock.

SJG

38

Allaire State Park

Total distance: 4 miles
Hiking time: 2.5 hours
Vertical rise: 120 feet
Rating: Easy to moderate
Maps: USGS Farmingdale, Asbury Park; DEP Allaire State
   Park

Allaire State Park (PO Box 220, Farmingdale, NJ 07727; 201-938-2371) began in 1941 as a gift to the people of the state of New Jersey from Arthur Brisbane, a prominent newspaper man. The original 1,000+ acres has now expanded to over 3,000 and includes a steam, narrow-gauge railroad, a golf course, a car camping area, and an entire historical village dating from the boom days of the bog iron industry—in the last two centuries. The park, located in one of the northernmost sections of the Pine Barrens, straddles the Manasquan River, which is popular with canoeists. The recent completion of I-195, which bisects the park, "pollutes" the park with sound denying it the isolation it once had. On the other hand, I-195 also makes the park more accessible to the public.

The park has within its boundaries a large number of sand and gravel roads and an abandoned railroad bed that are used for hiking and horseback riding. Some of these trails are marked with colored wooden plaques. Since the park is essentially quartered by the river and the freeway, a complete tour of the park is not possible, and we have chosen a route that takes the hiker through some wooded areas as well as the park's main attraction, the historic Allaire Village.

To reach the park, take exit 31B off I-195 and head east on County Road 524. The route is well marked with signs, and you should have no problem finding the park. The hike described here begins at an unmarked parking area on state land, .6 mile past (east of) the main entrance. This parking area is on the right and has two access points off the main road. By parking here the fee charged to cars entering the park by way of the main entrance need not be paid. You will also be avoiding the crowds that visit the park only to tour the historical village.

To begin the hike, cross the road and head west back toward the main entrance. You'll be walking past a small horse ranch with a split-rail fence. At the end of the rail fence, look for a gate leading into a field. Just to the right of the gate find a post that marks the entrance to a lane that runs between the ranch and the field. This pathway may be overgrown for the first hundred yards or so but soon widens and becomes

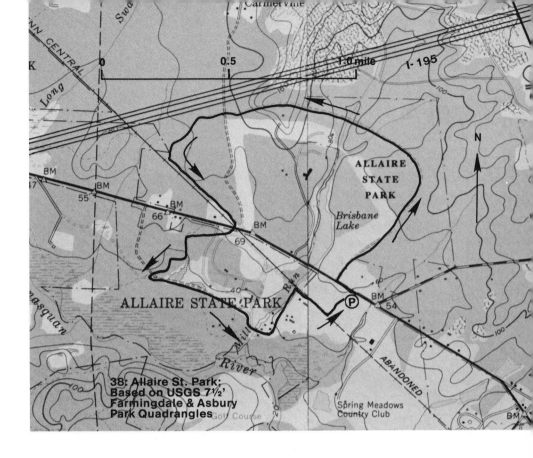

ALLAIRE STATE PARK

Brisbane Lake

ALLAIRE STATE PARK

38: Allaire St. Park; Based on USGS 7½' Farmingdale & Asbury Park Quadrangles

Golf Course

Spring Meadows Country Club

more comfortable for walking. The lane, which is very straight since it is the border of a farmed field, is shadowed by tall sumac trees and vines. There are also a few patches of holly along the trail. As you leave the highway and the sound of traffic, the sounds of birds, plentiful in this area of field and woods, are heard.

After about ten minutes of walking, enter a typical south Jersey forest. The pathway widens into a sand and gravel road common to the Pine Barrens, and the walking becomes very pleasant. Ferns and blueberry bushes form the ground cover, and huge clusters of mountain laurel rise up from the forest floor. At first some oaks and maples appear, then farther along come sassafras and the inevitable pitch pines. Keep to the left where the road you are on comes

to a fork. With the possible exception of a few puddles after a rain, the walking is easy and comfortable here, and there are no ups or downs.

The trail or, more accurately, sand road used in this first part of the hike makes a large horseshoe and eventually returns to the county road you started on, though a little farther west. As it swings to the left and west, it parallels I-195, which is always busy with cars heading to and from the Jersey shore, for about half a mile. In this section is a short uphill climb to a gravel quarry and water tower, and then a long downhill where the trail comes within sight of the highway. Stay on the main road, now quite wide, which eventually swings away from the noisy highway and heads south toward the main park entrance and a

Allaire State Park **191**

Allaire State Park.

quieter environment. The sounds of birds once again become more prominent. A wood thrush or two may resent your intrusion into their territory. In this section the trail parallels the bed of the former Freehold–Jamesburg railroad, used in other sections of the park as a hiking and horse trail.

The trail will bring you to the main road at a gate similar to the one at the beginning of the hike. Cross the road here, bear somewhat to the right, and follow the narrow-gauge railroad tracks toward where they enter the woods. Look for a sign saying "horse trail" and follow it, not the tracks, into the woods. This trail is marked occasionally with orange markers. After only a few yards, cross the park entrance road and reenter the woods still on the orange trail. The trail next crosses a gravel maintenance road, another bridle path, and eventually comes to a T intersection with a gravel road. Bear left here, cross a creek, and make another left on a gravel road known in the park as the "Raceway."

Follow the Raceway straight ahead keeping the water to your left. After a short distance, notice some red and green trail markers. Keep to the right and find a wooden bridge on your left. This bridge leads to the park nature center, which has some interesting displays and an accurate wall map of all the sand roads and trails in the park.

From the bridge, continue along the Raceway past the pond and through a large picnic area. This area is the developed section of the park, and one should expect to see many people here, especially on summer weekends. After passing the large parking lot on the left, enter the historic Allaire Village.

Back in the eighteenth century, this village site was known as Monmouth Furnace and, later, as the Howell Works, named for the first iron maker here. He leased the property to James P. Allaire of New York in 1822, who was already very much established as a brass worker. At the Howell Works, Allaire put together a community of over four hundred people to turn bog iron into pots, kettles, cauldrons, stoves, pipe, and other common items. The self-contained community included a wide variety of craftspersons both to run the industry and serve the population.

Bog iron, found in the Pine Barrens, is smelted from iron oxides leached from the sand and deposited in accumulations of decaying swamp vegetation. Interestingly, bog iron is a renewable source of iron as long as the vegetation decay cycle is not interfered with. The operation at Allaire's village prospered until around 1850, when competition from products made of higher-grade iron ore lowered profits. After its abandonment, the Allaire community was used for a time by the Boy Scouts as a headquarters, and in 1941, it was deeded to the state. Today, the village of Allaire is remarkably well preserved and nearly intact from its heyday a century ago.

The visitor's center, a long brick building, is on your left and offers a number of interesting displays about the park and the village. A map and guide to the village can be obtained here. A food concession is located in this area also. From here, continue straight ahead to the end of the visitor's center, make a right, and follow the main road that heads downhill, to the left, and out to the main buildings of the village. This route is marked in places with yellow markers. Follow this main road as it swings to the left at the general store, and head north, eventually leaving the village area through a gate.

Follow the gravel road, which ultimately leads to County Road 524, away from the village. To avoid walking back to your car on this busy road, bear right on a pathway that crosses the lane. Weeds may obscure this pathway at first, but it will soon widen out for it is the Freehold–Jamesburg abandoned railroad bed. After only a few minutes of walking, you'll find a trail coming in on the left that will lead you through a field to the parking area and your car.

BCS

39

Rancocas State Park

Total distance: 4.5 miles
Hiking time: 2.5 hours
Vertical rise: Minimal
Rating: Easy to moderate
Maps: USGS Mt. Holly; DEP Rancocas State Park

Rancocas State Park (c/o Lebanon State Forest, New Lisbon, NJ 08064; 609-726-1191) preserves a confluence of rivers at the western extreme of the Pine Barrens. Although the park is undeveloped, it receives a good amount of use, and abuse, from area residents. The best time to hike in this interesting park, and avoid bikers and hunters, would probably be on weekdays or during the off-season.

To reach the trailhead from NJ 206, take NJ 38 west to Mount Holly. Go 3.8 miles and turn right onto the Mount Holly Bypass, indicated by signs to County Route 541, Burlington, the Burlington Bristol Bridge, and the NJ Turnpike. Travel .5 mile and turn left at the light on Marne Highway, also County Road 537. The first right turn off Marne Highway, only .1 mile ahead, is Deacon Road. Take Deacon Road 1.3 miles to its terminus at a sand road, blocked by two wooden posts, that enters the woods. Although the barrier is obviously ignored by some, it is best to park here.

Enter the Rancocas woods heading west on the sand road directly in front of you. The woods, which have been hit hard by gypsy moths, are nonetheless pleasant, and walking on the soft sand is easy on the feet. The forest is mostly of oak with a rather sparse understory of sassafras and laurel. The park allowed the public to remove the trees killed by gypsy moths a few years ago, which accounts for the openness not usually found in such a forest. At your first junction with another sand road, bear to the right on the more distinct and well-traveled route. After a slight descent, the trail swings to the left through soft sand and heads west again.

Rancocas State Park has had a history dominated by politics. In the late 1970s, budget cuts forced the park actually to close to the public for a few years. This was the only state park in New Jersey that had to do so. Management of the park was transferred to Lebanon State Forest some twenty-five miles to the east and not directly accessible. This situation makes it virtually impossible for anyone to police the area, leading to vandalism and the free use of the park for off-road vehicles, beer parties, dumping, and illegal hunting. In recent years, portions of the park were leased to private groups— one section to the Audubon Society and another to the Rankokus Renape Indian

Council. An annual American Indian Arts Festival, which attracts Indian artists from North and Central America, is held here every October. The section of the park that contains this hike is now offically open to the public but is not actively patrolled or maintained by the state.

Here and there along the walkway the forest opens up into small grassy areas where the dead trees have been cleared. In some places, blueberries, ripe in July, line the trail. Continue straight ahead, ignoring the occasional sand roads that branch off from the more heavily traveled route you are on. After about a mile, the trail forks again. Bear right here, and almost immediately you'll find yourself on the banks of the North Branch of Rancocas Creek. Here are the remnants of an old dock leaning precariously out into the water. Enjoy the view and the dense aquatic vegetation on the other side. When you leave the area, return to the main sand road, from which you cannot see the river, and continue heading west. In just a few more minutes, you should

arrive near the point where the North and South branches of Rancocas Creek merge.

The view from this point is quite spectacular in its own way. Though you are not directly at the point of confluence, which is impossible to reach because of a dense marsh, you still sense the expansiveness of the area. In front of you are great stands of arrowroot and other fresh-water marsh plants. Notice that while the banks of the North Branch are muddy and slick, the banks of the South Branch are of sand. The orange color of the sand is from the iron present in the Pine Barrens, the source of the river. In fact, the Rancocas, which empties into the Delaware River, is the only major west-flowing river draining the Pine Barrens. The other great Pine Barren rivers, the Mullica, the Wading, and the Great Egg Harbour, drain directly, or indirectly, into the Atlantic Ocean.

Leave the area via the same trail you came in on. Club mosses carpet the damp forest floor, and sweet pepperbush

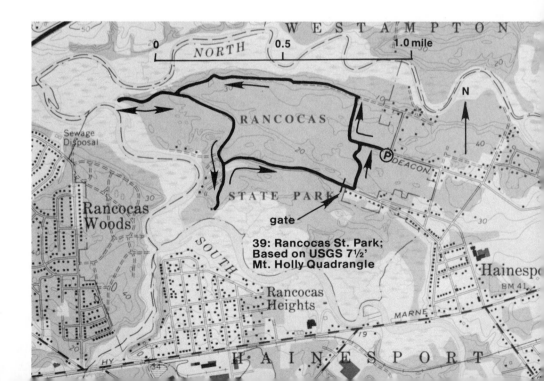

39: Rancocas St. Park;
Based on USGS 7½'
Mt. Holly Quadrangle

grows in abundance. Just past the dock area, the sand road swings to the right and forks. Take the path on the right and enter a stretch of pine barrens. For a time, you'll be walking through a pitch pine forest typical of those in Wharton and Lebanon State forests. During wet periods you'll have to navigate some huge puddles, which may be inhabited by frogs. Watch your footing as you detour around these small ponds—the banks of the sand road contain clay and may be slippery. When you come to a fork, bear to the left and keep to the left until you reach an intersection with a much larger sand road, which is obviously well used by vehicles. There may be a fifty-gallon drum for garbage located here.

If you desire to have another look at the South Branch of the Rancocas, bear right at this junction and walk straight ahead, ignoring the two sand roads leading off to the right, one of them to a residence. After walking around a large puddle you should come into an area on the banks of the river that is frequented by fishermen and the local public. Return to the junction the way you came.

At the junction, bear to the right on the well-used sand road, heading east. (If you have not taken the short trip to the river, turn left.) Walk down this straight lane with a swamp on your right and occasional wet areas on your left. You'll pass a few catalpa trees with their long seed pods and another sand road that heads out to the river on your right. After about half a mile of walking, come to a post and gate marking the boundary of the state park, with a paved road and some houses beyond.

Continue walking straight ahead on the paved road, and look for a small, barely noticeable footpath leading back into the woods on your left. It is found opposite the third house on your right. The path is unmarked but fairly easy to follow. It takes you slightly uphill to higher ground through the same moth-devastated oak and pine forest in which you began the hike. Stay on the main trail, which is grassy and very pleasant to walk on. After several minutes, you should meet the sand road you started on. Bear right here and walk out to your car.

BCS

The North Branch of Rancocas Creek.

Cattus Island

Total distance: 3 miles
Hiking time: 2 hours
Vertical rise: Minimal
Rating: Easy
Maps: USGS Toms River/Seaside Park; Cattus Island Ocean
 County Park map

Cattus Island Park preserves a small portion of the salt marshes and pine forests, now steadily being developed, on Barnegat Bay. Located in the midst of New Jersey's most popular summer vacation area, Cattus Island offers the hiker a variety of environments to explore, including pinelands, open marshes, holly forests, and bay beaches. The excellent views over vast marshes, across inlets, and out over the bay, plus the variety of wildlife found in the park, are further reasons to walk the trails found in this five hundred-acre Ocean County park.

To reach the park from Garden State Parkway exit 82 (Toms River/Route 37), take NJ 37 west 4.4 miles to Fisher Boulevard. Travel north on Fisher Boulevard for exactly 2 miles and turn right onto Cattus Island Boulevard. This turn is made just after the Bellcrest shopping plaza. The park entrance road is located .1 mile ahead on the left. Another .5 mile will bring you to the large parking area near the Cooper Environmental Center.

Before beginning the hike, follow the asphalt path to the nature center. Sign in, take a look around, and pick up a map of the park that shows both trails and terrain. The nature center has a number of displays, including a wall of all the USGS topographic maps for Ocean County. The center, which uses solar energy, is staffed by naturalists and a large number of volunteers, both young and old.

To begin the hike, walk around the center past the directory and bear to the right, through a wooden gate and onto a sandy road. This road, more like a causeway, penetrates the salt marsh that surrounds the slightly higher and dryer land ahead. Cattus Island is not an island in the true sense, but if it were not for this road, access would be very difficult. The body of water to the left is Mosquito Cove. The sand road leads straight ahead into the woods and eventually out to the tip of the island, which extends well into Barnegat Bay.

Make a left turn onto a footpath just after leaving the marsh. This path is the orange trail, marked by a combination of generous orange paint on trees and occasional concrete posts with arrows. The trail, winding through a pine forest, makes a right and swings out to the grassy shore of Mosquito Cove. A left turn at this point leads to a short counter-

Phragmites on Cattus Island.

clockwise circuit (also marked orange) to the cove, which may be confusing at first. Here, rising from the water, are the remains of an old dock. A white trail joins the orange at this spot also.

Leave the dock area, following orange markers through a forest of oak, pines, and enormous thickets of greenbrier. The walking through this aromatic woods is very pleasant. Pass a park bench near the gnarled trunk of an old cedar and enter a holly forest, green in all seasons. Notice that the red berries do not occur on all the holly trees—only the female trees bear fruit. These bright red berries are found on the tree year round and supply the bird population with a good source of food. Not far ahead, the orange trail meets the sand road again. Turn left here, heading northeast.

Walk the sand road causeway, bordered by salt marsh on the right and wet lowland forest on the left. Here are stands of pitch pine, red cedar, and other water-loving plants. Towering over the marsh to the right is an osprey nesting site. Other water birds, such as the white egret, may be seen feeding in this area. After about ten to fifteen minutes of walking, the road ends at the narrow, sandy beach that forms the northern tip of Cattus Island. You may wish to walk along this narrow strip of sand to the fina point of the island. After this short exploration, return to the sand road and retrace your steps to its junction with the orange trail.

From the sand road, bear left on the orange trail, which again penetrates the dryer woods of Cattus Island. The trail winds through a forest of holly and some rather large oaks. Two large, twisted, gnarled, and quite dead cedar trees are passed on the right. Deer are plentiful in this area, their footprints in the sand a common sight along this trail. After penetrating a dense pine forest, an extensive

vista of black, muddy salt marsh, sliced by drainage ditches, and the forest beyond it is reached. From this vista, the trail swings to the right, then to the left in an open area lined with bayberry bushes. The large clearing and the park benches under tall cedars mark the site where the island's former residents lived.

It was the Page family, who moved here in 1763, that first settled the island. Timothy Page, born on the island during that year, served in the local militia during the American Revolution. Most probably he was a privateer, essentially a pirate licensed by the Continental Congress. During the war, British ships were lured into Barnegat Bay through the Cranberry Inlet, only to be attacked and their cargos sold for profit. Cranberry Inlet, an opening to the Atlantic near present-day Ortley Beach, existed between 1750 and 1812. It was opened and closed by strong storms.

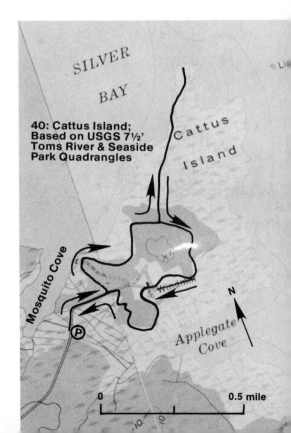

SILVER
BAY

40: Cattus Island;
Based on USGS 7½'
Toms River & Seaside
Park Quadrangles

Cattus
Island

Mosquito Cove

Applegate
Cove

N

0   0.5 mile

After the death of Timothy Page, the family house burned down, and the property was sold to Lewis Applegate. He moved there in 1842 and developed the southeastern section of the island, now named for him. He built a sawmill and a port for lumber boats. The island was sold again in 1867 and was slated to be developed as a resort, but the 1873 depression cancelled the project.

In 1895 the island was purchased by John V. A. Cattus, an importer and Olympic class athlete. He used the island and its buildings for weekend vacations, not as a full-time residence. Cattus loved boating, owned many boats, and also built a hunting lodge on the island. When he died, the land was sold in 1964 by his sons to developers. New state laws passed in the early 1970s limiting development in wetlands and along the coast discouraged the developers, and they sold the land to Ocean County in 1973. The property was acquired with county tax dollars and state "Green Acres" funds.

In 1976 the park opened to the public, and the following year trail development began.

From the clearing, continue following the orange markers to the left of a bench and back into the woods on a curving forest road. White trail markers are seen here also. The trail makes a series of tight turns through holly trees, only to re-emerge near the edge of the salt marsh. A few feet from where the trail turns right is a park bench. From here you will see Applegate Cove on the left and, to the right, the Cooper Environmental Center.

Return to the orange (and white) trail, which winds its way through a dense forest of oak, pine, and holly. After many small turns, the trail emerges onto the main sand road just to the west of the cleared mansion area. Make a left here, walk down the straight lane through the marsh, and journey back to the nature center and parking area.

BCS

41

Island Beach State Park

Total distance: 3.5 miles
Hiking time: 2.5 hours
Vertical rise: Minimal
Rating: Easy
Maps: USGS Barnegat Light; DEP Island Beach State Park

Along the 127-mile boundary between New Jersey and the Atlantic Ocean are a number of long, thin, barrier islands. Separated from the mainland by large bays, these islands are part of a chain that runs from New England to the Gulf coast of Mexico. The constant movement of sand pushed by the ocean waves, called littoral drift, both maintains and changes these relatively fragile land forms. Severe storms often open or close inlets, wash out beaches, and even extend barrier islands, creating new land. With the exception of Island Beach State Park (Seaside Park, NJ 08752; 201-793-0506), most of these islands have been developed with row after row of summer beach homes, boardwalks, and restaurants. If it were not for this park, many New Jerseyites would have no idea of what the shoreline in its natural state would look like.

To reach the park from exit 82 on the Garden State Parkway, take NJ 37 east through Toms River and over the Barnegat Bay Bridge. The entrance to the park is located 2.5 miles south of the bridge at the southern end of NJ 35. There are many signs directing one to the park along the way. Visitors to the

park will find that a fee is charged at the entrance gate, higher during peak season, less at other times, for each vehicle. Hikers should also know that, although there are a large number of parking spaces spread along the eight-mile road in the park, they often fill up quickly during peak season, and late arrivals are turned away at the gate. The best time to explore Island Beach State Park is during the off-season, especially during the week.

Island Beach State Park occupies the southern end of a long spit that is joined to the mainland near Point Pleasant. This section of the spit was an island at one time; an inlet connecting the ocean and Barnegat Bay was once located near present-day Ortley Beach. This inlet, known as Cranberry Inlet, was created and destroyed overnight by storms in 1750 and 1812. More recently, in 1935, a storm opened up an inlet just south of the present park entrance. Local rum runners wanted it to remain open, but the owners of the tract at the time had it closed.

The 2,694 acres of the park are divided into three sections, the northernmost and southernmost being natural

Back dunes at Island Beach State Park.

areas, the central section being public beaches and concessions. Located 1.2 miles south of the entrance are the park office and a nature center. A short, circular, self-guiding nature trail, which begins at the Aeolium, the nature center, is a good introduction to the park's vegetation. Farther ahead, on the left, is one of the original homes built in the 1920s as part of a planned development, this home now being used as a summer residence for New Jersey's governor. Beyond this house are the two large beach areas with their huge parking lots.

To begin the hike, drive the full 8 miles south from the park entrance to parking area A-23, the last parking area on the paved road. This parking area is very popular and may be filled on sunny days, even during the off-season. If it is, park at parking area A-22 or A-21 and walk the extra distance along the road.

From parking area A-23, walk through the gate toward the shoreline. You will be walking in a southern direction toward the Barnegat Inlet and Lighthouse. You can walk either on the beach buggy tracks or along the water's edge, both far easier to walk on than the soft sand. The compacted sand along the water is probably the most interesting choice since it offers the walker a fascinating variety of ocean debris that is constantly being reorganized by the tides and waves. Here are shells, dead fish, crabs, and driftwood. You will also encounter seagulls and fishermen with their beach buggies and campers. One is never bored walking along what may appear at first to be a monotonous stretch of beach.

After about 1.5 miles of walking, the southern tip of Island Beach is reached.

This is Barnegat Inlet, where the Atlantic Ocean meets Barnegat Bay. Barnegat Lighthouse, built in 1858, stands across the inlet at the northern tip of Long Beach Island. In Barnegat Inlet, the ocean currents are steadily moving sand southward toward Long Beach Island. The accumulation of sand from this drift is awesome when you consider that the end of the road, over a mile back, was once the end of the island. The Army Corps of Engineers struggles to keep this inlet, which is constantly filling with sand, open to navigation. It was hoped that the inlet would be stabilized by the two jetties, but even these structures don't prevent the sand from filling the inlet. During low tide, a sandbar or breaking waves are often visible between the two.

Walk west along the jetty toward Barnegat Bay. To your right is a protected bird nesting area and, beyond that, the dunes. The stability of the entire state park depends on these dunes, which are in turn stabilized by dune grass and other plants such as seaside goldenrod and Hudsonia or beach heather. These plants are very tolerant of the salty sea spray, which kills other species. Continue walking westward until nearly opposite the lighthouse across the inlet. Comparing the present topography with that of the geological survey map reveals the incredible changes constantly taking place here. To your right are the Sedge Islands, a large area of salt marsh inhabited by countless birds. Also to the right are the higher backdunes, separating the foredunes and the bay, which support a thick barrier of holly, bayberry, and other shrubs that cannot tolerate salt spray. There is also a residence visible from here, one of several located at the southern end of the park.

Originally, Island Beach was owned by Lord Stirling, owner of vast acreages in New Jersey during the seventeenth cen-

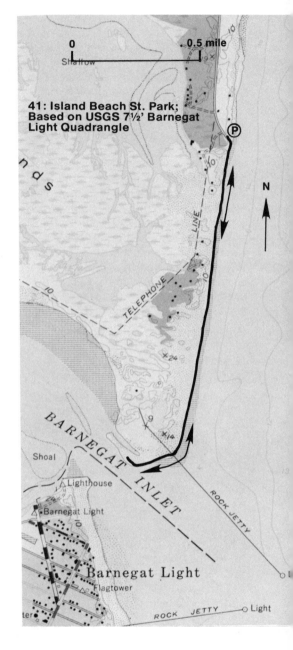

41: Island Beach St. Park; Based on USGS 7½' Barnegat Light Quadrangle

tury. During this period, the island was called Lord Stirling's Isle. Not much happened here during the next one hundred years. These beaches were remote from industrial areas and were occupied only by squatters who lived in part from materials washed ashore.

In 1926, Henry Phipps purchased the island with a shore resort in mind. He was able to build three large homes, one of which (mentioned earlier) is presently used by the governor of New Jersey as a summer residence, before his project was halted by the stock market crash and Depression. During World War II, Island Beach was used by the army for rocket experiments and, as such, was restricted to the public. The squatters and leaseholders who lived on the island were forced to leave, though they were allowed to return after the war. In 1953, after much talk about preserving the area, the state purchased the land from the Phipps estate and opened the park in 1959. The island residents who held leases were allowed to live there as long as they were alive. Of the original ninety leases, only thirteen remain.

There is a small promontory made of jetty stone that juts into the inlet, usually a private spot for lunch or simply for viewing the bay, ocean, and inlet all at once. To the south, the lighthouse and a steady parade of fishing and pleasure boats are a sharp contrast to the wild, inaccessible Sedge Islands to the northwest. When ready, retrace your steps from this spot back to the ocean shoreline and then back to the parking area. The first large gap in the dune fence that parallels the shore is the access to parking area A-23.

BCS

Lebanon State Forest

Total distance: 8.5 miles
Hiking time: 5 hours
Vertical rise: 50 feet
Rating: Moderately strenuous
Map: USGS Browns Mills; DEP Lebanon State Forest; DEP Batona Trail

Utilizing a section of the Batona Trail and the gravel and sand roads that crisscross the Pine Barrens, this hike takes in much of what Lebanon State Forest (New Lisbon, NJ 08064; 609-726-1191) has to offer. You can stop at Pakim Pond for lunch or a swim, you will cross a large cedar swamp twice, and you will follow the shores of reservoirs and cranberry bogs. Though long in mileage, this hike is not especially strenuous since the land is so flat; however, hot weather and biting deer flies could make it seem difficult, and, like most long hikes in the Pine Barrens, it should probably be hiked in cooler weather.

Lebanon State Forest is named after the Lebanon Glass Works, manufacturers of window glass and bottles, located here during the middle of the last century. The availability of sand and wood for charcoal supported the glassmaking industry until about 1867 when the wood supply became exhausted. About 150 men worked here, and a small town of sixty homes, a few shops, and a post office was established but later abandoned. In 1908 the state began to acquire land in the area.

The main entrance to Lebanon State Forest is located on NJ 72 one mile east of the traffic circle where NJ 70 intersects NJ 72. The entrance is located on the north side of the road and is well marked with a large sign. Proceed 0.3 mile on this entrance road and bear right at the first intersection. The park office is just ahead on the left. Park you car here.

To begin the hike, take the blue access trail to the Batona Trail found south of the parking area. This trail is labeled with a sign reading "Batona Trail." After a short walk, you will meet the true Batona Trail, which is marked with pink paint blazes. Bear left here, heading east. You'll be walking through a mixed pine and oak forest on a well-used footpath. The walking is pleasant and the trail surface, mostly sand, is soft and comfortable. After a short distance, the trail crosses a sand road and reenters the woods, continuing in an easterly direction. Here stands of scrub oak, sassafras, pink and white mountain laurel, and blueberry bushes close in on the trail. Tall ferns line the trail in darker places. Farther along, the Batona Trail crosses another sand road, this one larger than the

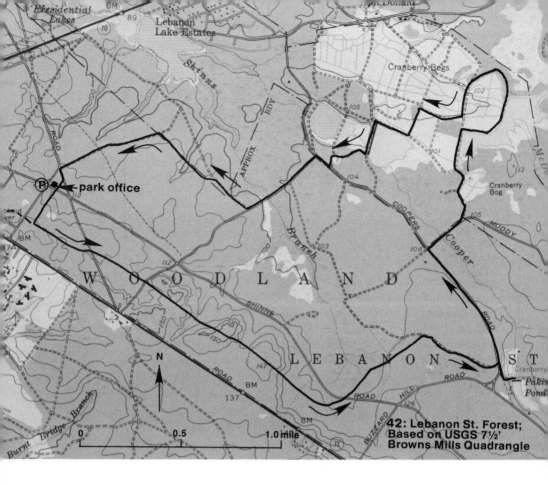

42: Lebanon St. Forest;
Based on USGS 7½'
Browns Mills Quadrangle

last, and reenters the woods on a small
sand road. Gradually the trail climbs to
its highest elevation, about 150 feet
above sea level. The land is dry here,
and blackjack oak, scrub oak, and pitch
pine dominate.

At about 2 miles into the hike, the trail
veers to the north and crosses a paved
park road. You may see some blue
markers after a short distance—disregard
these. Continue following the pink
markers of the Batona Trail and enter a
swampy area utilizing a corduroy log
footpath and boardwalks in some places.
This tract is the edge of the Cedar
Swamp Natural Area, a dense jungle of
Atlantic white cedars surrounded by the
pitch pine forest. The cedar wood, which

is soft but durable, is used in boat building and for some kinds of furniture, as
well as for shingles and stakes. The management of this tree is an important project in the forest. Below the tall cedars,
the vegetation is dense and the lighting,
dark. Plant life includes rare orchids,
curley grass ferns, pitcher plants, and
sundews. After leaving the swamp, you'll
come to a junction with a gravel road—
follow the markers and bear right through
an area where cedars have been harvested. After passing a few sand roads
leading off to the right, the road swings
to the left and meets an even larger
gravel road. Turn right and follow the
pink markers into the Pakim Pond area.

Pakim Pond is named from the Indian

word for cranberry. Its water is the reddish brown, acidic water typical of the Pine Barrens. The water, known as "cedar water," picks up its color and acidity as it moves very slowly through thick cedar swamps. Next to the pond is a swamp, a former cranberry bog. When the bog was actively cultivated, Pakim Pond was used as a reservoir to store water for the fall flooding of the bog. At Pakim Pond are rest rooms, picnic tables, and a swimming area.

If you have time, you may wish to take the one-mile nature trail located here, which explores both the pond and the swamp. This trail begins just off the Batona Trail at the southern part of the dam. An interpretation guidebook, which explains the points of interest located by numbered posts, is available at the park office. Carnivorous plants can be found here including the pitcher plant and at least two types of sundew. The pitcher plant has funnel-like leaves that are filled with water. Insects are attracted to the leaves by their odor and color and, should they fall in, are drowned and digested by the plant. The sundew is very small and grows in clumps in very wet but sunny areas. Its leaves have numerous sticky hairs that trap insects and then digest them.

After either exploring or resting at Pakim Pond, leave the way you came in and return to the gravel road. Do not turn left on the Batona Trail at the junction, but stay on the gravel road that, though not marked, is called Coopers Road. From now on you will be following unmarked sand and gravel roads and will need to pay attention to the text and map.

Coopers Road, like most of the gravel and sand roads in the Pine Barrens, is straight, flat, and lined with pines. It can be very hot here, and very buggy, during the summer. After about fifteen min-

utes of walking you'll come to a gate. Immediately past the gate, turn right on another, smaller gravel road known as Muddy Road. Along the side of the road are rhododendron, pepperbush, spicebush, and various species of blueberry. You will pass through a cedar swamp with towering Atlantic white cedars, densely packed, looking down on you from both sides of the road. Just where the road begins to swing to the right, look for, and then turn onto, a sand road coming in from the left. This road is a genuine sand road, and the going may be slow for a short distance. Farther along, you'll pass an open area that is, in fact, a former cranberry bog in various stages of regrowth. Follow the road as it swings around the bog and heads north (ignore the road going off to the left), then heading west again where it ends at a T intersection. Bear right here and head north towards the reservoir, which, like Pakim Pond, was used to flood cranberry bogs.

The scenery, as you walk along the dam, is beautiful with the backdrop of pines and the green shades of water lilies and other aquatic vegetation. Wildflowers, not found in the shady woods, thrive in this sunny and well-watered environment. When you come to the corner of the reservoir, bear right, following its perimeter. The walkway heads east, then swings to the north, eventually leaving the reservoir with its dark cedar water, standing dead trees, and elusive pickerel fish. The sand road now winds through a quiet and remote pine woods with a forest carpeting of pine needles.

When you come to a junction with another sand road, bear left, heading back into an immense and potentially confusing area of reservoirs, cranberry bogs, and sand roads. Stay on this sand road, heading south, for about 250 yards, then make a right turn on a sand road head-

Cooper's Road in Lebanon State Forest.

ing west. (From this junction, the edge of the first reservoir is visible.) Having made the turn, an overgrown bog will be on your right and an open swamp, with possibly some waterfowl activity, on your left. Don't be surprised if some large, military aircraft fly by as well, for these bogs are not far from Fort Dix and McGuire Air Force Base. Take the second left-hand turn, at a T intersection, and head south out to another reservoir. This reservoir was drained the last time we were here and presented an awesome sight of blackish mud and grey tree stumps. At this junction, another T intersection, bear right, heading west, along the shore of the reservoir. Next bear left at the end of the reservoir and head south along the dam.

Cranberries are still harvested in some sections of this area by farmers who lease the land from the state. The reservoirs are used to flood the bogs in the early fall for harvesting the cranberries. Machines are run through the bogs to shake the berries off the vines. The berries, which float, are scooped up and loaded, via conveyor belts, onto trucks that take them to processing plants. Those who find cranberry bog walking interesting and pleasant should explore Whitesbog, a turn-of-the-century agricultural village preserved as part of Lebanon State Forest. A map and information on Whitesbog can be obtained at the ranger's office.

Leaving the bog area at the end of the dam, turn right on a sand road that heads out to Coopers Road. This road winds around a bit and then comes to a small, but confusing, section where the road splits and then reunites. Bear to the left or center here, and you should find Coopers Road in less than 100 feet. Bear right on Coopers Road and then left on another gravel road only 200 yards ahead. Once again, a cedar swamp is crossed. Here the cedars are particularly tall and completely shade the road.

Just after leaving the swamp, bear right on a sand road heading west. After about 250 yards of walking, look for a small sand road on the left. Take this road south for about 200 feet and then bear right and west again on a very straight sand road that marks the boundary of Lebanon State Forest. This road is shady, surrounded by pine forest with an undercover of blueberries. Pass over a small mossy bog and then, after another ten minutes or so of walking, reach an intersection with a somewhat larger sand road. Bear left here, heading south. Another ten or fifteen minutes of walking will bring you to a paved road. Make a left here, walk about 150 yards, and, on the right, arrive at the park office and your car.

BCS

Batona to Ong's Hat

Total distance: 9 miles
Hiking time: 5 hours
Vertical rise: Minimal
Rating: Moderately strenuous
Maps: USGS Browns Mills; DEP Lebanon State Forest; DEP
  Batona Trail

This hike, like the previous Lebanon State Forest hike, begins from the ranger's office, which has a large parking area. To find the office from NJ 72 one mile east of its intersection with NJ 70, take the forest entrance road .3 mile north and bear right at the first intersection.

Begin the hike by taking the blue-marked trail directly across from the entrance to the ranger's office. A sign reading "Batona Trail" marks the path. Head south for only .1 mile to the junction with the actual Batona Trail, which is marked with pink blazes. Turn right here, heading west. You'll cross over two paved roads before you reach the Lebanon fire tower, about 100 yards in front of you.

Only from the highest reaches of this fire tower does one get a bird's-eye view of the terrain through which you will be walking for the next few hours. The green of the pines extends in all directions, unbroken to the horizon except for a few man-made objects. In the distance to the northwest, the low hill is Mount Holly, a remnant of the original sea floor, which, after uplifting, has survived millions of years of erosion.

Return to the Batona Trail, which follows a paved road for a short distance until it reenters the woods at a T-junction with a road in poor condition. This section of pine and oak forest is particularly beautiful. The trail, a white, sandy ribbon bordered by soft green moss, enters a forest penetrated by the sounds of cicadas and distant motor traffic. After crossing two more sand roads, pay careful attention to the markers since the trail, which has been relocated, can easily be lost. Immediately after this section you'll come to NJ 70, which the trail crosses to reenter the woods on the other side.

The trail in this section is wider, probably due to off-road vehicle abuse, and composed of loose sand, which makes for some extra work. Where the trail splits, keep to the left following the pink blazes onto a footpath. After a few minutes of walking, the trail leads to a small paved road and then to Deep Hollow. To the left are the remains of what was once Deep Hollow Pond, the recreational centerpiece of an early public campground in the state forest. The large residential development to the immediate northeast of the area created an overuse situation for the campground and lake, and during the early 1970s the campground was relocated. The lake, which never received enough water from its meager watershed anyway and tended to get polluted with overuse, was left to return to nature.

The trail leads over the drainage of the pond on the road and then immediately reenters the woods on the right. For the next mile or so, the Batona Trail parallels the course of Bisphams Mill Creek. Beginning in a mixed oak forest, the trail descends a few feet into a forest dominated by pitch pines. The footpath, which rises up and down over the next mile, never comes within sight of the stream but grazes the edge of the swampy wetland that surrounds it. Where the trail closely approaches the wetter areas, which are dominated by ferns, you can feel the temperature drop. After about a mile of walking along the stream bank, the Batona Trail makes a sharp left and heads for higher ground. This turnoff appears abruptly and, because the footpath you have been walking on continues straight toward Carpenter Spring, can easily be missed.

Now, back into a dryer forest, the Batona Trail crosses gravel Four Mile Road and enters an area where, during the late 1970s, the trees were cut and sold for lumber. The regrowth of both pine and oak gives one an idea of how fast these forests can recover from such a cutting. After crossing a small sand road, you'll enter an area containing mostly young pitch pines and, not long after that, cross the paved highway New Lisbon Road. After a brief walk through the woods, the trail bears left onto an open and sunny sand road for only 200 yards or so until it turns off to the right on a footpath. This turn is not clearly marked.

Although the next section of trail, a fairly recent relocation, may be difficult to follow in places, you'll be walking through a particularly beautiful pine forest. The trail makes a left turn onto a sand road and then, after only 100 yards, makes another left back into the woods. Now on the final stretch to its terminus at Ong's Hat, the Batona Trail snakes its way through another cleared area, crosses a sand road, then emerges on NJ 72 near a market and a restaurant. After 4.6 miles of walking, you will reach Ong's Hat.

Here, at the northern terminus of the fifty-mile-long Batona Trail, is a convenient place to fill your stomach or just get a drink. It makes good sense to locate a major trailhead near a food source. Ong's Hat Restaurant even has an outside counter from which you can buy soft ice cream and sodas. If you don't care to buy your lunch or eat it in civilization, simply follow the pink blazes down a gravel road opposite the restaurant a few feet to the Batona parking area, which is grassy and has a few places to sit.

But what, you must be asking, is Ong's Hat? Ong's Hat is the name of this very, very small town (town?) facing you. The story of its name begins in the early 1700s when Jacob Ong built a tavern here. He was a Quaker from Pennsylvania who apparently strayed from the steady course and took a liking to dancing and flirting. The tavern, which made an excellent halfway stop for stage-coaches traveling between Philadelphia and the Jersey shore, soon became the scene of some wild goings-on, and in 1715 the history-making event occurred. Jacob got into a fight with one of his girl-friends who, in the midst of a jealous rage, grabbed the hat off his head and threw it high into a huge oak tree beside the tavern. For years the hat remained caught in the high branches, and passersby would frequently say, "Look, there's Ong's Hat." It took a while, but in 1828 the town got recognition on the offi-

Deep Hollow Pond.

cial New Jersey maps, and it is also shown on the USGS Browns Mills quad. As for the tree, well, it was cut down in 1978 by the county highway department. The present "Ong's Hat Family Restaurant" and the market next door mark the spot where all this action took place.

After your stop, follow the pink markers to the Batona Trail parking area, directly across from Ong's Hat on the gravel road. Continue past the parking area for a short distance until you come to a junction with a sand road paralleling NJ 72. Turn right here, heading east on a very straight, soft sand road lined with pines. In just a short distance, you will pass the Batona Trail and farther on come to a fork where you should continue straight ahead. A large, cleared area will appear on your left. During 1986 and 1987 this area was cleared by a commercial lumber company that bought the wood, mostly oaks, from the state. As you can see, it doesn't take long for the forest to begin regeneration. One of the advantages of periodically cutting the forest and creating open areas, which occurs naturally in nature due to forest fires, is that habitats for certain animals are created. Deer love to brouse in cleared areas, and birds, such as the red-headed and red-bellied woodpeckers, summer tanagers, and bluebirds, thrive there also. Bluebirds, quite rare in New Jersey these days, make homes here—aided in part by the placing of nesting boxes by the forest service.

At the end of the sand road, cross NJ 70 and follow the asphalt as it swings to the left and then down a lane lined with utility poles. A highway department maintenance shed will be on your left. The walkway is sandy and heads gradually downhill. Immediately after crossing a low, wet area, look for the pink markers of the Batona Trail. Turn right here and follow the trail back to the state forest office. Remember, after passing the area of the fire tower, be alert for the junction with the blue-marked access trail to the office. This junction is indicated by signs for Pakim Pond on a tree.

BCS

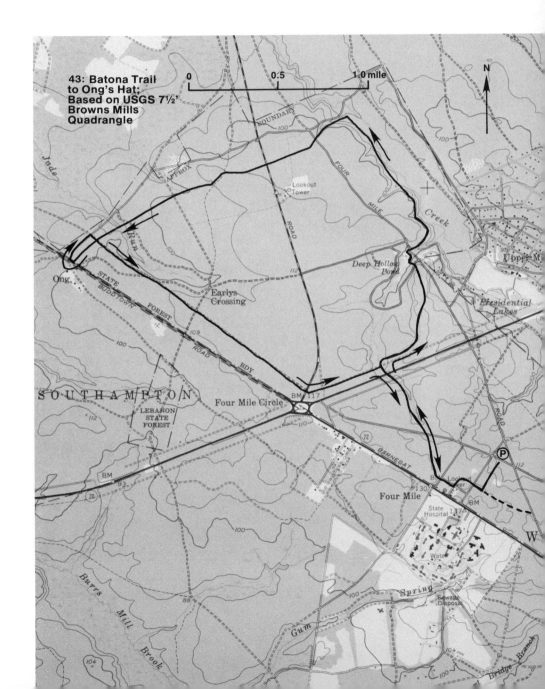

43: Batona Trail to Ong's Hat; Based on USGS 7½' Browns Mills Quadrangle

Carranza to Apple Pie Hill

Total distance: 8 miles
Hiking time: 4.5 hours
Vertical rise: 166 feet
Rating: Moderately strenuous
Maps: USGS Chatsworth, Indian Mills; WB #19; DEP Batona
   Trail; DEP Wharton State Forest

Walking uphill in the Pine Barrens is very unusual. The entire region is just above sea level, and the very few "hills" are usually only twenty-five or thirty feet above everything else. There are a few exceptions, however, and this hike leads to the highest elevation in the Pines, a dizzying 205 feet above sea level and about 125 feet above the land around it. This is Apple Pie Hill, on which a fire tower is located. En route the hike will take you over another hill, 139 feet above sea level, as a warm-up for the big climb.

To reach the parking area at the Carranza Memorial, turn left (east) off US 206 just south of its junction with NJ 70. The sign here directs you to the town of Tabernacle and the Carranza Memorial. You'll reach the little town of Tabernacle and cross County Road 532 in 2.3 miles. Continue straight ahead through farms and a residential area into Wharton State Forest (Batsto, RD 4, Hammonton, NJ 08037; 609-561-3262). Seven miles from Tabernacle, you will find the Carranza Memorial, which has ample parking, on the right.

The Carranza Memorial commemorates the tragic crash and death of Mexican pilot Emilio Carranza. Carranza, only twenty-three at the time of his death, had been a Mexican hero for five years, his fame resting on both his aviation and military accomplishments. On June 11, 1928, he took off from Mexico in a Ryan monoplane, the same as Lindbergh's, and attempted a nonstop flight to Washington. He was grounded by fog in North Carolina but was still received with speeches and parades in both Washington and New York. Carranza was on the return leg of this goodwill flight when he flew into a thunderstorm over this remote section of the Pines and crashed. The local American Legion holds an annual observance of this event the first Saturday after the Fourth of July. Each year on this day wreaths are placed around the memorial, a stone marker made in Mexico that portrays a diving Aztec eagle.

From the memorial, cross the paved road and head north into the Batona Camp. There is a sign here indicating the campsite. After about 200 yards, you'll meet the pink-blazed Batona Trail, which connects with the camp access road from the right. From here to Apple Pie Hill and back you'll be following these pink markers.

Batona Camp is one of several primi-

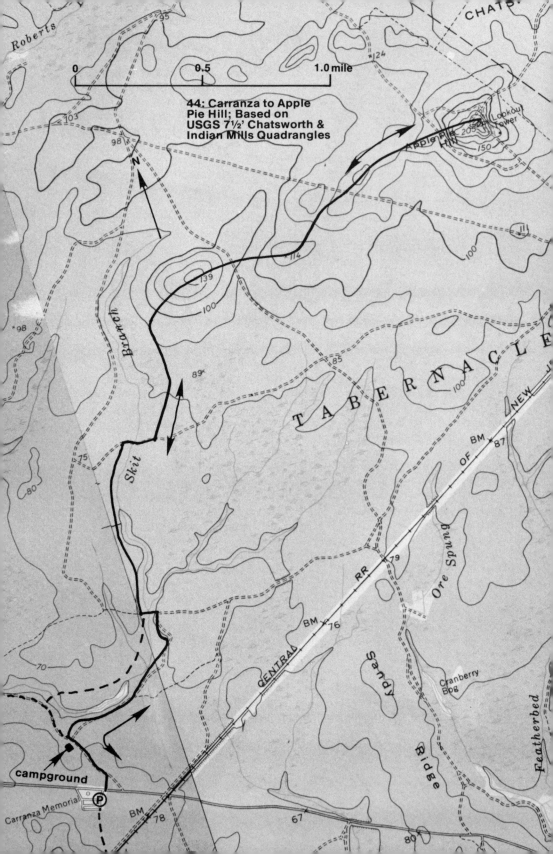

44: Carranza to Apple
Pie Hill; Based on
USGS 7½' Chatsworth &
Indian Mills Quadrangles

N

TABERNACLE

campground

Carranza Memorial

Roberts

CHATS

Apple Pie Hill

Lookout Tower

Branch

Skit

NEW

Ore Spring

RR

CENTRAL

BM

Sandy

Cranberry Bog

Ridge

Featherbed

tive camping areas located in Wharton State Forest. The site is accessible by car and offers numerous spaces to pitch a tent, also providing a water pump and several pit toilets. If you wish to camp here, you'll need a permit, available from the Atsion Ranger Headquarters farther south on US 206 or from the office in Batsto. At the time of this writing, the fee was $5.00 per night. Pets are not permitted in the campsite for overnight camping.

When you reach the end of the camping area, the trail veers to the right past a toilet and enters the woods on a footpath. Immediately, the typical flora of the Pinelands surrounds you. Highbush blueberries, which are found along the trail over much of this hike, make their first appearance. Blackjack oak and, of course, pitch pine surround you. Within a few hundred feet, the trail emerges onto a wide sand road, which it follows for a short distance. For the next half mile, the trail parallels this road, playing "tag" by using it for short stretches then cutting back into the woods on a footpath.

After a section that skirts the edge of a cedar swamp, the trail emerges onto the road for a final time to use its bridge. The brook you are crossing is the Skit Branch of the Batsto River. Like all Pine Barrens water, it is tea colored from the cedar wood that grows in it. From the bridge is a good view of the swampy brook and its plant life. If you look closely at the clumps of grasses growing in and around the water, you'll see hundreds of tiny sundew plants. If you look even closer, you may find a few miniature pitcher plants as well. These plants survive in this nutrient-poor environment by digesting insects that get trapped in their sticky leaves or no-exit entrances.

After crossing the bridge, the trail turns right and back into the woods on a footpath, this time for good. For the next half

mile, Skit Branch and its white cedar swamp will be on the right. The many dead cedars, still standing tall in the water, were killed by fire. Unlike the pitch pine and the shortleaf pine, the Atlantic white cedars do not regenerate after a burn; only the water protects them from fire. In this section, the trail crosses a wet area on loose logs. Be careful, or you may sink into deep, black mud. The next crossing is of the stream itself, again on logs and, once more, potentially perilous for your shoes.

The Batona Trail now leaves the wet area surrounding Skit Branch and heads into dryer, and higher, territory. About 2 miles from the start of the hike the first climb begins. The ascent is first noticeable by the change from soft, white sand as a walkway to a harder gravel path. After a "climb" of about 40 feet, you'll reach the tablelike summit of this unnamed hill and, before you know it, begin heading downhill. Pay close attention ahead as the trail veers left off the path, crosses a sand road, and then reenters the woods.

One of the creatures of the Pines you may encounter on this hike, particularly in the dryer areas, is the aptly named fence swift lizard. You may see a blur and hear the rustle of leaves, yet not get a look at this speedster unless you catch him sunning on a piece of dead wood. This rather attractive lizard has a grey-brown body and some very jagged scales along its head and back. The males have a dark marking under their lower jaws.

After crossing three more sand roads, the Batona begins another climb, this one more serious. Some views out to the horizon in the south appear between the trees. The trail winds along the hill until the summit and its fire tower appear. This rise is Apple Pie Hill, at 205 feet, the highest summit in the Pine Barrens.

Carranza Memorial.

Although the hill, which is accessible by car or truck, is the scene of many a wild party, the view from its tower is spectacular. To the south, a wilderness of green pines extends as far as the eye can see. To the west, in the distance, is the slight rise of Mount Holly. To the north are pines and, far in the distance, a water tower and a few other protrusions of civilization. In the east is a cranberry field—and more pines. To the southeast, a sand road runs from the hill in a perfectly straight line. For the most part, the view is one of vastness and wilderness and gives the hiker an idea of the magnitude of the Pine Barrens.

Fire towers, which are frequently manned, play an important role in controlling the frequent fires (about four hundred a year) in the Pine Barrens. The soil in the Pinelands drains the water so well that the oil and resin-rich pine needles and dead branches are nearly always dry as tinder. There are no earthworms or bacteria to digest the dead materials on the forest floor, so the tinder accumulates year after year until it burns in a fire. The shortleaf pine and the pitch pine, the most common pines here, are two of only three pines in the United States that can sprout from buds lying deep within their trunks or large limbs, thereby assuring their quick recovery following a fire. The persistence of fires, many of them started by arsonists, in the Pine Barrens has insured the dominance of these two pines in the forest. Ecologists believe that without regular fires, oaks would probably make up the bulk of a climax forest.

Because it is somewhat abused and there is much broken glass, Apple Pie Hill may not be the best place for a rest or lunch. We suggest that you find a resting place nearer to the first hill you climbed, which shows little sign of use other than from hikers. Whatever you decide to do, the way back to your car is the way you came.

BCS

Penn State Forest

Total distance: 8.5 miles
Hiking time: 5 hours
Vertical rise: 125 feet
Rating: Moderately strenuous
Maps: USGS Woodmansie/Oswego Lake; DEP Penn State
   Forest

Penn State Forest (c/o Bass River State Forest, PO Box 118, New Gretna, NJ 08224; 609-296-1114), located northeast of the huge Wharton tract, contains a number of sand roads, a beautiful lake, and even a hill with a view. The forest is, for the present, undeveloped, though it is administered through Bass River State Forest just to the south. There are no designated hiking trails here, but the sand roads, as elsewhere in the Pinelands, make for good hiking. Unlike the other state forests located within the general region known as the Pine Barrens, the acreage in Penn State Forest includes an area of dwarf pines called the Plains.

To reach the parking area near Oswego Lake from County Road 563, turn east onto Chatsworth–New Gretna Road and proceed 3.2 miles to Lake Oswego. This turnoff is located .4 mile north of Mick's Canoe Rental and 1.4 miles north of the junction with County Road 679. The parking area is on the right, just over the bridge, and may be filled during summer weekends. Lake Oswego is a very popular swimming area in season.

Begin the hike at the parking area lo-cated at the northwestern end of Lake Oswego. Proceed east for a few hundred feet, then bear left onto a sand road. At the first fork, bear left on what is known as Lost Lane Road. Follow the lane through an open forest of small to me-dium-height pitch pines. After about a mile of walking, a sand road called Penn Place will turn off on the right. Ignore this turn and continue straight ahead on Lost Lane Road.

Just past the junction with Penn Place, Lost Lane enters a swampy area that is quite picturesque. Tall cedars line the road, which is high and dry in most places. Farther on, Lost Lane, which is fairly solid, easy to walk on, and re-markably white, continues to penetrate the pine forest, gradually swinging around to the right. On a clear, bright day, the contrast of white sand road, green pines, and blue sky is magnificent.

Two miles into the hike, come to paved Chatsworth Road. Cross Chatsworth and continue on Lost Lane, heading north-east. After about fifteen more minutes of walking, enter another swampy area con-taining many dead cedars. As vistas open up, the terrain becomes stranger

and wilder. The expansiveness of these relatively open areas is a prelude to what is ahead. With the exception of an occasional military transport plane taking off from McGuire Air Force Base to the north, this section of the forest is about as remote as you get in the Pine Barrens. You may spot deer or, more likely,

the common fence swift lizard skirting its way across the road.

In less than a mile from its junction with Chatsworth Road, Lost Lane makes a sharp right and begins a straight course, heading southeast along the boundary of Penn State Forest. After passing Sooey Road, which turns off to

Dwarf pines in the "Plains."

the right, Lost Lane climbs a small hill and then descends, flanked by some beautiful specimens of pitch pine and scrub oak. Notice that the bark of the trees is charred, a fire having occurred here not long ago. Just ahead are the Plains.

There is nothing else in New Jersey that compares with the incredibly expansive vistas created by five-foot-tall, stunted pine trees. The chaparral-like combination of white sand and clumps of green is reminiscent of both the high southwest deserts and the Cape Cod dunes. Many explanations have been offered for the dwarfed size of the pines in the Plains. One theory states that aluminum in the sand stunts the trees, though

aluminum is found in other areas where normal trees are found. Another theory holds that the trees are stunted by strong winds that blow on the generally high ground of the area. This theory fails because equally strong winds blow elsewhere and, even at the highest elevations such as at Apple Pie Hill, those trees are of normal height. Other explanations include poor soil, shallow soil, and pine-eating moths, none of which have held up when tested.

The only explanation for the dwarf pines that has consistently held up amidst all the debate is simply the frequency of fires in the area. On average, a major fire occurs in the Plains every seven years. Once burned, the pine roots tend to spread horizontally, forming a ground mat that can extend up to thirty feet from the original taproot. It is still not known exactly how the fires cause stunting, however. One other interesting aspect of the stunted pines is relevant here and supports the fire theory. The pitch pine tree is capable of producing both closed and open pine cones. Closed pine cones can survive fires, in fact, they need fire to open up. In the Plains, the pitch pines tend to produce closed cones, though in other sections of the Pine Barrens, the open type is more prevalent.

Continue walking through the Plains on Lost Lane, passing a road turning off to the left, until a triangular junction with Stave Road is reached. Turn right here, heading southwest. You are still in the Plains, about 4.5 miles from Oswego Lake. In another mile, the Plains are left behind, and paved Chatsworth Road is reached. Bear right here, but only for .2 mile. Next, make a left on Sooey Road, which is paved but in terrible shape. You should be heading southwest again.

In just a tenth of a mile look for a paved turnoff on the left that leads to Bear Swamp Hill. After a short climb of 50 feet, something rare in the Pine Barrens, come to a parking area and, to the right, the site of a former fire tower. There is a partial view to the west that gives one a feeling for the vastness of the area. Bear Swamp Hill abounds in mountain laurel, beautiful when blooming in late spring. The wooden structure off to the left of the parking area housed rest rooms when the area was maintained. After your visit, retrace your steps downhill and bear left on Sooey Road, now a sand and gravel road.

After about ten minutes of walking, come to an intersection with Cabin Road and turn left, heading southeast. This road is narrow and receives less use than those traveled so far. The road will widen after a distance and swing around to the right. At a T-junction, bear to the left on Penn Place Road. In over a mile from Bear Swamp Hill, a junction with paved Jenkins Road, one of the main roads through the forest, is reached. At this junction, find a sand road on the right that parallels Jenkins Road. This road, which avoids motor traffic and has better footing and scenery to offer, is the preferred walkway. The gravel and sand on this road is particularly reddish, probably due to its high iron content.

After a walk of just over half a mile, the sand road will reconnect with paved Jenkins Road. Do not take the sand road heading off to the right. Walk straight ahead on the pavement, or, more accurately, on what's left of the pavement, to the parking area about a half mile ahead. En route are some excellent views of Lake Oswego on the left.

BCS

Batsto

Total distance: 2 miles
Hiking time: 1.5 hours
Vertical rise: Minimal
Rating: Easy
Map: USGS Atsion; DEP Wharton State Forest

The restored bog-iron town of Batsto, in Wharton State Forest (Batsto, RD 4, Hammonton, NJ 08037; 609-561-3262), makes an excellent introduction to both the history and the natural environment of the Pine Barrens. The hike described below is short and very easy, yet it provides a good sampling of the typical flora found throughout the entire region. After wallking through part of the village, the hike follows the shore of beautiful Batsto Lake, then returns via one of the frequent sand roads that crisscross the Pines. The Batsto Village section of Wharton State Forest is a major tourist attraction in south Jersey and can be crowded on sunny summer and fall weekends.

Batsto is located on County Road 542 between New Gretna near the Garden State Parkway and Hammonton on NJ 206. Signs directing you to Batsto, which is #1 on the New Jersey historical site listing, are found coming from either direction. Enter the historic area (you may have to pay a parking fee during peak season), and park your car near the ranger's office and souvenir shop. You can purchase USGS topographic maps here. Begin your hike by walking through or around the office and shop, then turn-

ing right on the main concourse through the restored village. Some artifacts relating to the iron industry, and the mansion, will be on the left.

Batsto was the site of an iron forge that produced kettles, stoves, cannon, pipes, and other iron products during the latter part of the eighteenth and the early nineteenth centuries. Like Allaire Village in the northern extremes of the Pine Barrens, the iron was made from bog iron—accumulations of iron-oxides leached from the sand by water and deposited in decaying vegetation. During the Revolutionary War, Batsto was a major source of military iron, and its workers were exempt from military service.

At its peak, the village that developed around the furnace had a population of nearly a thousand. When the iron industry declined, a glassmaking factory was built, and the town produced window panes and other flat glass products for a few years. In 1876, after a major fire in the village, Joseph Wharton bought the property as part of his plan to own the Pine Barrens and sell its water to the city of Philadelphia. The state of New Jersey responded by passing a law prohibiting the export of water, effectively halting this project. Eventually the Wharton holdings were acquired by the state, forming the present-day Wharton State Forest.

Walk past the Batsto Mansion towards the lake and turn right (north) on the lane that parallels its eastern shore. The lake, its spillage used to turn millstones and to pump bellows for the forge, was created by damming the Batsto River. Where the lane swings around to the right, look for a footpath near a split-rail fence leading straight ahead into the woods. The nature center, which is staffed with interpreters of the region's ecology, is to your right just before the footpath begins.

The footpath is marked with a combination of yellow, red, blue, and green discs, each being the color code for a particular nature trail described in a guide available from the nature center. Along these four trails, posted numbers point out relevant features. This hike utilizes the full length of the Pond Trail, which is marked with yellow tags.

The footpath soon narrows and crosses a wet area on a wooden bridge. Keep to the left where the red trail veers off to the right. At the time of this writing, the trail was very overgrown in places, no doubt due to budget cuts as much as to lack of use. Along the trail notice the dense brush that rises to about three or four feet in height. This growth, mostly blueberry, huckleberry, and dangleberry, makes up the understory of much of the Pine Barrens. Mountain laurel and azalea also fill in the understory in places.

About half a mile into the hike, arrive at an open area with good views of Batsto Lake. A bench located here invites a rest or meditation. Farther along, the Pond Trail dips into another wet area only to emerge along the shoreline of the lake again. A few large cedars, the source of the tea-colored water typical of the Pinelands, are found here.

As you approach the end of the .66-

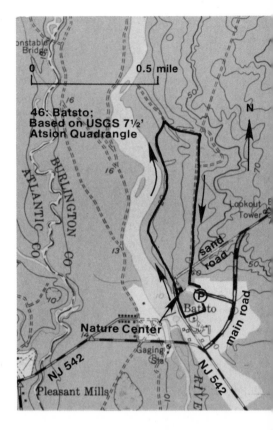

46: Batsto; Based on USGS 7½' Atsion Quadrangle

mile-long Pond Trail, it swings away from the lake and onto higher ground. The path is now a sand road and is subject to some vehicle traffic. Keep to the right and find a lesser-used sand road that heads in an eastern direction, away from the lake. This last segment of the Pond Trail is not well marked.

The sand road, which leads through a very typical Pinelands forest, is lined with green moss and covered with brown pine needles. This road, and the next, give one a very good idea of what hiking throughout the Pine Barrens is like. The scenery varies little, except when near water, but the tones of white sand, green leaves, and brown needles are very pleasing to the eye. After a short walk,

Upper Batsto Lake.

another sand road, this one more frequently used, is encountered. Turn right here and begin your walk back to Batsto.

The sand is softer here, due to use, but the walking is not that difficult. Stay on the main road until you come to where it swings to the left at a fence and gate. A view of the Batsto fire tower is to your left at this junction. Walk around the fence, effectively making a right turn, and then make the first left. A walk down this lane will lead to the parking area behind the ranger's office and your car.

BCS

Mullica River Wilderness

Total distance: 8 miles (from Batsto—6 miles from trailhead)
Hiking time: 5 hours
Vertical rise: Minimal
Rating: Moderately strenuous
Maps: USGS Atsion; DEP Wharton State Forest

Backpacking in the Pine Barrens is a unique experience for those more familiar with mountainous areas. The pines are not so dense or tall that they shut out a good view of a starlit sky. In fact, the effect is more like camping in a desert than in a forest. The pine needle cover on the sandy ground makes for a comfortable bed and great sleeping. From Batsto, in the heart of the Pinelands, a four-mile walk leads to the Mullica Wilderness Campsite, a good choice for such an experience. This primitive camping area, which is monitored by the rangers, is expansive enough for private folks, is right on the Mullica River, and has a water pump and pit toilet. You'll have to get a permit from the office in Batsto to camp here, which at the time of this writing cost $5.00 per night. Pets are not allowed.

Batsto, which is on County Road 542, is easy to find—signs directing you to it (it is a major historical site) are found frequently within a radius of twenty miles. If you plan to backpack, it is advisable to leave your car overnight at the parking area behind the state forest office in Batsto. After registering and picking up your permit, walk east on the main walk-

way through Batsto Village, across the dam on Batsto Lake, and turn right onto a footpath found just past the last building on your right. This path will take you to the gravel road onto which you should turn right. A walk of about .2 mile will bring you to where the road divides.

If you plan to day-hike the area, you should probably park your car at the end of a gravel road found .6 mile east of the main entrace to Batsto on County Road 542. Drive north on this road for about .4 mile and park near the lake on the left, just before the road divides.

The entire hike is on sand roads that are unmarked and perhaps confusing in places; however, since the entire hike is on the land between the Mullica and Batsto rivers, getting lost would be very difficult. Until you reach the actual Mullica Wilderness Area, these sand roads are open to motor vehicles. Don't be surprised if a huge four-wheeler or a truck towing canoes passes you. Because of all this traffic, sections of the sand roads are very soft, with poor traction. Wear appropriate shoes.

At the fork, take the sand road on the left and enter the Pinelands. Where the sand road swings sharply to the left and

Mullica River.

enters a maze of trails to the Mullica, keep to the right to stay on course. After about a mile of walking, you'll come to Constable Bridge over the Mullica River. If you're hiking on a busy summer week-end, expect regular deliveries of canoes to this popular boat launching point.

The Mullica, along with the Batsto, Wading, Great Egg Harbour, and Rancocas, is one of the major rivers draining the vast water reserves lying just below the sands and forests of the Pine Barrens. Though the river widens considerably farther downstream, the Mullica here in the forest is typical of other rivers in the Pines. There are no rapids, but the current is strong. The river is not wide, but it can be very deep. The fact that it runs all year long and through droughts at a constant water level indicates the extent of the aquifer underlying the Pine Barrens.

Continue hiking north on the main sand road (do not cross the bridge). The walking gets easier, for this section suffers less abuse from motor vehicles. After another mile, the entrance to the wilderness area is reached, a section of the forest where no vehicles (except the ranger's) are allowed. There is a sign here marking the boundary.

Almost immediately after entering the wilderness area, the forest becomes cleaner, the sand road harder, and the insects (in summer) more aggressive. Wildlife, including deer and flying squirrels, becomes more abundant. The red wasp, which looks like a giant ant, may be spotted alongside the trail. In another half mile, the sand road swings close to the Mullica River, offering another view of its dark and narrow passageway through the tall cedars and pines. As you continue farther north, these encounters with the river become more frequent. This section of the Mullica has been designated a wild and scenic river by the state of New Jersey.

About a mile from the beginning of the wilderness area is the Mullica River Wilderness Campsite, a good place for lunch—or for the night. There's a pump for good water here and plenty of camp-

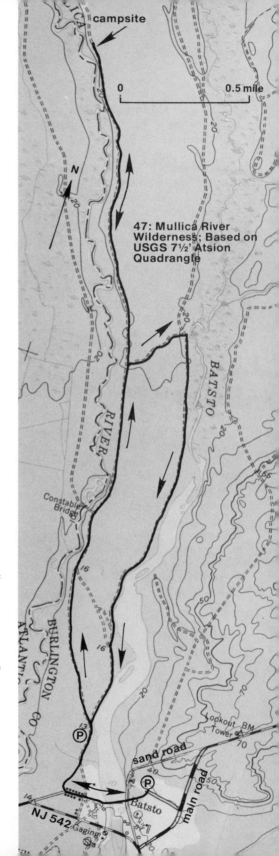

campsite

0   0.5 mile

N

47: Mullica River Wilderness; Based on USGS 7½' Atsion Quadrangle

sites within the limits posted and marked by a ditch. Along the banks of the Mullica are several beachlike areas and even a rope swing.

The water of the Pine Barrens is dark, the color of tea. "Cedar water" is the usual name for it. The color comes in part from the tannins in the cedar trees that grow in the water and in part from the iron in the ground water. Because the water in the Pine Barrens tends to stay fresher longer, sea captains used to sail up the rivers that drain the Pinelands and take on barrels of what they called "sweet water."

The water table in the Pinelands is shallow, but the reserve of water is vast. As an aquifer, there is no equal to the Pinelands in the northeastern United States. Because the water lies so close to the surface and the sand, which takes in the rain that falls on it, is not a good filter, the Pine Barrens aquifer is extremely vulnerable to pollution. For this reason, development, which constantly threatens this area, has until now been kept at bay.

After a lunch, a rest, or possibly an overnight, leave the campsite area and walk south, retracing your steps to the sign marking the entrance to the wilderness area. At this point, make a left onto a sand road that heads northeast and leads in about one-fourth mile to a sand road running north/south along the Batsto River. Make a right (south) on this road and begin the 2.5-mile walk back to your car. The sand is very soft in places, necessitating walking on the shoulder or on lesser-used trails parallel to the main sand road. Though it may not be immediately apparent to you, the Batsto River, on the left, is not far away. Perhaps the sound of paddles banging on the sides of aluminum canoes will alert you to its presence.

Along the banks of the Batsto are tall cedars and highbush blueberries, ripe in August. Soon the northern end of Batsto Lake, which is mostly a large swamp, appears. Where the road swings to the right, the hiker is finally rewarded with a wide panorama of the entire lake, right down to the village at its far end. When you come to another maze of sand roads, keep to the left and continue heading south. In this area, vehicular traffic may be encountered, more likely if you are hiking on a beautiful summer weekend.

After about an hour of walking along the western banks of Batsto River and Batsto Lake, you should arrive at the junction where you originally turned left toward the Mullica. If you day-hiked, your car is just ahead. If you backpacked, continue along the gravel road to the small opening in the split-rail fence. A left turn here will lead you through the village and back to the ranger's office and the parking area.

BCS

48

Parvin State Park

Total distance: 5 miles
Hiking time: 3 hours
Vertical rise: Minimal
Rating: Easy to moderate
Maps: USGS Elmer; DEP Parvin State Park

[handwritten note at top: 7/30/89 Typical S. Jersey. Some of trail nice, but much around Muddy Creek is close, buggy, + many thorns. Very Muddy, & bridge mostly out.]

In 1930, the New Jersey Legislature began the acquisition of Parvin State Park with an appropriation of just under $74,000. Nine years later, following nineteen separate transactions, Parvin entered the state park system. During the Depression, a Civilian Conservation Corps (CCC) branch was established in the park. The men hacked out trails through the dense forest, using the wood to build bridges across the swamps. They cleared the main beach and picnic area and constructed the cabins (each with its own boat landing) along the shore of Thundergust Lake.

A German prisoner of war camp was located in a section of the park in 1942. When the European hostilities ended, the camp was converted for use by interned Japanese-Americans from the West Coast. 1952 saw the last, nontraditional use of Parvin. Six years earlier, Stalin had had the Kalmyck people and some other Tartar groups transported to Siberia in retaliation for their revolt against the Communist government. Only about a quarter of the 400,000 people involved survived the ordeal, with some of them escaping to the United States. They came to Parvin in three groups but stayed only a few months. Some are now settled in the Philadelphia area and in Howell township in New Jersey.

Parvin State Park is located in south Salem County along the Cumberland County border. The park entrance is on County Road 540, slightly over a mile east of Centerton or six miles west of Vineland. The office (RD 1, Elmer, New Jersey 08318; 609-692-7039) is located in one end of the park bathhouse, with a large parking lot across County Road 540. In season, there is a small parking fee. The surrounding area has many road signs to point you in the right direction. Stop in the office for a free map and booklet.

The hike starts just outside the park office. Facing Parvin Lake and the bathhouse, walk to the right (west) along a brown dirt path, through, and then beside, a split-rail fence. This hike is over flat terrain, and the walking is easy. The trail travels between the highway and the lake, passing some picnic areas. Holly trees and mountain laurel abound.

A few minutes after crossing a small brook on a tiny stone bridge, a small, open clearing is reached. Avoid both the small trail to the left (which soon fades

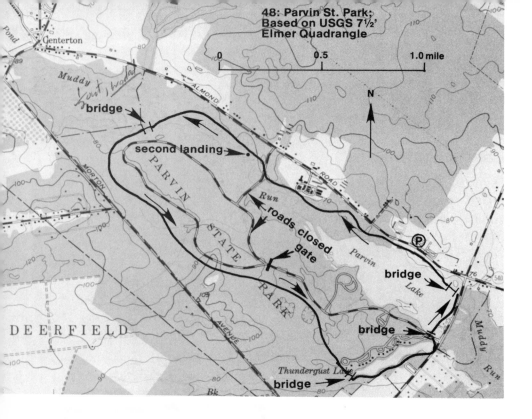

out) and the wider, but overgrown, trail to the right. Continue ahead as the route swings closer to both the road and a few houses seen through the woods. Large pitch pines with their distinctive, thick, shingle bark are much in evidence.

Soon, a short side trail leads left down to the edge of Muddy Run. Continue straight ahead, also avoiding the trail to the right. Shortly afterwards, there is another path to the water's edge. Muddy run is a typical slow-moving stream of south Jersey. A tributary of the Maurice River, its water eventually empties into Delaware Bay. In the 1800s, small ponds were formed by damming to provide power for gristmills and sawmills. One of these was owned by a family named Parvin.

Proceed ahead, crossing a series of small plank bridges to meet a paved crossroad. This road forms the main boundary between the developed and the designated natural area of Parvin State Park—the latter section to be left in a "forever wild" condition. A short walk left along this road leads to Muddy Run and an interesting jagged bridge allegedly so designed to keep away motor bikes. Once again back on the main trail, continue straight ahead as the path gets a little sandier. In a few minutes, an area known as Second Landing is reached. Uphill to the right, there is a picnic area with a rain shelter and rest rooms. The shore of Muddy Run is just to the left. Since the way now enters the heart of the designated "natural area," the trail is basically unmaintained and less obvious. There are some blowdowns to climb under and over, and the footway may be wet in spots—a minor price to pay for the peace, solitude, and natural dignity encountered here.

The League for Conservation Legislation, the New Jersey Chapter of the Sierra Club, and then Assemblyman (now Governor) Thomas Kean can take credit for passage, in 1976, of the Natural Areas System Act. This landmark legislation, which followed in the footsteps of the Forest Preserve article of the New York State Constitution, allows designations of certain areas to be left, forever, in their natural state. Except for trails, they are left fundamentally undeveloped, and the trees remain uncut.

Continuing ahead, avoid the trail forking to the right and proceed over two small wooden bridges, onto the footway now on land slightly raised from the surrounding marsh. This part of the trail has many small plank bridges but has otherwise not been maintained in many years. This path, and most of those in Parvin, were built during the 1930s by the CCC. Considering more than fifty years have passed, it is easy to praise them for their fine, long-lasting work.

The route through the natural area is obvious, even though indistinct in a spot or two. Don't worry, steps can always be retraced easily; but it is much more likely that, with just brief hunting and pecking, the path can quickly be regained. In one wet, open area, it does bend somewhat to the right, but otherwise it is mostly straight with gentle curves.

Cross three or four small, feeder inlets as the course winds out and bends slowly left towards Muddy Run. Be sure to take time to observe the forest around you. Being left alone by man, it has developed a distinct wild feel. The birds seem to like the area—you will hear many, see few. In about twenty minutes, a substantial bridge over Muddy Run is reached. It has seen better days but is still sturdy. Shortly after crossing it, just as the main trail takes a distinctive turn to left, watch for a fainter path on the right

through some blowdowns. If you miss this spot, you'll soon climb gently to a paved interior road of the park—just retrace your steps, find the correct path, and resume the hike.

Going ahead on the *fainter* trail, almost immediately a huge, downed tree with exposed roots is conspicuous. It's interesting to observe the complex web of the root system and large ground hole left by its fall. Many times we have seen these otherwise unexplained dips in the forest floor, after the tree has rotted or been carried away.

The trail continues as before with many two- and three-plank bridges. It soon arrives at, then parallels, a small inlet creek flowing through the dense brush and forest. After crossing a woods road, the trees begin to open up a little, and the trail resumes the wide and groomed look it had in the beginning of the hike. Through the trees to the right, there are glimpses of some houses as the trail nears the southern border of the park.

This part of New Jersey is known to have a considerable tick population. If you hike here during the warmer months (June - September), be especially alert for the little monsters. The Introduction to this book provides some basic advice on ticks and Lyme disease.

The footway becomes more distinct again, and the walking very easy. The plant community has resumed the character of that encountered early in the hike. The large pitch pines attest to the years the area has been undisturbed by logging. Young white pine trees add to the gentle feel, with their long, light-green needles. Holly trees canopy the now wide trail in one area. The holly is an evergreen tree that, like mountain laurel, keeps its leaves throughout the year. The trees can be either male or female, and both sexes are needed before berries develop.

As the trail comes to a T-junction, proceed right, crossing over a sandy road after a minute or so. Continuing ahead, the path passes some indistinct trails, one on the right and one just beyond it on the left. About fifteen minutes past the T-junction, at another junction, take a ninety-degree right turn over a small mound of dirt. Should you miss this turn, you'll shortly be at a paved road with two posts in the ground and can retrace your steps.

After taking the right turn, the path is again raised from the surrounding forest floor. Crossing yet another trail, continue straight as the path gets a little narrower. In less than five minutes, the main trail swings sharply to the left, while a fainter trail goes straight. Take the latter one ahead. Off to the left, through the woods, observe some of the cabins in the Thundergust Lake area. The route quickly arrives at a nice wooden footbridge over Thundergust Brook, a pleasurable place to pause as the hike draws to a close.

After crossing the bridge, the trail swings left as it heads along the east shore of the lake. At a U-shaped inlet, a little side trail goes uphill to the right, connecting with a play field. Continue along the shore, passing a playground and picnic area. Although the trail occasionally becomes indistinct in this developed and sometimes open area, just stay near the shore, and it soon becomes apparent again.

Fifteen minutes from the bridge, as the trail approaches Parvin Mill Road, swing left, staying along the shoreline as before. Close to the road, the trail passes the outlet of Thundergust Lake—a large, rectangular, cement spillway. The path, still sticking to the shoreline, parallels the entrance road for the camping area and then takes the first fork, crossing the entrance road at a sign that says "Hikers Only." On the left is the park nature center, certainly worth a visit if it happens to be open. The booth to the right is a gatehouse for the campers.

Crossing the road, the trail comes to the shore of Parvin Lake on a spit of land between the main section of the lake and a small cove. Cross the bridge; there is a clear view across the water to the beach and bathhouse where the hike began.

From here, no formal directions are required. Just continue through the more-developed part of the park, always remaining close to the shoreline. The outlet dam of Parvin Lake is especially interesting, with its art deco lines and unusual, curved spillway. Two small bridges, crossing what appear to be streams, actually take you on and off Flag Island, a tiny section in the corner of the park.

You will be back to your car before long. Stop at the office (nice rest rooms!) and tell the staff there of your excursion through the outer areas of Parvin. They don't get many hikers in the area and may enjoy hearing your anecdotes.

HNZ

Belleplain State Forest—East Creek Trail

Total distance: 6.5 miles
Hiking time: 4.5 hours
Vertical rise: Minimal
Rating: Moderate
Maps: USGS Woodbine/Heislerville; DEP Belleplain State
  Forest

Located in the southern tip of the Pine-lands, Belleplain State Forest (Box 450, Woodbine, NJ 08270; 609-861-2404) is a popular camping forest containing 194 family camping sites, eleven all-season cabins, two group campsites (which can each accommodate fifty persons), hot showers, and flush toilets. Belleplain has, in fact, the largest number of campsites of any forest in the New Jersey state forest system. Central to the camping areas in this approximately twelve thousand-acre forest, ninety percent of which is part of the Pinelands National Reserve, is Lake Nummy, a transformed cranberry bog with white sand beaches. The lake was named in honor of King Nummy, chief of the Kechemeche Tribe and the last to rule in the Cape May area. For hikers, the forest offers two short trails in the camping area and the East Creek Trail, a 6.5-mile footpath that will be utilized in the hike described below.

To reach the Belleplain State Forest, take exit 17 (Woodbine/Sea Isle City) off the Garden State Parkway. Bear right following signs to Woodbine, turn right onto NJ 9 for .6 mile, and then turn left onto County Road 550. After 6.3 miles, reach the town of Woodbine (historically a sanctuary for European and Russian Jews) where 550 makes a left and then a right. From Woodbine, it is 1.4 miles to the state forest. Turn left at the entrance and drive .5 mile to an intersection. At the intersection, a right turn will lead in .5 mile to Lake Nummy on the right and the park office on the left. If you are hiking during the summer peak season, make a right at the end of the lake, drive over the dam, and make the first right. A large parking area is located here. Parking is available during the off-season at the park office itself.

Begin the hike from the woodyard located about 100 yards west of the park office just to the left of the main road. If you parked your car at the main parking area on the north side of Lake Nummy, walk back over the dam and make a right turn onto the paved road. The woodyard will be on your left. A post with two white markers is found at the entrance to the woodyard, and a sign marking the trailhead is found in the yard itself.

The East Creek Trail, which begins here, is a 6.5-mile, circular trail marked with white paint markings on trees. A cut trail for nearly its entire length, it encircles the area drained by Savages Run between Lake Nummy and East Creek Pond. The trail generally traverses dry, oak/pine forests but frequently descends into the deep, dark, cedar brooks and swamps so characteristic of the Pine Barrens to the north. Unlike the Pine Barrens, shore vegetation, particularly greenbriar and holly trees, is found throughout the forest, revealing the transitional nature of the region. Hikers should be warned that the forest is located in an area that abounds in mosquitos, ticks, and deer lice. These insects are common during much of the year, and strong insect repellents may prevent unnecessary problems. At the time of this writing, the East Creek Trail was well marked but not well maintained.

Following the white markers, begin hiking in a southward direction from the woodyard. The trail, a moss-covered footpath, penetrates first an open forest of young oaks and then a pitch pine forest, reminiscent of the Pine Barrens. Parts of this forest were cut six to eight years ago. Where the trail parallels a fire ditch, the first of many found along the trail, be alert for a sudden right turn where the ditch swings to the left. Clumps of mountain laurel, small pine trees, and, in places, bracken ferns form the typical ground cover seen here and throughout the hike. About a mile into the hike, and in sharp contrast to the openness of the pine/oak forest, the trail crosses a cedar creek in the dark shadows of tall cedars. Here are the first of many holly groves and tangles of greenbriar that threaten to overwhelm the trail. After crossing the small brook, paved Sunset Road is reached and crossed.

The trail now follows the perimeter of an abandoned field filled with wildflowers in season. The transition from field to for-est is evident here, and wildlife, including deer and game birds, is often encountered. After reentering the woods, the trail joins an old sand road, following it through pine forest for only a hundred yards or so before turning sharply left. Here is an old boardwalk, the first of many that aid the hiker through the wet sections ahead. The narrow trail now penetrates an older, deeper, and darker forest, some of the pine trees being very large. In the wetter areas, huge holly trees are found.

After passing through this low and wet area, the trail crosses on planks another stream at the edge of a dense stand of cedars. The trail then recrosses the same stream where it is wider and the cedars denser. Here, the trees seem to be standing on their roots to keep out of the wet, green earth. Be careful while crossing on the planks, which are moss covered and may be slippery.

The next section of trail is very green, dominated by pine, holly, and laurel. This forest must be quite striking with a snow cover. After traversing two more sections of boardwalk, the trail winds through an open section of forest filled with trees killed by the gypsy moth. An old woods road is followed through a forest of young pines before the trail comes to an open area. Walk straight ahead, following markers, toward the building located at the southern end of East Creek Pond. The building is the East Creek Lodge, a former hunting lodge that is available from the state forest for use by groups. In front of the lodge is a dock and a picnic table, which, if unused, makes a good spot for a snack or lunch. This point is the halfway mark in the hike, about 3 miles from the forest office.

Today, the view out over East Creek Pond is one of calm, blue water lined by tall, green pines. If anything, the pond is underused, yet it is regarded as an ex-

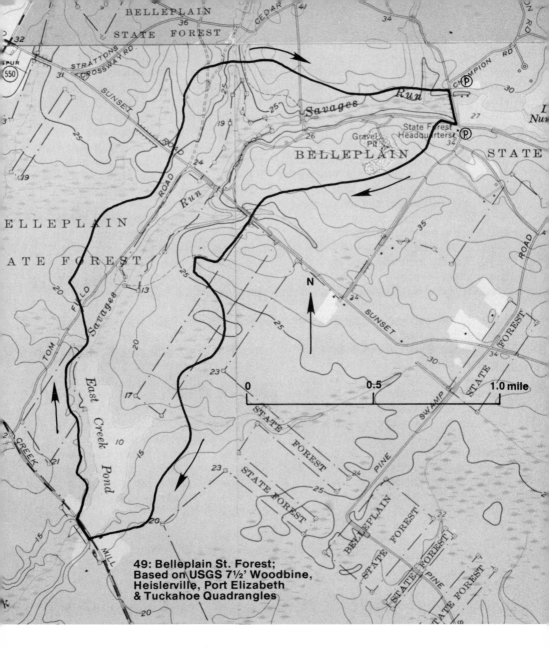

49: Belleplain St. Forest;
Based on USGS 7½' Woodbine,
Heislerville, Port Elizabeth
& Tuckahoe Quadrangles

cellent pickerel lake and does attract some fishermen. A hundred years ago, this area was the scene of much activity; a lumber and gristmill were located here.

When ready to continue, walk to the other side of the lake via the road, following white markers, and reenter the woods. A sign indicating the trail is located here. Now heading north, the trail parallels the lake for a distance before it actually comes out to the shoreline near an inlet. Here is a wilderness vista of the lake. With the possible exception of fishermen in boats, the entire visual panorama is of water and forest. From this point, the trail turns left, skirting a wet section, and then heads toward higher ground.

The trail now traverses a forest filled with young pines on both cut trail and woods road. As the trail nears the northern end of East Creek Pond, it meanders through a very dense cedar forest and, farther on, crosses a swamp on planks. Here, at the swampy, northern end of the lake, the trail makes a sharp left and meets, in 100 feet, a woods road. The trail utilizes this road for only a short distance, bears left at the fork (a right turn here will lead to a last look at the pond), and then almost immediately turns left again, off the road and cutting back into the woods on a footpath. After a short walk, the trail arrives at Tom Field Road, a gravel road open to vehicles.

After crossing the road, the trail heads back into the woods, making a sharp right turn after about 200 yards. For the next half mile, the trail penetrates some very dense growth in a low area, in places utilizing fire ditches. Eventually, Tom Field Road will be seen on the right, and then paved Sunset Road will be crossed for the second time in the hike. Here, on the northern side of Sunset Road, the trail traverses some higher and more open land making for easier hiking. After about a quarter of a mile, the trail,

now heading northeast, descends and crosses Tom Field Road and, after that, a smaller sand road.

From here the trail once again enters a cedar swamp, crossing its brook on a wooden bridge and a wet area on a boardwalk. After crossing a grassy road, the trail travels through a mature white pine forest, where some large holly trees may be found as well. Ahead, the trail makes a final road crossing and begins the last stretch toward Lake Nummy. This last section begins on fairly high ground, but then the trail descends toward a very large stand of cedars. In the heart of this river of cedars lies Savages Run, the stream that drains Lake Nummy and feeds East Creek Pond. After keeping its distance from the cedars, the trail finally enters what may be the darkest and wettest of all the cedar brooks encountered on the trail so far. Be careful here, for the trail can be slippery and very muddy in places. After emerging from the cedars, the trail bears left and then right on a utility line cut and meets, in a very short distance, the paved road that crosses Lake Nummy's dam. If you parked at the main parking area, bear left and then right on paved roads. If you parked at the forest office area, turn right, then left.

BCS

50

Cape May Point State Park

Total distance: 2 miles
Hiking time: 1 hour
Vertical rise: Minimal
Rating: Easy
Maps: USGS Cape May; DEP Cape May Point State Park

The land that makes up this small, 190-acre state park was once used by the navy to defend Delaware Bay. In 1942, huge bunkers (containing large guns) were erected here and across the bay in Delaware. At the time, these bunkers were located about nine hundred feet from the waters edge, but today, due to beach erosion, one bunker stands precariously just offshore. The lighthouse located here was built in 1859, constructed well to the north of the two earlier lights. It stands 170 feet tall. Cape May Point State Park (Box 107, Cape May Point, NJ 08212; 609-884-2159), which came into being in 1974, preserves both the military and natural history of the area and is especially popular with birders.

Cape May is located on the Atlantic Flyway, the main path for birds migrating from north to south. Many birds that summer in the Northeast migrate to Central and even South America for the winter via New Jersey. The birds, which utilize the New Jersey coast as a guide in this migration, converge on Cape May Point before the relatively long flight over the waters of Delaware Bay. Fall is considered the best time to observe birds in the park, particularly for hawks that mi-

grate south in large numbers from September to November each year.

To reach the park, take the Garden State Parkway to its terminus just before the town of Cape May and follow signs to Center City. Make a right at the T-junction, Sunset Boulevard (Route 606), following signs to Cape May Point. After 2.2 miles, make a left onto Route 629 and travel .7 mile to the park entrance, which is on the left. Park toward the far end of the large parking area, near the covered picnic area if possible.

Cape May Point State Park, although very small, offers about 2 miles of trail through a variety of habitats where both northern and southern species of plants exist together. Portions of the pathways are covered with boardwalk, and there is even a trail for wheelchairs. Three trails are color coded and marked with large arrows. The hike described below utilizes the entire blue trail, with a return walk via the beach. The trailhead is located near a directory at the far end of the parking area and begins on a boardwalk. There is a sign here indicating the entrance to the nature area. Pets are not permitted on these trails, though they are permitted on the beach.

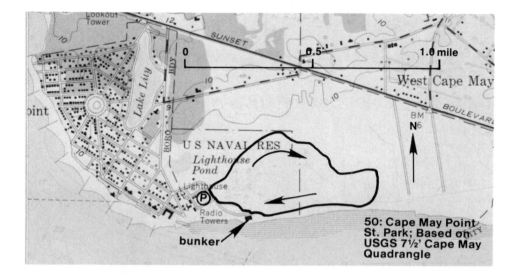

50: Cape May Point
St. Park; Based on
USGS 7½' Cape May
Quadrangle

Begin hiking on the boardwalk, over which rise tall red cedars and phragmites. Phragmites, the common marsh reeds seen all over New Jersey, originated in the Old World but have now taken over the habitats formerly filled by the native cattails. The red cedar is the source of the aromatic cedar wood used to make cedar chests. Almost immediately, the boardwalk divides. To the left is the red trail, suitable for wheelchairs, which leads to a fresh-water pond. There are observation platforms here, and those interested in birds may wish to take this side trail, which reconnects with the blue (and yellow) trail about .1 mile ahead. To the right, the blue (and yellow) trail crosses a wet area on a well-constructed bridge, goes through a wooded area, and soon meets the red trail coming in from the left.

Continue along the trail in the direction indicated by occasional blue and yellow arrows, now a narrow footpath meandering through a tangle of greenbriar, holly, and other shore vegetation. The scenery changes to phragmites again where the trail enters a marsh but soon returns to woodland. After crossing another marsh on a straight causeway, the trail comes to a junction where a left turn will lead to an observation platform overlooking Al's Pond, a habitat for muskrat and a food source for migrating birds. Return to the main trail where, just ahead, the yellow and blue trails separate. Bear to the left on the blue trail, which crosses over water on a wooden bridge and winds its way through a cedar and shadbush swamp, mostly on boardwalk. Ahead, the trail passes along the edge of a marsh where especially tall phragmites are growing. After reentering a particularly viney woods, the trail bears to the right, climbs a dune, and meets the ocean.

On the beach, turn right and head back toward the lighthouse in the distance. Foredunes stabilized by dunegrass protect from the encroaching sea the marshes and woods traversed by the trails. As you walk along the beach, look for the small, clear, and very polished pebbles known locally as Cape May Diamonds. These pebbles, pieces of clear quartz, have been tumbled by the waters of the ocean and bay for countless

Cape May Lighthouse.

years. The original source of this quartz was probably northern New Jersey, New York, or Pennsylvania, the material being washed down to the Cape May area by the ancient Delaware River. The largest Cape May Diamonds ever found were reported to weigh about a pound, though most are much smaller than these.

Just before reaching the lighthouse area, a huge concrete bunker stands on wooden pilings in shallow water. Built during World War II to protect Delaware Bay, the bunker has turrets that once held six-inch guns and 155-mm coast artillery guns. Originally located far from the ocean, the bunker was covered over with earth. The amount of erosion in just over forty years is staggering, and it seems inevitable that this heavy construction will soon topple from its wooden perch.

Just opposite the bunker, a path leads through the dune fence into a shallow pond area, which is a wildlife sanctuary. The path leads along the shore and up to the path from the parking area. A right turn here will lead past a bird observation platform overlooking the pond and to the parking area.

BCS

Guidebooks from The Countryman Press and Backcountry Publications

Written for people of all ages and experience, these popular and carefully prepared books feature detailed trail and tour directions, notes on points of interest and natural phenomena, maps and photographs.

Walks and Rambles Series

Walks and Rambles on the Delmarva Peninsula $8.95
Walks and Rambles in Westchester (NY) and Fairfield (CT) Counties $7.95
Walks and Rambles in Rhode Island $8.95

Biking Series

25 Bicycle Tours in New Jersey $8.95
25 Bicycle Tours on Delmarva $8.95
25 Bicycle Tours in Maine $8.95
25 Bicycle Tours in Vermont $7.95
25 Bicycle Tours in New Hampshire $6.95
20 Bicycle Tours in the Finger Lakes $7.95
20 Bicycle Tours in and around New York City $6.95
25 Bicycle Tours in Eastern Pennsylvania $7.95

Canoeing Series

Canoe Camping Vermont and New Hampshire Rivers $6.95
Canoeing Central New York $9.95
Canoeing Massachusetts, Rhode Island and Connecticut $7.95

Hiking Series

50 Hikes in New Jersey $10.95
50 Hikes in the Adirondacks $9.95
50 Hikes in Central New York $8.95
50 Hikes in the Hudson Valley $9.95
50 Hikes in Central Pennsylvania $9.95
50 Hikes in Eastern Pennsylvania $9.95
50 Hikes in Western Pennsylvania $9.95
50 Hikes in Maine $8.95
50 Hikes in the White Mountains $9.95
50 More Hikes in New Hampshire $9.95
50 Hikes in Vermont, 3rd edition $9.95

50 Hikes in Massachusetts $9.95
50 Hikes in Connecticut $8.95
50 Hikes in West Virginia $9.95

Adirondack Series

Discover the Southern Adirondacks $9.95
Discover the South Central Adirondacks $8.95
Discover the Southeastern Adirondacks $8.95
Discover the Central Adirondacks $8.95
Discover the Southwestern Adirondacks $9.95
Discover the Northeastern Adirondacks $9.95
Discover the Eastern Adirondacks $9.95
Discover the West Central Adirondacks $13.95

Ski-Touring Series

25 Ski Tours in Central New York $7.95
25 Ski Tours in Maine $5.95
25 Ski Tours in the Adirondacks $5.95
25 Ski Tours in the White Mountains (revised edition available fall 1988)
25 Ski Tours in Vermont (revised edition available fall 1988)

Other Guides

State Parks and Campgrounds in Northern New York $9.95
The Complete Boating Guide to the Connecticut River $9.95
The Other Massachusetts: An Explorer's Guide $12.95
Maine: An Explorer's Guide $13.95
Vermont: An Explorer's Guide, 3rd edition, $14.95
New England's Special Places $10.95
New York's Special Places, $12.95

The above titles are available at bookstores and at certain sporting goods stores or may be ordered directly from the publisher. For complete descriptions of these and other guides, write: The Countryman Press, P.O. Box 175, Woodstock, VT 05091.